Foreign Exchange Management
in Multinational Firms

WITHDRAWN

Research for Business Decisions, No. 26

Gunter Dufey, Series Editor
Professor of International Business and Finance
The University of Michigan

Other Titles in This Series

Foreign Exchange Management in Multinational Firms

by
Vinh Quang Tran

Produced and distributed by
UMI Research Press
an imprint of
University Microfilms International
Ann Arbor, Michigan 48106

Library of Congress Cataloging in Publication Data

Tran, Vinh Quang, 1946-
Foreign exchange management in multinational
firms.

(Research for business decisions ; no. 26)
Bibliography: p.
Includes index.
1. Foreign exchange problem. 2. International business
enterprises—Finance. I. Title. II. Series.
HG3851.T7   658.1'5   80-23986
ISBN 0-8357-1133-1

KÍNH DÂNG HUONG HỒN CÂU
in memory of my loving father

Contents

Figures

Tables

Acknowledgments

This work is the result of the efforts of many individuals. While all the remaining errors are mine, its completion would not have been possible without this support and cooperation. In this recognition, special thanks are extended to Professor Jack Zwick, Chairman of the Research Advisory Committee, whose knowledge and suggestions have provided much insight and kindled my interest in this international financial area. I am also grateful for the moral support, encouragement, and advice from Drs. J. Minor Sachlis and Rodney Eldridge of the Committee.

Of the many executives and consultants/bankers who participated in this study, all have cooperated beyond the call of courtesy and professional consideration; their contribution was simply indispensible to the completion of this research project. For this, I am most appreciative, regretting that their efforts cannot be acknowledged individually.

I am also grateful for the support from my employer, Acuity Systems, Inc. who allowed extended leave of absence for the research and writing, and my staff whose cooperation has been beyond the call of duty.

Lastly, but by no means least, I am grateful for the unending and untiring support and encouragement from my wife, Nhung, who provides a home environment where creative work can be accomplished, in addition to her spending countless hours in the library collecting research materials for me.

Chapter I

Introduction

General

The foreign exchange risk has long been an inherent part of doing business overseas and an area of concern for firms which venture across national boundaries. Many firms have found themselves caught up in a devaluation, and have discovered that profits remitted to their home countries were worth less than they had expected. Under these circumstances, firms naturally have devised ways to contain their foreign exchange losses and reduce their exposures to this risk. Their efforts were partly aided by the relative infrequency of currency devaluations and the security of "one-way bet" in the exchange rate system of par values and relatively narrow margins which had prevailed since World War II.

The emergence of floating exchange rates after the break up of the Bretton Woods system in the early 1970s, however, has presented new dimensions to the task of managing foreign exchange risks. From the viewpoint of multinational firms, the frequent changes in exchange rate relationships, often of substantial magnitudes and in difficult-to-predict directions, represent new challenges with which they must cope. Not only one-time losses in cross-border transfers of funds, but also long-term and potentially permanent business decisions, such as those related to plant location, sourcing, purchasing, or subsidiary financing, which underlie the very survival of a business, are subject to this increased uncertainty in the international financial environment. As a matter of fact, the ways that firms would respond to this environmental change were a key issue in the long debate over the pros and cons of floating exchange rates. It was questioned whether the private sector, of which multinational firms are prominent participants, was

> . . . sufficiently equipped to ensure a reasonable stability in the foreign exchange markets in order not to expose international trade to the vicissitudes and uncertainties which had hitherto been confined to commodity markets and stock exchanges.[1]

In 1975, the Financial Accounting Standards Board introduced the Statement of Financial Accounting Standards No. 8 (FASB 8) which prescribed new currency accounting rules to be applied by U.S. firms doing business overseas. For many companies, these requirements represent an important departure from the ways they had previously reported the effects of exchange rate fluctuations. As a result, a number of them reported the significant impact of FASB 8 on their earnings. This has created concern that companies may react to FASB 8 such that they take actions which may be inconsistent with their economic objectives, and thus further complicate a complex situation with potential effects on resource allocation in the economy.

However, notwithstanding significant progress in conceptually understanding the management of foreign exchange in multinational firms, empirical data on their behavior under conditions of foreign exchange risks in the environment of floating exchange rates are scant. Unavailable is the empirical evidence on the effects of FASB 8 on firms and how they react to it.

In view of the importance of these issues and the lack of adequate understanding thereof, this research is undertaken in an attempt to (1) shed more light on them, and (2) to formulate a model descriptive of the behavior of the subject companies under conditions of foreign exchange risks in the environment of floating exchange rates.

Toward this broad objective, this study has investigated and analyzed: (1) the process of and the factors involved in foreign exchange management of large U.S. multinational manufacturing firms; (2) the changes in their defensive strategies due to greater exchange rate variations; and (3) the effects of FASB 8 on their currency exposure measurement and defensive strategies.

The data on these foreign exchange management aspects were collected by in-depth interviews with the financial officers in charge of this function at a sample of companies. For various reasons, these companies do not constitute a representative sample in the strictly statistical sense of the word. However, this sample contains a cross-section of large U.S. multinational firms subject to this study.

Hopefully, this research will: (1) contribute to a better understanding of the foreign exchange management process and the factors involved in it; (2) help the development of accounting rules and the regulation of firms' public disclosure by regulatory agencies, and the assessment of the effects of floating exchange rates on multinational firms and vice versa; and (3) improve the effectiveness of multinational firms' management of their foreign exchange.

This study is divided into three major parts. The first two chapters deal with the theoretical aspects of the subject matter and delineate the objectives, scope, and study design. Chapters III to V constitute a report of the empirical findings. The two remaining chapters focus on the applications and implications of the findings.

In the balance of Chapter I, there will be a detailed discussion of the implications of floating exchange rates and FASB 8 on multinational firms insofar as the defensive strategies are concerned. It is then followed by a review of the literature which provides an analysis of the issues that have been con-

ceptually and empirically studied before this research. This chapter thus fur-
nishes a rationale for this research project. A conceptual model of foreign exchange management is formulated in Chapter II to depict the major elements of
the foreign exchange management process and thus provides a conceptual framework for the empirical research. In the remainder of Chapter II, the objectives
and scope, the limitations of this research project, and the methodology of
research will be delineated.

Chapter III presents and analyzes the empirical findings on four factors
in the foreign exchange management process: currency exposures, objectives,
defensive strategies, and constraints. Chapter IV concentrates on relationships:
information systems, risk analysis, and selection of defensive strategies. Chapter
V discusses the changes in the defensive strategies due to floating exchange
rates and the effects of FASB 8 on currency exposure measurement and
defensive strategies.

Based on the empirical results, Chapter VI presents a model descriptive
of the foreign exchange management process and also contains a discussion
of some of the implications of the findings. Finally, the study results are sum-
marized in the concluding chapter which also suggests areas for additional
research.

Definition of Terms

To clarify the discussion, hereafter "foreign exchange management"
refers to the financial activity which aims at protecting a company against
adverse effects of exchange rate fluctuations. "Hedging" connotes the use of
defensive strategies for this purpose. "Defensive Strategy" indicates the actions
that a company can take for hedging against foreign exchange risks. "Currency
exposure" is a quantitative measure of the extent that a company is exposed
or subject to the effects of a change in the exchange rate of a currency.

Elsewhere, the terms "foreign exchange management," "exposure management," and "hedging" have been used either as synonyms or to indicate specific
meanings which underlie the viewpoints of the users about the objective(s) or
purpose(s) of this financial activity. For example, Jilling and Folks defined
"foreign exchange (risk) management" as:

> . . . the orderly incorporation of potential exchange rate changes into the opera-
> tional and long-range planning process of the multinational corporation. Viewed in
> this fashion, potential exchange rate changes represent an opportunity for profitable
> redirection of corporate resources.[2]

However, "such an expansive view of the exchange risk management task is
relatively new, theoretically, and difficult to discover in practice." In this study,
the terms "foreign exchange management" and "hedging" are to have the

indicated meanings. Furthermore, the terms "foreign exchange management" and "exposure management" will be used interchangeably.

Following are some other terms which are sometimes used in this study:

> current rate: in accounting terms, the exchange rate in effect at the balance sheet date of a reporting company
> historical rate: the exchange rate at which foreign currency could be exchanged for the reporting currency at the date a specific transaction or event occurred
> spot rate: the rate quoted for sale/purchase of one currency against another for immediate delivery (normally two days hence in Western markets)[3]

Implications of Floating Exchange Rates and FASB 8

These are implications of greater uncertainty in exchange rate movements and FASB 8's earnings impact on multinational firms' defensive strategies against foreign exchange risks.

Floating Exchange Rates and Uncertainty

The decade of the 1970s has been marked with uncertainty and upheaval in the environment in which corporate international financial affairs are conducted. It started out with massive realignments of major world currencies and was followed by violent fluctuations in foreign exchange markets. The end result was the break up of the exchange rate system established at Bretton Woods since the end of World War II.

The events that culminated in the emergence of the floating rate regime began with a heavy influx of speculative capital into European foreign exchange markets in the early days of May, 1971. These capital flows caused the monetary authorities of Germany, the Netherlands, Belgium, Austria, and Switzerland to cease official intervention in support of their currencies parities against the U.S. dollar. Three months later, the United States announced the suspension of U.S. dollar-gold convertibility in official transactions. The ensuing Smithsonian Agreement in December, 1971, which led to major realignments for the currencies of 10 industrialized countries, proved to be short-lived as the basis for an alternative regime of exchange rate relationships.

In June, 1972, after a massive speculative attack directed against the pound sterling, England decided not to maintain the exchange rate for its currency within announced margins; the pound began to float. Then, in January and February of 1973, outflows of funds from Italy, largely into Switzerland, and heavy speculative sales of U.S. dollars brought the worst exchange crisis in at least 25 years to its final phase, ending with the U.S. dollar devalued by 10 percent in terms of special drawing rights, and the introduction of generalized floating exchange rates.

In the floating rate regime, exchange rate movements have been large. For example, during the early months of the floating period, some European currencies appreciated against the U.S. dollar by as much as 4 percent in a single day, and by as much as 10 percent in little more than one week, only to decline sharply thereafter. These sizable swings occurred again in 1974 and 1975. More significantly to multinational firms, the heavy up-and-down movements of exchange rates since the adoption of generalized floating have lasted for sustained lengths of time, from three to six months. Thus, the regime of floating exchange rates seems to have introduced greater foreign exchange risks to multinational firms in their international transactions.

The foreign exchange risk refers to the uncertainty in the direction, the frequency, and the magnitude of the changes in the external value of a currency. Characteristic of the floating regime is the removal of the security of "one-way bet" and the greater frequency of the changes in exchange rates. Figure 1 shows the patterns of exchange rate movements of the currencies of selected major European countries from 1974 to 1976. Table 1 expresses in numerals the movements of six European currencies for the 1974-1977 period. These statistics were in sharp contrast to the three devaluations of the French franc and the two devaluations of the pound sterling in the 19 years from 1949 to 1967.[4] During this period, after a devaluation in 1949, both the Dutch guilder and the Deutsche mark were revalued once, in 1961. On the other hand, the Swiss franc's exchange rate did not change at all during this period.

For an indicator of the uncertainty with respect to the direction and magnitude of exchange rate movements, variances (a measure of dispersion) are computed on the quarter-to-quarter changes in the spot rates of six major European currencies. The eight quarters from 1971 to 1972 represent the fixed exchange rate period. In another study of the 1973 and 1974 years of floating rates, the choice of the 1971-1972 fixed rate period was justified as follows:

> From January, 1971 through December, 1972, this period was hardly one of stable, fixed parities, such as those in the early 1960's. It was, however, a fixed rate period where instabilities due to disequilibrium exchange rates make it attractive for comparison to a subsequent flexible rate period. For the relevant question is not how the 1973-74 flexible rate system performed compared to a fixed exchange rate system in a world of stable international financial markets, but how it performed relative to how a system with less variable exchange rates would have performed in the same markets.[5]

In other words, if there is any bias in the selection of the fixed rate period, it is in favor of the fixed exchange rate system. For floating rates, three periods are studied: 1974-1975; 1976-1977; and 1974-1977. F tests are performed to determine statistical significance at the 95% confidence level. The quarterly percentage changes are shown in Table 1. The variances and F values are shown in Table 2.

Figure 1
Exchange Rates Against the U.S. Dollar, January 1974 to June 1976.

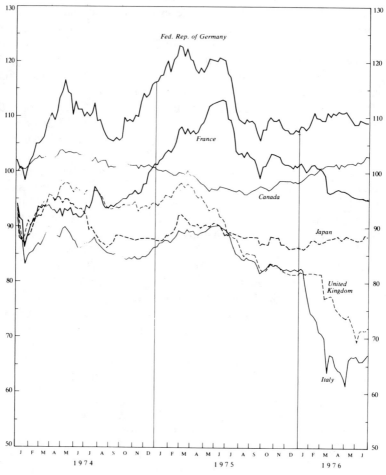

¹ Based on Wednesday noon spot quotations in New York.

Source: International Monetary Fund, *Annual Report of the Executive Directors for the Fiscal Year Ended April 30, 1976* (Washington, D.C.: International Monetary Fund, 1976), p. 26.

Table 1
Exchange Rate Movements of Selected Currencies (1974-1977)

End of Quarter	French Franc	Deutsche Mark	Swiss Franc	Dutch Guilder	Italian Lira	British Pound Sterling
	Percent Change from Previous Quarter					
1971						
1st	.0939	.3827	.4315	.0288	.4625	.9855
2nd	- 2.2261	3.6818	4.9319	.7370	- .4230	.0331
3rd	.2101	3.6176	2.5507	- 3.6949	1.5869	1.8222
4th	- .0883	3.4169	2.1399	4.4820	.6642	1.4802
1972						
1st	3.3348	3.0452	1.5479	1.7258	1.8829	2.3411
2nd	.3029	.0794	1.4356	- .0480	- .0058	- .8707
3rd	.6039	- .5011	- .1750	.6982	.3148	- 5.4789
4th	- 1.0805	- .1817	.1890	- .0161	- .5928	- 4.0752
1974						
1st	- 1.3031	6.2228	2.4620	4.9596	- 2.2083	2.0739
2nd	- 2.7746	1.3598	.8280	.6560	- 4.4541	1.1640
3rd	1.9583	- 5.4872	- .5874	- 2.5297	- 1.4755	- 3.2126
4th	4.1984	7.2630	11.0444	5.6369	- .5500	.5201
1975						
1st	5.8389	3.7150	.9981	5.5747	3.3333	3.2292
2nd	5.3570	- .2141	.2420	- .8852	.8064	- 5.8527
3rd	- 9.4907	- 9.7075	- 7.4361	- 9.2529	- 6.8750	- 7.3140
4th	- .9304	- 1.3303	.7435	- 1.4234	- 1.7651	- 4.1925
1976						
1st	- 4.9773	2.2811	2.1713	- .6734	- 19.3154	- 5.5460
2nd	- 1.2088	- 1.1610	2.2956	- 1.7326	- .8788	- 7.5471
3rd	- 3.6517	2.9004	.4329	4.6816	1.3810	- 1.6385
4th	- 1.5554	4.1554	.9958	4.4042	- 2.8422	- 4.5652
1977						
1st	- .5146	- 1.5992	- 3.9333	- 1.7682	- 1.4865	.8165
2nd	.6367	1.4077	2.0803	.1596	.2840	.0454
3rd	.2076	1.2844	4.4798	.4250	.1327	1.3813
4th	- 1.9206	6.2802	12.0300	3.8745	.8309	- 1.5784

Source: Department of Financial Markets, Federal Reserve Board, Washington, D.C.

Table 2
Exchange Rate Variability of Selected Currencies (1971-1977)

Period	French Franc	Deutsche Mark	Swiss Franc	Dutch Guilder	Italian Lira	British Pound Sterling
Percent Change from Previous Quarter						
Mean						
1971-72	.1438	1.6926	1.6752	.3146	.4862	.9652
1972-75	.3567	1.3198	1.0543	.3420	- 1.6485	- 1.6981
1976-77	- 1.6230	1.9436	2.6366	1.1713	- 2.7367	- 2.3290
Variance						
1971-72	2.5137	3.5870	2.5240	5.2802	.7796	1.4265[a]
1974-75	26.2242	18.0082	25.2654	25.9671	9.6567	15.5619
1976-77	3.6168	6.8056	19.4548	7.4483	46.7034	10.4167
1974-77	14.9709	19.4858	17.4840	21.2017	26.6171	12.2950
F Tests						
1974-75	10.4325	5.0204	10.0101	4.9178	12.3866	10.9115
1976-77	1.4388[b]	1.8973[b]	7.9020	1.4106[b]	59.9016	7.3023
1974-77	5.9557	5.4323	6.9271	4.0153	34.1416	8.6190

Source: Table 1

[a] The pound sterling began to float in June, 1972. Therefore, for this period, the variance is computed only on the first six quarters.

[b] A sufficiently small F value indicates that statistically at the 95% confidence level, the difference between the variance for the period 1971-72 and that for 1974-76 is not significantly different from zero.

It is clear from Table 2 that during the 1974-1975 floating period, these six European currencies exhibited greater volatility in their movements than that experienced during the 1971-1972 period of the fixed exchange rate system. This condition continued to exist during the period of 1976-1977 for the currencies of Italy, Switzerland, and England, whereas the fluctuations of the Deutsche mark, Dutch guilder, and French franc somewhat abated to the extent that their volatility was not significantly greater (statistically) than that during the fixed rate period. Overall, the uncertainty in the movements of these currencies has been significantly greater in the floating rate period. (This is indicated by the F values computed for the 1974-1977 period).[6]

Another way to look at the uncertainty aspect under floating exchange rates is the difference between the forward rate and the spot rate which prevails at the (forward) contract maturity date. The meaning of this measure is explained as follows:

> In their decisions on the use of the forward market for covering exchange risks, market participants compare the present spot and forward rates with their expectation of the future spot rate at the time when the forward contract matures and the interest rate differential prevailing in the relevant markets. The actions of market participants taken together result in a tendency for the forward rate to be drawn toward the future spot rate collectively expected by the market, with both of these rates tending to differ from the present spot rate by the differences in short-term interest rates in the two money markets in question. These tendencies may, of course, be prevented from fully manifesting themselves by the thinness of the forward market for many currencies and in some instances also by official intervention in this market.
>
> To the extent that the forward rate reflects the market's expectation of the future spot rate on the date on which the forward contract matures, the gap, observed *ex post*, between the forward rate as quoted three months earlier and the actual spot rate on this date can serve as an indicator of market participants' errors in forecasting exchange rate developments.[7]

Figure 2 shows the spread between the three-month forward rate and the actual spot rate observed three months later for eight major currencies. It is calculated as a nine-month moving average of the absolute deviations, whether positive or negative, between the two rates. The results indicate that, when combined with Kohlhagen's findings,[8] the exchange rate movements of the French franc, the Deutsche mark, the Swiss franc, and possibly the British pound sterling (Kohlhagen did not use nine-month moving averages) have exhibited greater uncertainty under floating exchange rates than in the fixed rate system.

Thus, the weight of the evidence as presented lends strong support to the contention that exchange rate movements under floating exchange rates have exhibited greater uncertainty than in the fixed exchange rate system.

In view of the volatile movements of exchange rates, it is not surprising that even a number of the largest multinational firms have experienced large

10   Foreign Exchange Management in Multinational Firms

Figure 2
**Indicator of Uncertainty of Future Exchange Rates Against the U.S. Dollar,
January 1973 to December 1976.**

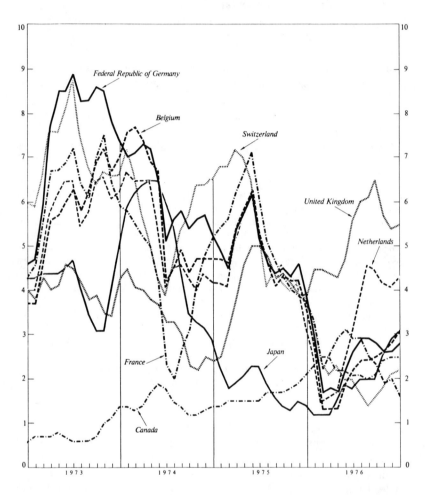

¹ End-of-month data; nine-month moving averages of the absolute difference between the spot rate on a given date and the three-month forward rate for currency to be delivered on the same date.

Source: International Monetary Fund, *Annual Report of the Executive Directors for the Fiscal Year Ended April 30, 1977* (Washington, D.C.: International Monetary Fund, 1977), p. 29.

swings in their reported earnings due to foreign exchange adjustments. For example, Union Carbide—ranked twenty-first on the 1977 Fortune 500 List of the 500 largest industrial enterprises—reported a gain of $9.6 million in 1976, but a loss of $26.5 million in 1977, a swing of 400 percent. Warner-Lambert recorded a loss of $7.9 million in 1975, then $20.8 million in 1976, and another loss of $20.8 million in 1976, an increase of almost 200 percent.[9] While these earnings impacts are considerable, these companies' experiences are not unique among the multinational firms on the 1977 "Fortune 500 List." Given that the geographical diversification of these firms' international operations do not shift significantly from year to year, and that they are equally effective in managing foreign exchange risks, these earnings fluctuations can only be attributed to the volatility of exchange rate movements.

An implication of greater uncertainty in exchange rate movements is that companies would seek to hedge more of their foreign exchange exposures, i.e., would seek to "insure" against greater foreign exchange risks. To the extent that greater demand for hedging leads to higher hedging costs, companies would devise new ways to hedge and/or increase the use of the existing defensive strategies if they incur less direct costs. Examples of defensive strategies which, according to preliminary evidence,[10] have gained wider acceptance are "extend/ receive more generous credit terms" in trade transactions, "lead/lag local currency receivables," and "specify currency denomination" in hedging of import and export transactions. However, this comparison is obviously inadequate to understand the effects of floating exchange rates on multinational firms' defensive strategies due to incomparability of samples and methods of data measurement and collection.[11]

Another defensive strategy that companies could use is inter-currency netting. This strategy recognizes the fact that exposures to foreign exchange risks of a multinational firm are diversified across a number of currencies and assumes that the global foreign exchange loss from exposures in all currencies combined is a greater concern than losses in individual currencies. Since the global exchange loss is a linear combination of the gains and losses in the individual currencies, this strategy implies the management of exposures in the individual currencies—or individual currency exposures—such that the global loss does not exceed a target amount or is limited to an acceptable range, or some other pre-defined objective.

To the extent that companies increase hedging to protect themselves against greater foreign exchange risks, their actions would have profound effects on foreign exchange markets. These effects may be direct or indirect. The direct effects take place when a firm uses foreign exchange markets, such as when it contracts forward buying or selling of foreign currencies. The direct effects also occur even when the firm does not use exchange markets, such as when a foreign currency payment is delayed in anticipation of a depreciation. In both cases, the demand and supply forces in the foreign exchange markets are affected. The indirect effects operate through the financial system of a foreign country. Again, to delay a foreign currency payment may lead to an increase in demand for funds in the foreign country. This may affect its domestic interest rates, and therefore the external value of its currency.

Thus, in view of the greater uncertainty in exchange rate movements, the observed impact on multinational firms, their resultant actions and the implications of their increased hedging on foreign exchange markets, and a lack of adequate practical understanding thereof, it is necessary to re-examine the multinational firms' defensive strategies against greater foreign exchange risks.

FASB 8

Until the issuance of FASB 8 in December, 1975, multinational firms had a number of options as to what extent unrealized gains/losses from translation of a foreign subsidiary's assets and liabilities were to be reported as a part of current income from ordinary operations. This was possible because they could elect to translate inventory and long-term debts at either the historical or the current rate of exchange between the local currency and home currency, and to treat translation gains/losses as either ordinary revenue/expense items or credits/charges against a reserve account.[12]

FASB 8 now requires among others things that cash, receivables and payables of the foreign subsidiary that are carried at present or future prices be translated at the current rate of exchange, i.e., the rate prevailing at the balance sheet date, and assets and liabilities carried at past prices at applicable historical rates. When the foreign statements are prepared in conformity with U.S. generally accepted accounting principles, this translation method produces results that are the same as those of the monetary-nonmonetary method. Unlike past practices, FASB 8 rules that the resulting adjustments from translation are to be included in net operating income of the current period.

For multinational manufacturing firms among the largest 100 companies on the 1977 Fortune 500 List, FASB's currency accounting rules represent an important departure from their past practices.

With regard to the translation of the balance sheet, only a small number of this group of companies followed the monetary/nonmonetary method. Of the thirty-one 1977 Fortune 100 multinational manufacturing companies in Pakkala's sample,[13] only six used this translation method before FASB 8. While researching for this study, this researcher examined 10-K reports of 25 such companies and found only 7 which had used the monetary/nonmonetary method for translation. By combining this list and Pakkala's sample, appropriately retaining the names which appear on either list, the sample amounts to 44 companies. (The population of 1977 Fortune 100 multinational manufacturing companies was estimated to consist of 62 companies.) Out of this sample, only seven were found to have used the monetary-nonmonetary method.

As to recognition of adjustment for foreign exchange gains/losses, none of these seven companies followed the practice that was later prescribed by FASB 8. The practice closest to FASB 8's provisions was that of Pepsico which deferred gains and losses on foreign currency long-term debts in a reserve account. (Eastman Kodak did not disclose its policy in this regard.)

For some companies which did not use currency accounting rules similar to those prescribed by FASB 8, restatement of their foreign currency financial statements has resulted in substantial adjustments. At Union Carbide, restatement of earnings in accordance with the new accounting rules resulted in an increase of $10.3 million in 1975, whereas its 1974 results were adjusted downward by $5.0 million. The currency accounting change also affected the Warner-Lambert Company's earnings. Its 1973 earnings showed an increase of $7.0 million, whereas its 1974 income was reduced by $7.5 million.[14] However, these adjustments were unrealized gains/losses (i.e., dollar cash flows were not affected when the adjustments were recorded).

Impact on earnings of this magnitude has prompted suggestions that because

> ... typically management doesn't like to have volatile earnings . . . faced with State-ment No. 8, they will devise ways to dampen the potential effect of translation gains and losses on the volatility of earnings.[15]

These actions could be taken regardless of a large amount of empirical evidence suggesting that the capital market is quite efficient in getting at economic values of financial statements.[16] This is due to a number of possible reasons, one of which is related to the behavior of corporate managers.

> Corporate managers may not believe that the market is efficient. Alternatively, they may believe that the issue is irrelevant. Or, they may be unaware of the issue, but act as if it were irrelevant. Or, they may think that the owners are not con-cerned about market inefficiency. Or, they may not believe that the owners will read the footnotes that seek to distinguish accounting data and economic data. Furthermore, even if owners do read the footnotes, they might not be able to dis-tinguish accounting data and economic data.[17]

And, if indeed stock prices react negatively to earnings volatility caused by FASB 8, corporate managers would be motivated to take actions to reduce fluctuations in their companies' reported earnings.

Given that FASB 8's impact is sufficiently significant to motivate com-panies to change their behavior, one of the defensive strategies that they would be motivated to abandon is to forward cover expected payments or receipts of foreign currencies which cannot be considered fixed foreign currency commitments (for example, confirmed, but not shipped, orders). The reason is that under FASB 8, such forward contracts are deemed speculative, therefore, the resulting gains/losses are required to be recognized currently in every accounting period. However, in the periods before the contracts mature these (unrealized) gains/losses are not offset by losses/gains for the expected payments or receipts. The latter, which are realized (i.e., dollar cash flows are affected), will not be recorded until the expected transactions are actually made. However, failure to forward cover these payments or receipts will necessitate the recognition of the (realized) losses (when these transactions are made) without being offset by gains from the forward contracts.

Furthermore, the requirement of translating inventory at the historical rate of exchange would motivate companies to exclude inventory from the computation of their currency exposures. This is because if the currency is depreciated, exclusion of inventory would decrease the impact on reported earnings. In other words, if companies previously hedged their exposed inventories in the foreign exchange markets, because of FASB 8, they would be motivated to avoid the forward cover of this component of their currency exposures to save the fees on the forward contracts. Thus, this FASB 8 requirement contains a motivation for companies to change the method of computing their currency exposures. Once this change is made, if price adjustment is not feasible (possibly because of local price controls, competitive pressures, or desire to maintain price stability in the local markets[18]), the decline in sales revenue (translated into dollars at current rates) will lead to profit erosion.

In both of these examples, FASB 8 could lead companies to change their behavior with respect to currency exposure measurement and defensive strategies such that their (real) economic performance is adversely affected, although their reported earnings may be improved. Conversely, if companies disregard FASB 8, their reported earnings (not their economic performance) will be affected. To the extent that the securities markets respond to these data on reported earnings—or corporate managers so believe—allocation of resources in the economy will be adversely affected.

This discussion suggests that potential changes in multinational firms' behavior due to FASB 8 depend on:

1. The magnitude of FASB 8's impact on their earnings. (An impact of ± 5% can be considered significant.[19]) Other things being equal, the greater the exchange rate changes, the greater the impact. Putting this differently, the greater the exchange rate variations, the greater the volatility of reported earnings.
2. The translation method which was used. In other words, FASB 8

should not have an impact on companies which used the monetary/ nonmonetary method of translation, insofar as the method of computing exposures is concerned.

In view of the magnitude of FASB 8's impact on earnings of multinational firms and the implications of their reaction on the resource allocation in the economy, it thus seems necessary to seek a practical understanding of the changes in currency exposure measurement and defensive strategies by multinational firms in response to FASB 8.

Summary

This and the previous section deal with the potential effects of floating exchange rates and FASB 8 on multinational firms. These effects can take place in two ways: (1) firms could change their method of currency exposure measurement and avoid certain defensive strategies that they used before FASB 8 in response to its impact on their reported earnings; and (2) firms could devise new defensive strategies and/or increase the use of existing ones to protect themselves against greater foreign exchange risks. If multinational firms' behavior is so affected, this would have profound repercussions on resource allocation in the economy and foreign exchange markets.

Review of Literature: Foreign Exchange
Management in Theory and Practice

This section will provide an analysis of the issues in foreign exchange management that have been theoretically explored and empirically studied in the literature. This literature can be classified into conceptual, normative, and empirical studies. This classification will show emphatically the state of research in this subject area.

Conceptual Studies: Accounting versus Economic

These studies are addressed to the related questions: (1) What is foreign exchange risk? (2) What constitutes a foreign exchange exposure? (3) What are the effects of an exchange rate change on a foreign subsidiary?

There are two basic approaches: accounting and economic. Accounting studies seek to identify those items/accounts on the balance sheet of a foreign subsidiary which can be considered as exposed to foreign exchange risks and those which should not be. Leading these studies is the article by Cecil Ashdown which distinguished current from non-current assets and liabilities.[20] In 1956, Hepworth introduced the distinction between monetary and non-monetary items.[21] In 1972, Lorensen espoused the temporal principle of currency translation.[22] A study by Parkinson, however, presented arguments for the current rate method.[23] The following quote summarizes the balance sheet items that each of the above translation methodologies treats as exposed to foreign exchange risks (i.e., they are to be translated into U.S. dollars at the current exchange rate) and those that are considered unexposed (i.e., they are to be translated at the exchange rates prevailing at the dates that these assets are acquired—historical rates).

> (a) The temporal method translates cash, receivables and payables, and assets and liabilities carried at present or future prices at the current rate and assets and liabilities carried at past prices at applicable historical rates.
>
> (b) The monetary/nonmonetary method generally translates monetary assets and liabilities at the current rate and nonmonetary assets and liabilities at applicable historical rates. For translation purposes, assets and liabilities are monetary if they are expressed in terms of a fixed number of foreign currency units. All other balance sheet items are classified as nonmonetary.
>
> (c) The current-noncurrent method generally translates current assets and liabilities at the current rate and noncurrent assets and liabilities at applicable historical rates.
>
> (d) The current rate method translates all assets and liabilities at the current rate.[24]

For the purpose of translation, a foreign subsidiary's balance sheet consists of the following major items:

A. Monetary assets consist of cash, marketable securities, and accounts receivable. Marketable securities can be valued at cost or market prices.

B. Current assets consists of monetary assets plus inventories and prepaid expenses. Inventories can also be carried at cost or market prices.

C. Current liabilities consist of all liabilities due currently, i.e., within 12 months. Accountingwise, they are also classified as monetary liabilities.

D. Monetary liabilities consist of current liabilities plus long-term debts and deferred income (charges).

E. Fixed assets.

F. Stockholders' equity consists of capital stock and retained earnings.

For ease of exposition, hereafter prepaid expenses and deferred income (charges) will be excluded from the discussion because of the differences in translation methods applicable to them; yet they are of relative insignificance in the total assets/liabilities.

The temporal and monetary-nonmonetary methods differ more in their conceptual bases than in practice. When U.S. generally accepted accounting principles which embody the principle of historical cost accounting are applied, the two methods give the same results. For this reason, hereafter they will be considered one and the same. The monetary-nonmonetary method is different from the current-noncurrent method in that it translates inventories at historical rates but long term debts at the current rate of exchange.

The current rate method does not distinguish monetary from nonmonetary and current from noncurrent items. Instead, it translates all assets and liabilities at the current rate. As to the temporal versus monetary-nonmonetary method, if the U.S. generally accepted accounting principles are used, they yield the same results. With regard to the revenue and expense items recorded on the statement of income (operations or profit and loss), it is accepted by all but the current rate method that they are to be translated into U.S. dollars at the rates of exchange prevailing on the dates that they are realized, except those revenues and expenses derived from the assets and liabilities that are translated at historical rates, e.g., depreciation expenses. The current rate method translates all revenues and expenses at the current rate. Table 3 summarizes the rates of exchange that are used to translate a foreign subsidiary's balance sheet.

The result of the distinction between historical and current exchange rates in translating balance sheet items is the exclusion of those items translated at the historical rate from the foreign subsidiary's exposure to foreign exchange risks. In other words, those items translated at the current exchange rate are considered exposed to foreign exchange risks because their dollar values change with exchange rates. Conversely, those items translated at historical rates are unaffected. Since the four mentioned translation methods differ in the items translated at historical rates, they yield different results as to the effects of exchange rate changes on a foreign subsidiary—and, therefore, its exposure to foreign exchange risks—yet none of which are accepted by economists as correct.

Part of the problem is that the choice of a particular translation method has been a reflection of the circumstances of the time rather than was based on theoretical consistency.[25] Thus, the current-noncurrent method gained acceptance during a period when the U.S. dollar strength was undoubted and when the U.S. involvement was skewed toward import and export transactions. As U.S. companies began to increase their international operations via the foreign direct investment route, the monetary-nonmonetary method was developed to better reflect this change.[26] The current rate method was a further attempt by the British accounting profession to incorporate the view that to the extent that a foreign subsidiary is an operationally independent entity, its individual assets and liabilities are not exposed to foreign exchange risks; the entire operation is. Alternatively, it was argued that the foreign exchange risk

Table 3
Translation Rates for Balance Sheet Items of a Foreign Subsidiary

Balance Sheet Item	Temporal	Monetary-Nonmonetary	Current-Noncurrent	Current
Cash	C*	C	C	C
Marketable Securities				
Carried at cost	H**	C	C	C
Carried at market	C	C	C	C
Accounts Receivable	C	C	C	C
Inventories				
Carried at cost	H	H	C	C
Carried at market	C	H	C	C
Prepaid Expenses	H	H	C	C
Fixed Assets	H	H	H	C
Current Liabilities	C	C	C	C
Long-term Debts	C	C	H	C
Deferred Income (charges)	H	H	H	C
Stockholders' equity				
Capital stock	H	H	H	C
Retained earnings	***	***	***	C

*C: Current exchange rate
**H: Applicable historical exchange rates
*** Retained earnings consist of the residual of the net of revenues over expenses in the current period plus the dollar balance brought forward from the end of the preceding period.

should be viewed from the perspective of the local currency rather than from the viewpoint of the reporting currency of the parent company, because an asset acquired by a foreign subsidiary has no historical cost in U.S. dollars and therefore can be measured only in the local currency.

Aliber and Stickney suggested that the distinction of monetary versus nonmonetary and current versus noncurrent assets and liabilities should not be a critical variable in the measurement of the foreign exchange exposure of a foreign subsidiary. In fact, they argued that the assumption underlying the monetary-nonmonetary method is logically inconsistent and empirically unjustifiable.[27]

> If prices are stable within each country, exchange rates should remain unchanged. The money interest rates in each country should be approximately equal as a result of arbitrage. If one country then follows inflationary monetary policies, its currency will depreciate in the exchange market in proportion to increases in its prices relative to those in other countries. Interest rates denominated in its currency will increase to reflect the anticipated change in the exchange rate. The increase in its relative price level and in its interest rate should equal, in terms of percentage points, the expected change in the exchange rate, unless expectations and realizations differ significantly.[28]

The assumption underlying the monetary-nonmonetary method is divergent from the above described relationships between price levels, exchange rate changes, and interest rates. This method assumes that exchange gains or losses on nonmonetary items are largely offset by changes in the local prices of the assets. It thus implicitly accepts that the Purchasing Power Parity theory is valid. On the other hand, in translating monetary items at the current rate, it rejects the proposition that exchange rate changes are reflected in the relative interest rate differentials on similar assets denominated in several currencies. This proposition is called the Fisher Effect.

Empirically, the authors examined the data on prices, exchange rate changes, and interest rates in six developed countries for the 1960-1971 period and seven less developed countries for the period from 1966-1971. They found that for the developed countries the deviations from the Fisher Effect were all smaller than the deviations from the Purchasing Power Parity theory. They therefore suggested that if the validity of the Purchasing Power Parity theory was accepted as it was implicitly in the monetary-nonmonetary translation method, then the Fisher Effect should have been accepted as well. The implication is that monetary items should be translated at historical rates and therefore considered unexposed to foreign exchange risks—the same as nonmonetary items. For the less developed countries, the deviations from the Fisher Effect were in all but one country larger than the deviations from the Purchasing Power Parity theory. In this connection, it is interesting to note Giddy's tests of the Purchasing Power Parity theory and the Fisher Effect. This author ran tests of the 2 theories for 4 developed countries (Canada, Britain, France, and Italy) over a 24 year span consisting of periods of various lengths, from one to 24 years. In all cases, he found that the deviations from the Fisher Effect were all very much larger than the deviations from the Purchasing Power Parity theory. Both studies, however, confirmed marked deviations from the two theories in the short run.[29] In Aliber and Stickney's study, the deviations were large enough for them to conclude that for periods of two to three years, all assets and liabilities tend to be exposed to foreign exchange risk.[30] In Giddy's tests, the deviations did not appear to diminish with the length of the period.[31]

The above two studies and other tests of the Purchasing Power Parity Theory and the Fisher Effect tend to support the conclusion that in the short run the two theories are less reliable as predictors of exchange rates than they are in the long run.[32] The implication is that in the short run, all assets and liabilities are exposed to exchange risks.

This conclusion notwithstanding, economists are of the viewpoint that the accounting approach to measuring a foreign exchange exposure is not correct, for it places emphasis on the valuation of the stock of assets and liabilities of the foreign subsidiary that exist at the valuation (balance sheet) date and on current period accounting income, but excludes the future cash flows. Principally, these future flows consist of revenues from sales of the subsidiary's products and costs of its production inputs. To the extent that the exchange rate change causes revenues to increase more/less rapidly than the increase in costs, the change in the exchange rate would be more/less beneficial to the foreign operation than the accounting measurement would indicate. In other words, economic theory seeks to define a foreign operation's exposure as change in its dollar value as consequences of exchange rate changes; the dollar value of foreign subsidiary is defined as the discounted net present value of all future cash flows. This discrepancy between accounting and economic data has been observed by Robbins and Stobaugh,[33] and Vernon.[34] Its implications on financial policies were analyzed in great detail by Dufey.[35] Dufey pointed out that the effects of a devaluation on a foreign operation go beyond its assets and liabilities.

First, as a going concern, the subsidiary needs a certain minimum amount of financial assets

> . . . for continuing profitable operations as (much as) the brick and mortar for its buildings. Therefore, it is illogical to act as if certain parts of that bundle of assets, the subsidiary, were subject to the full devaluation loss, while other equally necessary parts are treated as automatically "self-hedging."[36]

Second, in addition to the cash flows generated by the liquidation of its assets/liabilities—if they are liquidated at all—which may be more or less than the amounts realized in the event that the devaluation had not occurred, depending on whether it is a net debtor or creditor, the going foreign operation would enjoy additional benefits or suffer additional detriments from the devaluation. These incremental gains or losses arise from the changes in the structure of its revenue and cost streams induced by the devaluation. Dufey gave some examples:

> Devaluation should improve the LC revenues that result from a firm's export sales. The firm may either maintain its product prices in terms of foreign currency, thereby increasing its LC receipts by the devaluation percentage, or it may lower the foreign currency price and presumably increase its sales volume . . . If the firm is producing goods for a sector of the domestic market where import competition is not a factor, LC revenues will suffer because demand is weakened by falling real income attributable to more costly imports and the rise of domestic cost of exports benefiting from devaluation . . . In any event, the devaluation will cause a rise in the LC cost of inputs of most firms. Obviously, those companies whose expenses include a high proportion of imported materials will be hardest hit.[37]

The author then concluded: "Any final effect of a devaluation on the profits received by the parent company can be computed only *after* the expected LC revenue and expense streams have been adjusted."[38]

This analysis thus suggests that the computation of a foreign exchange exposure should be derived from the foreign operation's future cash flows rather than from the balance sheet. It is worthy to observe in this connection that if a firm's planning horizon is fairly short, e.g., one year, its fixed assets *per se* do not generate any cash flows, therefore should not be considered exposed. On the other hand, as its current assets and liabilities normally have a turn-over rate of less than one year, they should be considered exposed. This suggests the critical role of a firm's planning horizon in the computation of its foreign exchange exposure, although for a reason different from that cited by Aliber and Stickney.[39] This observation is injected to point out the widespread disagreement between economists, corporate practitioners, and the accounting profession in arriving at an acceptable conceptual basis to measure a foreign operation's exposure to foreign exchange risks. In fact, Aliber and Stickney's data indicated that the Purchasing Power Parity theory and the Fisher Effect were "valid" only in certain periods and in certain countries (currency denominations).

Under these circumstances, it is no surprise that there is as yet no economic formulation of foreign exchange exposure that is acceptable, even to economists. Before the article by Dufey, cited above, was published, Heckerman attempted to formulate a quantitative definition of a foreign operation's exposure to foreign exchange risks.[40] This formulation follows the future cash flows approach to compute the discounted present value of a foreign operation's income stream due to price and exchange rate changes. It therefore includes a residual over and above the balance sheet items. Heckerman, however, assumed that real sales and costs remain constant over time. Repeating Dufey,[41] Shapiro criticized that this assumption is unrealistic. He then proceeded to quantitatively demonstrate that the effects of an exchange rate change on a foreign operation depend on (1) the distribution of the foreign subsidiary's local and export markets, (2) the amount of import competition it faces locally, (3) the degree of substitutability between its local and imported factors of production, and (4) import and export demand elasticities for its products.[42] Hendershott, however, pointed out that this analysis regrettably lacks the elementary distinction between the movements along the demand curve and shifts in demand. In addition, Shapiro's conclusion that the multinational firm is less affected by inflation and exchange rate changes than a traditional export firm because it can shift its production and exporting activities from one country to another is not warranted by his assumptions. These assumptions state that the price level in the home country (where the parent company is located) is held constant and that profits are denominated in the home currency. These assumed conditions should have led to the conclusion that there is no effect on production in the home country by changes in the price level in the local country (where its foreign subsidiary is located) and exchange rate changes, Hendershott argued.[43]

The difficulty in arriving at a formulation of economic exposure does not negate the validity of the proposition that a foreign exchange exposure should be measured by the foreign operation's future cash flows. Reflecting this line of economic reasoning, Ankrom, an executive with Chrysler Corporation, suggested that the monetary-nonmonetary measure be modified to include future sales and purchases.[44] He noted the following, however:

> While it is easy to recognize the importance of transaction exposure on future sales and purchases, it is much more difficult to define it quantitatively. The problem is one of deciding how many months of sales and purchases should be included in the transaction exposure position . . . It depends on each company's pricing flexibility, and how fast it can increase selling prices to offset the effects of a currency change. For most companies, it is virtually impossible to predict reaction time.[45]

Earlier, Shulman proposed to add future earnings plus depreciation to the exposure measured by the current-noncurrent method.[46]

From the foregoing discussion, it can be concluded that the accounting approach tends to misstate the exposure to foreign exchange risks of a foreign operation for it excludes the effects of an exchange rate change on the subsidiary's revenue and cost streams. Additional research is, however, needed to account fully for these effects.

Given the discrepancies between accounting and economic data in the measurement of foreign exchange exposures, should corporate managers be concerned with (accounting) exchange losses and therefore undertake actions to reduce/eliminate these losses? This question becomes particularly relevant since the adoption of FASB 8. As it is now well-known, this accounting ruling eliminates the latitude that companies used to have in translating their foreign currency financial statements. To the extent that the old standards were closer approximates to individual firms' economic exposures, FASB 8 would only widen the existing gap between accounting and economic data. Additionally, the new standards would lead to—as it actually did—fluctuations in these firms' reported earnings due to large translation gains and losses. To the extent that the stock market discounts their share prices as a result, these firms would be induced to make uneconomic alterations of their economic exposures.

Some writers have argued that the stock market should not react negatively to share prices of firms that are adversely affected by FASB 8, and therefore, they should not be concerned with the accounting exposure measured by this accounting convention. The basis for this conclusion is the efficient market hypothesis. This hypothesis states, among other things, that the stock market is quite efficient in filtering through accounting information to arrive at the true economic condition of a company. Earlier proponents of this view are Giddy and Shapiro.

Giddy suggested

> The implication is that any increase in the variability of net reported earnings resulting from FAS No. 8 should *not* affect a firm's stock prices, *except* when it reflects a fundamental instability in the firm's condition, arising from exchange rate fluctuations.
>
> This argument is reinforced by the fact that FAS No. 8 provides the financial community with more, not less, information, since the alternative to immediate recognition of exchange gains and losses is to place translation effects in a reserve account.[47]

In Shapiro's words,

> In an efficient capital market, knowledgeable investors should be able to understand detailed financial statements and to properly interpret various accounting conventions behind corporate balance sheets and income statements. Thus, the existence of sophisticated traders should preclude a firm's ability to change its stock's market value by massaging account information.[48]

There exists a large amount of empirical evidence supporting the efficient market hypothesis, although there is some evidence to the contrary.[49] Additionally, Burns added a word of caution:

> If . . . the new accounting standards produce a greater volatility of reported earnings than existed under the previous standards, and if credit rating companies reacted to this greater volatility by lowering the ratings of the companies involved, the market's efficiency might be impaired.[50]

The early empirical work by Makin, however, provides some evidence about the reaction of the stock market on share prices of those companies which have been adversely affected by FASB 8.[51] Using the Capital Asset Pricing model, he examined the returns on securities of three groups of companies over five time periods. These time periods were segregated to isolate the effects of floating exchange rates from those of FASB 8. The three groups of companies include a control group of non-multinational firms, a group of multinational firms insignificantly affected by FASB 8, and the third group consisting of companies whose earnings were significantly impacted by FASB 8. The results suggest that after FASB 8, for the third group of companies, there was a reduction in the *ex post* annual rate of return of about one-half of one percent below that for a typical portfolio with the same market risk. Makin therefore concluded that the hypothesis that FASB 8 induces a depression in the share prices of those companies which are significantly affected by FASB 8 could not be rejected.

Given the potential economic consequences of FASB 8, or a lack thereof, it seems certain that additional research will be conducted to provide better insight into the reaction of the stock market to share prices of those companies whose earnings have been adversely affected by FASB 8. In fact, the Financial Accounting Standards Board and the Financial Executives Institute have commissioned studies to address this issue. At the time of this writing, November, 1978, these studies, however, are not yet released.

Normative Studies: How to Hedge

Existing normative studies are concerned with two main issues: hedging methods and risk analysis (decision models).

Hedging Methods

Hedging methods can be classified into financial hedge and real hedge. The financial hedge consists of those defensive strategies which are aimed at altering the foreign exchange exposure by manipulating the balance sheet accounts or by "buying insurance" against the foreign risk on a cash receipt/payment via the forward exchange market. It can also be distinguished from the real hedge by its short-term nature although it is not always so. In contrast, the real hedge is necessarily long-term and more permanent in nature. It seeks to alter the very structure of a firm's international operations by diversification, expansion, and even contraction of its overseas investments.

Studies in financial hedges are numerous and most of these methods and their variation have been discussed at length in textbooks on international financial management. Better known texts are *International Financial Management* by Zenoff and Zwick;[52] *Manager in the International Economy* by Vernon;[53] and *Money in the Multinational Enterprise* by Robbins and Stobaugh.[54] Most recent is the text *International Financial Management* by Rodriguez and Carter.[55] A recent book by Prindl, *Foreign Exchange Risk,* was devoted exclusively to a discussion of the various aspects of foreign exchange management in which most of the financial hedging methods were examined in detail.[56] Earlier, Business International Corporation published a monograph on these hedging methods.[57] There are also other sources which devote attention to specific hedging methods.[58] Table 4 summarizes the hedging methods from these sources that will be empirically investigated in this study.

In addition, there has been some attention directed to policies and organization of the foreign exchange management function. Most notably, Ankrom advocated the use of committees in foreign exchange management decision-making and argued for central control and direction at the parent headquarters.[59]

Some writers have suggested that while financial hedging may be effective in smoothing out period-to-period fluctuations in reported earnings, it may be a misdirection of corporate resources.[60] First, as the Sharpe-Lintner-Mossin capital asset pricing model suggests, the cost of equity to a firm is dependent on its systematic risk which it cannot reduce unless, carrying the argument to the extreme, it converts all assets into some risk-free investment. Therefore, the best a company could do to protect itself against foreign exchange risks is through foreign currency diversification (in order to reduce the unsystematic risk). However, an investor can accomplish this risk reduction without some sacrifice of expected return by holding a diversified portfolio of securities. This conclusion is based on the assumptions that investors are well informed of international investment opportunities and that barriers to international investment are no greater for individuals than for corporations. Second, under conditions of efficiency in the markets for foreign exchange, securities, and goods, changes in the exchange rates are reflected in the prices of goods and money. Therefore, corporate hedging against the foreign exchange risk becomes superfluous. Furthermore, to the extent that foreign exchange markets are efficient, hedging in the forward exchange markets might be even costly. In fact, some evidence now exists that the cost of forward contract hedging over a one to three year period averaged about seven tenths of one percent.[61]

Under these conditions, companies should be concentrated in what they are presumed to do best: manufacturing and marketing.[62] Therefore, the tasks of management in multinational firms should be directed to planning, production, and marketing strategies in anticipation of exchange rate fluctuations so as to alter pricing, product, credit, and market selection strategies on which plant locations, materials sourcing, and investment decisions depend.

However, these authors are aware that market imperfections do exist.

Table 4
Hedging Methods

1. Timing of Payments and Receipts
    1.1   Lead/lag local foreign currency receivables from/payables to third parties
    1.2   Lead/lag inter-subsidiary receivables/payables
    1.3   Accelerate/delay remittances to parent company
    1.4   Pre-payment of bank borrowings and like commitments to third parties

2. Price Adjustments
    2.1   Increase export prices
    2.2   Increase billing prices to local customers
    2.3   Increase/decrease inter-subsidiary transfer prices

3. Credit Policy
    3.1   Specify currency of billing in import and export transactions
    3.2   Extend/request more/less generous credit terms

4. Inventory Adjustments
    4.1   Increase/decrease investment in local/foreign currency inventories

5. Money and Foreign Exchange Market Operations
    5.1   Local currency borrowings
    5.2   Foreign currency borrowings
    5.3   Forward exchange contracts on payments/receipts arising from import and export transactions
    5.4   Forward exchange contracts on payments/receipts for commitments not recorded on the books
    5.5   Forward exchange contracts on net exposed balance sheet positions

6. Rearrange Inter-Subsidiary Cash Flows
    6.1   Adjust the flows of remittances to parent company
    6.2   Adjust planned parent company's dollar investments
    6.3   Negotiate foreign currency and/or credit swaps

7. Asset and Liability Management
    7.1   Reduce short-term assets and increase short-term liabilities denominated in depreciating currencies, and vice versa
    7.2   Adjust local/foreign currency long-term debt

8. Inter-Subsidiary Netting

9. Inter-Currency Netting (Leave open the exposure in one currency anticipating that its loss will be offset by the gain from the exposure in another currency)

These imperfections may be investors' unequal access to capital markets due to lack of information or knowledge and that prices do not move together. In addition, creditors may be concerned with total variability in returns from operations or even with variability in cash flows where default is possible. Therefore, hedging and foreign currency diversification may be useful. In fact, there is evidence suggesting that geographically diversified corporations have contributed to the integration of international securities markets.[63]

When hedging is undertaken for profiting from exchange rate fluctuations due to market imperfections or to reduce variability in returns or cash flows, economic theory suggests that companies should aim at reducing cash flow fluctuations rather than balance sheet exposure. In the latter case, the overall foreign exchange management strategy should be to match cash inflows with cash outflows rather than assets and liabilities matching. In this connection, Makin suggested that attention should be paid to the total return of the portfolio of exposures in all currencies rather than inflow-outflow matching on a currency-by-currency basis.[64] This is the portfolio approach to foreign exchange management. It is, in fact, akin to what is called inter-currency netting in this study.

Risk Analysis

Many studies on risk in foreign exchange management are modeled after the mean-variance framework pioneered by Markowitz.[65] And like the Markowitz model, they all require the specification of a potentially large number of covariances. They also require quadratic utility function for deterministic solutions. However, it has been pointed out that this utility function is subject to some serious limitations.[66] First, it must be bounded; beyond the bounded range, it may not represent rational economic behavior. Second, it implies increasing absolute risk aversion which is empirically implausible. The only alternative to quadratic utility—for using this approach—is the assumption of normal probability distribution of exchange rates. Given the available evidence in this regard,[67] this assumption is difficult to defend. In addition, the existing studies using this approach are focused only on the foreign exchange risk as it is connected with financing and remittances of funds across borders, but ignore the other hedging methods, such as leading/lagging, local/foreign currency borrowing, or billing currency denomination.[68]

An early application of the mean-variance framework to calculate an efficient risk-return frontier was proposed by Lietaer for evaluation of investment alternatives in two-country situations.[69] The decision variables are interest rate, exchange rate risk, and the firm's risk preference curve. The latter is assumed to be equal to a quadratic utility function. The same approach was used by Yutaka Imai to deal with exchange risks in fund transfers, balance sheet hedging through borrowings, and currency swaps;[70] and by Jucker and de Faro in sourcing debt funds.[71]

Markowitz' theory has also been applied to analyze risk in the context of currency speculation such as in the works by Feldstein[72] and Leland.[73] The latter's analysis of speculative behavior in the forward exchange markets was an extension of Feldstein's, without restrictions on the form of the prior profitability distribution of future spot rates and with inclusion of initial wealth and other risky investment opportunities. Again, using the same analytical approach, Folks sought to determine the optimal level of forward exchange purchases as a hedge against foreign exchange risks in fund transfers between two countries.[74]

Another type of optimization models which has been used in practice to aid decision-making in financial hedging uses mathematical programming techniques. This approach requires a careful modelling of the firm's behavior and seeks to maximize an objective function within assumptions of uncertainty, subject to a set of constraints. Necessarily, these models require the analysis of a fairly large number of variables, including exchange rates.

An early application of dynamic programming to international financial management was Rutenberg's analysis of inter-subsidiary transfer of funds as a network problem.[75] Shapiro provided a comprehensive analysis of various hedging problems, from forward cover to pricing strategies.[76] A joint effort by these authors produced a multi-period analysis of the problem of forward exchange contract hedging under four different conditions, using a dynamic programming formulation.[77]

In contrast to the deterministic nature of the decision models described in the above, heuristic models seek to simulate the decision-making process, but leaving the choice of objectives—or risk-return trade-off—to the decision-maker(s). Of this type are the criteria of expected monetary value, minimax, minimum variance suggested by Folks,[78] or the decision-tree formulation by Wheelwright.[79] The concept of "breakeven" rate has also been used to compute the costs of alternative financing/hedging strategies, such as the analysis of a specific swap transaction by Zenoff and Zwick.[80] A more general methodology, using the same concept, was developed by Folks to calculate the breakeven exchange rate in cross-border financing operations.[81] This model also allows for the incorporation of the decision-maker's risk preference—by using probabilistic statements—into the analysis.

As a concluding remark for this part of the review, it is worthy to cite the results from a survey of the use of management models for hedging in practice.[82] This survey's results indicate that of the 40 firms in the sample, only 9 used a model. The models that were used, however, were of the simulation variety; none involved mathematical programming. The reasons for this lack of appeal were several, but the complexity and excessive data requirements of the models, and the corporate managers' disbelief in their usefulness, seemed to be the major drawbacks.

Empirical Studies: Foreign Exchange Management in Practice

Empirical research into the problems of foreign exchange management under floating exchange rates and FASB 8 are rare. A few early empirical studies were directed to the translation practices by companies before FASB 8.[83] A recent study of annual reports of 70 multinational firms was conducted by Rodriguez to examine as to how widespread was the impact of FASB 8 on the reported earnings of these companies in the 1975 fiscal year.[84] The results indicate that only 13 companies reported an impact greater than 5 percent of their net income. There are also a few anecdotal papers by corporate officers for description of their companies' foreign exchange management practices.[85] A number of executives have taken advantage of the availability of seminars on foreign exchange management to express their views about this subject matter or describe their companies' practices.[86]

However, as compared to the amount of attention directed to the conceptual and normative aspects, there are few sampling studies in this subject area. An early sample survey was conducted by Jadwani to study the hedging practices of U.S. firms with subsidiaries in Britain in the wake of the 1967 pound sterling devaluation. The data were collected by interviewing a non-random sample of 25 companies, 20 of which were manufacturing firms.[87] A later sample survey by Robbins and Stobaugh provided a comprehensive analysis of financing foreign operations and thus gave valuable insight into aspects of foreign exchange management.[88] Their treatment of hedging itself was, however, rather sketchy.[89]

In the early period of the floating rate regime, Fieleke conducted two mail surveys to examine whether or not the flotation of the Canadian dollar in 1970 and the Deutsche mark in 1971 inhibited U.S. firms in hedging their transactions in the forward exchange markets.[90] The results of these two studies indicate that none of the respondent firms had foregone any transactions with Canadian or German residents due to difficulties in the forward exchange markets of the two currencies or were unable to engage in forward exchange transactions in either market.

A recent paper by Rodriguez sought to categorize the attitude towards risk into three major groups: risk paranoid, neutral risk aversion, and asymetrical risk aversion. The author then proceeded to relate these risk attitudes to foreign exchange management strategies of a sample of 36 companies. The data were obtained by sampling interviews. The results indicate that the syndrom of risk paranoid did not appear to dominate management policies, i.e., a strategy of always reducing exposure to zero did not appear to prevail. Neither the data support the hypothesis that companies ignore foreign exchange risks (that is, companies have a neutral risk aversion). Instead, the attitude towards risk in each currency was found to be either selective or random. Overall, risk asymmetry seemed to prevail. The degree of asymmetry appeared to be dependent on the currency and access to domestic financial markets. These two variables were found to help determine the signs (positive or negative) of the exposures.[91]

"The first comprehensive survey of how corporations actually are attempting to manage the exchange risk"[92] was a mail survey by the University of South Carolina in 1975. Of the 107 companies which responded to the questionnaire (a response rate of twenty-seven percent), fifty had sales of one billion dollars or more, and twenty-six were not on the 1974 Fortune 500 List. The questionnaire covered exchange rate forecasting procedures, translation methodology and balance sheet exposure management, identification of defensive strategies and cost comparison among them, and problems encountered by the companies under floating exchange rates. However, being characteristic of mail surveys, the number of "no response" was uncomfortably high in several important issues, such as the following: division of responsibility (72 percent); cost comparison among defensive strategies (30 percent); the use of various defensive strategies (ranging from 16.8 percent to 69.2 percent); or the inclusion of certain future transactions in the computation of the currency exposure (ranging from 71 percent to 91.6 percent).[93] In addition, several important issues were not sufficiently dealt with in this study. For example, it focused on how the respondent companies measure their exposures according to the accounting approach, and not how the economic exposure was computed; or how they ranked the usefulness of various defensive strategies, not how infrequently these strategies were used. In addition, the objective "minimization of foreign exchange losses" was not clearly defined. Whereas these weaknesses do not negate the significant contribution of Jilling's study, they suggest a need for additional research in this subject area.

Summary

This literature review indicates that significant progress has been made to understand conceptually and empirically the various aspects of foreign exchange management. However, at least empirically, certain areas need further investigation:

1. How do multinational firms recognize the economic effects of foreign exchange risks in their currency exposure measurement?
2. What are their foreign exchange management objectives?
3. How extensively do they use the various defensive strategies for protection against exchange risks?

The following aspects have not received any investigation:

1.   The information systems that help multinational firms assess the effects of exchange rate changes on their exposures and to analyze and evaluate defensive strategies
2.   The procedures to analyze the risk-return trade-offs of the defensive strategies
3.   The organization and/or procedures to select defensive strategies which are consistent with a firm's risk acceptance level or attitude towards risk
4.   Effects of FASB 8 on multinational firms' currency exposure measurement and defensive strategies
5.   Changes in defensive strategies due to greater uncertainty in exchange rate movements

The conceptualization of the foreign exchange management process in Chapter II will highlight the importance of these issues.

Chapter II

Conceptual Framework, Study Objectives,
Sample Design, and Methodology

This chapter will discuss the conceptual framework of the study, specifically set forth the objectives of the research, and delineate its scope and limitations. It will also establish the methodology whereby the data were collected, the kinds of companies to be included in the sample, and how the data were analyzed and interpreted.

A Conceptual Model of Foreign Exchange Management

This conceptualization of the foreign exchange management function and process serves to guide the empirical research and provides a conceptual basis for the interpretation of the data.

Figure 3 depicts the model. This model has three interactive components: the internal and external environments; diagnosis of the effects of the external environment; and response.

The internal and external environments. Two aspects of the external environment have been discussed: foreign exchange risks under floating exchange rates, and FASB 8. The internal environment of the firm is the very business it is in and which characterizes its organizational structures, the financial structures of its subsidiaries, inter-subsidiary relationships, the source of its supplies, the markets where it sells its products, and the competitive pressures with which it has to contend. These internal factors delineate the kinds of exposures to foreign exchange risks that the firm seeks to protect. They also constrain the kinds of actions or strategies that the firm can employ to protect its exposures. The last statement is made on the assumption that firms view foreign exchange management as a reactive response to effects of exchange rate changes, i.e., firms seek to eliminate, minimize, or reduce these effects, not as an opportunity for profit-making. In addition, the firm is also constrained by FASB 8 with respect to translation methodology and timing of income recognition. However, these rulings may affect the firm in ways that it may elect to define its exposures differently, i.e., different from the exposures that would be defined solely in terms of its internal factors, or take actions that it would not otherwise. These implications of FASB 8 were discussed earlier.

Other external environmental factors may also constrain the firm's actions, such as local rules and regulations, or desire to be a "good corporate citizen."[1]

Figure 3

A Conceptual Model of Foreign Exchange Management

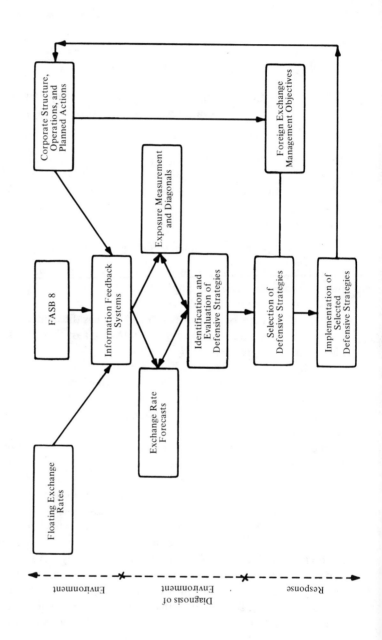

Diagnosis of the environments. This is a process by which the firm seeks to determine the effects of foreign exchange risks. It implies information systems which are used to collect, process, and analyze the data on the firm's exposures, the effects of foreign exchange risks on these exposures, and the risk/cost consequences of actions that can be taken within the internal and external constraints to eliminate, minimize, or reduce these effects.

Response. This is the phase when actions that the firm can take within its internal and external constraints will be identified, and the risk/cost consequences of these actions are analyzed and evaluated, so that, given the firm's foreign exchange management objective(s) and its risk acceptance level, the most acceptable action(s) can be selected. The final step in the response phase is implementing the selected action(s).

This conceptualization of the foreign exchange management function and process thus projects foreign exchange management as a process reactive to one aspect of the external environment, namely, exchange rate changes for the purpose of eliminating, minimizing, or reducing the effects of foreign exchange risks on the firm. It consists of the following elements:

1. A definition of the firm's currency exposures to foreign exchange risks

2. A delineation of the internal and external constraints on the firm's defensive actions or strategies

3. In the light of the internal and external constraints, identification of the firm's foreign exchange management objective(s) and its risk acceptance level

4. Information systems to collect the data on future exchange rates, currency exposures, and risk/cost consequences of any defensive strategies that the firm may take

5. Identification of the alternative defensive strategies that satisfy the internal and external constraints

6. A set of procedures to analyze and evaluate the risk/cost consequences of the identified feasible defensive strategies

7. An organization or a set of procedures to select a defensive strategy such that its risk/cost consequences meet the firm's objective(s) and the firm's risk acceptance level

8. Implementation of the selected defensive strategy

Item (1) needs some clarification. This discussion will indicate the major components of a currency exposure and certain areas of discrepancy between two alternatives of defining currency exposures: retrospective accounting versus future cash flows. These major components are monetary and non-monetary assets/liabilities, and inventory.

Regarding monetary assets and liabilities, for firms whose international involvement consists solely of import and export transactions, the assets and liabilities that are exposed to the risk of exchange rate changes are their foreign currency denominated receivables and payables. Upon conversion of funds, if the foreign currency is depreciated/appreciated, the value in terms of the home currency of the net exposed assets will be reduced/increased to the extent of the depreciation/appreciation. Thus, given an exchange rate change, the translation loss will reflect the one-time economic loss on the exposed assets.

The above is also true with respect to foreign currency long-term debts. There seems to be no question that the home currency value of a long-term debt changes with every change in the exchange rate. That is, unless changes in exchange rates are reflected in interest differentials. Then, it could be considered that long-term debt is unexposed to the foreign exchange risk. On the other hand, as empirical data suggest, whether or not long-term debt is exposed depends on the planning horizon of the firm, the currency denomination of the debt,[2] and the time period under consideration.[3] These factors may explain why some firms used historical rates to translate long-term debts, while others used the current rate. Now, FASB 8 requires that the current rate be used to translate foreign currency denominated long-term debts.

However, if the analysis is focused on the foreign currency cash flows, the potential effects of an exchange rate are even less clearcut. Here, if the foreign currency receivables are viewed as the necessary investment for the firm to maintain a permanent export market in the foreign country (i.e., a certain level of receivables is required for ongoing business operations), it can be argued that as long as the foreign currency receivables remain unchanged after the exchange rate depreciation, the exporting firm with a permanent market overseas does not incur any loss on its assets—the receivables.[4] On the other hand, *ceteris paribus,* the firm's home currency export revenue will decline unless it can raise the foreign currency selling price proportionately with the depreciation percentage. Nonetheless, under these circumstances, application of translation procedures required by either FASB 8 or past rulings will result in a loss on the receivables, and the revenue losses will be recognized when the transactions giving rise to them actually occur.

The differences in information provided by accounting data and economic data are even more pronounced in the case of a manufacturing subsidiary.

Again, focusing on the foreign currency cash flows, the analysis pertaining to foreign currency receivables of an exporting firm with a permanent market overseas is also applied to the monetary assets and liabilities of a manufacturing subsidiary.[5] Thus, for such a subsidiary's local currency cash, receivables, and payables, the losses created by a depreciation of the local currency's exchange rate occur only when additional funds are required from the parent company. Conversely, if the exchange rate change is to alter the subsidiary's operations in such a way that less cash and receivables, and/or more payables are required, the freed local currency funds would provide the parent company with additional home currency funds—which are profits.

Moving to the nonmonetary assets of the foreign subsidiary, the situation is more complex. The exact impact of an exchange rate change on its future cash flows can only be arrived at after a complete analysis of its operations' characteristics. Among the factors that affect the economic exposure of a subsidiary's nonmonetary assets are: (1) the distribution of its sales between local and export markets; (2) the amount of import competition it faces locally; (3) the degree of substitutability between local and imported factors of production; and (4) price elasticity of demand for its exports.[6] Thus, for an export-oriented firm, an exchange rate depreciation may sufficiently help increase its revenue so that its profitability will be enhanced. On the other hand, a depreciation will likely be detrimental to a firm which sells most of its output locally and faces little or no foreign competition in the local market.

The above analysis of non-monetary assets also pertains to inventory, although inventories with a very high turn-over rate represent a less significant exposure problem. Here, the treatment of FASB 8 differs from past practices in that inventory will be translated at the historical rate. This ruling introduces potentially misleading reporting of earnings by allowing exchange gains/losses associated with inventory to pass through the income statement over time rather than be reflected in the period in which the rate change occurs.

In view of these potential discrepancies, the definition of a currency exposure is important to assess the effects of exchange rate changes on a firm. It is also needed to analyze a firm's foreign exchange management objective(s)— does the firm seek to, say, minimize foreign exchange losses on an economic basis? On an accounting basis?

Items (3), (4), (6), and (7) also deserve some elaboration. At these stages of the foreign exchange management process, the selection of a defensive strategy becomes a problem of choice under risk.

In this kind of problem the decision-maker has a number of choice alternatives, each of which entails an amount of expected costs or (negative) return and a risk that the actual outcome is variant from the expectation. How much variance can be accepted? It depends on the decision-maker's attitude toward risk.

For the analysis of risk, several criteria can be used. One is to choose the choice alternative for which the lowest possible return is greatest. This approach assumes a very conservative attitude towards risk on the part of the decision-maker. On the other hand, one could choose the alternative for which the highest possible return is greatest, thus demonstrating a very aggressive risk attitude. Another approach is to rank order the choice alternatives in terms of their expected returns. Under this method, it is necessary to compute the mathematical expectation of return for each alternative and choose that alternative which yields the greatest expected return. A choice criterion based on central measures such as expected return, however, has been criticized for not recognizing the spread of potential outcomes (i.e., the risk factor).

To explicitly recognize risk without any *a priori* assumption of the risk attitude, it is necessary to incorporate both the central tendency measure and variance of the probability distribution of return into the analysis. This approach has been used in selected problems of foreign exchange management as they were discussed earlier.

Once risk is recognized, it becomes a critical decision variable in the sense that among the (feasible) choice alternatives which have the same expected return, the one which has the lowest level of risk will be the efficient one. Conversely, among the alternatives which have the same degree of risk, the efficient choice will be the alternative which has the highest expected return. Thus, there may exist a set of efficient alternatives compared to any one of which there is no other alternative which gives either (a) a higher expected return and the same degree of risk, or (b) a lower degree of risk and the same expected return. The problem then is to select the efficient alternative which is consistent with the decision-maker's attitude towards risk.

It was shown earlier that Lietaer had used the mean-variance framework in his analysis and had described the firm's attitude towards risk by way of a quadratic utility function on the assumption that an individual—such as the Treasurer—would make foreign exchange decisions.[7] However, it has been pointed out that quadratic utility is subject to some serious limitations as to its description of rational economic behavior. In addition, it is an empirical question as to whether a firm's attitude towards risk—if it has one—can be equated to any individual's attitude. If it cannot, or should not, then, how can it be incorporated into the analysis?

Obviously, this analytical process requires reliable data and information systems to collect and communicate them to the decision-maker(s) in the firm. It is axiomatic that the value of a defensive strategy depends on the data input and the analytical process that generates it.

The above discussion of the various elements of the conceptual model depicted in Figure 1 points to the importance of their roles and the relationships among them in the foreign exchange management process.

Study Objectives

In the foregoing discussion, it has been shown that floating exchange rates and FASB 8 have important implications on defensive strategies and currency exposure measurement of multinational firms. In addition, a conceptual model descriptive of the process and the factors in foreign exchange management was outlined. Some of these factors have not received sufficient empirical investigation, while the others—most notably, effects of FASB 8, the information systems, and the analysis of risk-return trade-off—have not been explored empirically. Given the potential effects of multinational firms on national economies and foreign exchange markets, a better understanding of these aspects is urgently needed.

Therefore, the purpose of this research is to investigate and analyze these aspects of foreign exchange management, so that a model descriptive of the behavior of multinational firms under conditions of foreign exchange risks within the constraints of its environments can be formulated.

Toward this broad objective, the study investigates and analyzes (1) the process of and the factors involved in foreign exchange management of large U.S. multinational manufacturing firms; (2) the changes in their defensive strategies due to greater exchange rate variations; and (3) the effects of FASB 8 on their currency exposure measurement and defensive strategies. The limitation of the study to large U.S. multinational manufacturing firms will be discussed shortly.

More specifically, the research seeks to investigate and analyze:

1. The items included in the computation of currency exposures and the reasons for such inclusion
2. The foreign exchange management objective(s)
3. The factors which constrain defensive strategies
4. The defensive strategies employed to achieve the objective(s), and changes in defensive strategies due to greater exchange rate variations
5. The items that had/had not been included in the computation of currency exposures and the defensive strategies that had/had not been used but now are/are not as a result of FASB 8
6. The information systems to collect the data on future exchange rates, currency exposures, and risk/cost consequences of the defensive strategies
7. The procedures and/or organization to analyze, evaluate, and select defensive strategies with consideration for their risk-return trade-offs

To express the study's objectives more specifically, the following research questions are posed.

Main Research Questions

1. What are the factors involved in the foreign exchange management of large U.S. multinational manufacturing firms, and how are these factors related?
2. What are the changes in their defensive strategies due to greater exchange rate variations?
3. What are the effects of FASB 8 on their currency exposure measurement and defensive strategies?

Subsidiary Research Questions

1. What are the items included in the computation of currency exposures and the reasons for such inclusion?
2. What are the transactions covered?
3. What are their foreign exchange management objectives?
4. What are the factors which constrain their defensive strategies?
5. What are the defensive strategies employed to achieve these objectives?
6. What are the defensive strategies which had/had not been used in the fixed exchange rate system but were/were not under floating exchange rates?
7. What are the defensive strategies which had been used in the fixed exchange rate system and which were also used under floating exchange rates, but more/less frequently?
8. What are the items that were/were not included in the computation of currency exposures and the defensive strategies that were/were not used, but now are/are not, as a result of FASB 8?
9. What are the information systems to collect the data on future exchange rates, currency exposures, and risk/cost consequences of the defensive strategies?
10. What are the procedures and/or organization used to analyze, evaluate, and select defensive strategies with consideration for their risk/return trade-offs?

Scope and Limitations

So that the effects of floating exchange rates and FASB 8 can be isolated and that the study is of a manageable size, the variables "firm size" and "firm activity" are held constant. For various reasons, they may exert influence on foreign exchange management of U.S. multinational firms.

Firm size. Past studies indicated that size of a company affects its financial actions and defensive strategies in a number of ways.

In a study by Stobaugh concerning the factors which influence the organization of the financial function and the practices of subsidiary financing, it was found that the "medium" firms made greater use of the system optimization approach than the "small" and "large" firms. This was evidenced by the continuous stream of instructions to the subsidiaries on both short- and long-term financing problems. In contrast, the "large" firms leaned toward system optimization but were too large to implement this strategy. The relative independence of the "small" firms seemed to stem from the fact that they had limited central staff. Also, there was a marked difference between the "medium" firms, on the one hand, and "small" and "large" firms on the other, with respect to the methods of subsidiary financing. For example, the "medium" firms were less likely to use intra-company accounts as an instrument of subsidiary financing.[8]

In Stobaugh's study, it was also found that there was a high correlation between total sales and the ratio of foreign sales to total sales.[9] In Jadwani's study, the data indicated that firms with a high ratio of foreign sales to total sales tended to make greater use of forward contracts as a defensive strategy.[10]

Furthermore, since large companies possess greater resources than smaller firms (for example, size of staff), any possible effects of resource constraints can be excluded by holding firm size constant.

Under these circumstances, it seems appropriate to concentrate the investigation on large multinational firms. The terms "large" and "multinational" will be defined in the section on Research Methodology.

Firm activity. The research questions addressed in this study are not to be directed to companies in the extractive industries or those engaged in trade and service activities. The latter companies are excluded because some of the problems discussed do not concern them as much as the manufacturing companies. For example, their nonmonetary assets overseas do not form a sizable part of their total foreign assets. On the other hand, companies in the extractive industries are subject to a higher overall risk (e.g., political, expropriation, nationalization, etc.), and pricing for their products (e.g., copper, petroleum) is often subject to international political pressures. Any of these factors could interfere with their defensive strategies. In addition, U.S. overseas investments have been heavily concentrated in the manufacturing sector. In Europe, U.S. investments in manufacturing at year-end of 1975 accounted for over 50 percent of the total while the investments in the extractive industries, including petroleum and mining, were less than 25 percent.[11]

For these reasons, the emphasis in this research will be placed on multinational firms engaged in manufacturing activities.

Other restrictions on the scope of the study are FASB 8 and hypotheses.

FASB 8. This study does not seek to question the validity or the merits of FASB 8's currency accounting rules. Only their effects on the subject companies are analyzed.

Hypotheses. This study is not aimed at testing hypotheses. Actually, its objective is to discover the relevant variables and the relationships among them so that hypotheses can be generated.

In addition, the study is subject to the following limitations: data, data measurement, and sampling methodology.

Data. The data obtained for this study were collected in personal interviews with the financial officers at the headquarters of a sample of the subject companies. To the extent that their subsidiaries' actions are not communicated to the headquarters, the data do not reflect this discrepancy.

Furthermore, the data may contain "noise." However, attempts were made to reduce this "noise" to a minimum by using probing questions, interviewing with more than one executive where possible, personal interviews with foreign exchange consultants and international bankers, and by comparing the findings with past empirical studies.

Data measurement. Part of this study is addressed to the frequency in the use of defensive strategies, by using the four-category scale (i.e., always, usually, occasionally, never). While this measurement is not completely unambiguous, given the unavailability of the dollar amounts, there is no real solution to this problem. However, the findings in this study are combined with past research to provide an indication of the use of such strategies.

Sampling methodology. The sample of companies is not selected randomly. Therefore, the findings may not be representative of the population of large multinational manufacturing firms. However, care has been taken to include in the sample a cross-section of companies in the sample, and where possible, writings and/or seminar lectures of financial executives of other firms in the population were consulted to verify the data. Additionally, the frequency distribution was discussed with the consultants and international bankers. This last procedure was found to be very useful in several areas of the study. In fact, several executives were subsequently re-interviewed resulting in some changes in the data.

In conclusion, thanks to these supplemental procedures, these limitations are believed to have no significant effect on the findings, insofar as the objectives of the study are concerned.

Importance of the Study

Problems of foreign exchange have always been a concern to multinational firms. However, with the emergence of floating exchange rates, foreign exchange risks with associated greater uncertainty have become more of a problem and attendance to it has absorbed a greater amount of companies' resources.

Multinational firms' response to these problems, on the other hand, have been a key issue in the debate over the advantages and disadvantages of the fixed exchange rate system versus those under floating exchange rates. Monetary authorities and participants in international monetary affairs have been concerned over the effects of alternative exchange rate regimes on international trade in which multinational firms have a substantial share. And the actions of multinational firms in response to foreign exchange risks in turn have profound effects on foreign exchange markets.

Now the Financial Accounting Standards Board prescribed changes in the ways multinational firms report and account for the effects of foreign exchange on their earnings to their shareholders. These currency accounting rule changes could lead companies to take actions which may not be consistent with their economic objectives, therefore affecting resource allocation in the economy.

Notwithstanding the concern over foreign exchange risks on the part of multinational firms, and the profound implications of their actions, the previous detailed review of the existing literature specific to foreign exchange management reveals an extensive attention to conceptual and normative issues, yet a severe lack of empirical knowledge of the process and factors involved in this financial activity. Although this gap between theoretical and empirical understanding has been somewhat reduced in recent years, much remains to be learned in several important areas. Most notable are (1) How companies measure their economic exposure; (2) What are their economic (transaction) objectives, not just accounting; (3) How frequently they use a certain defensive strategy (all companies may use a defensive strategy, but if they only use it occasionally, the impact might be less significant than when a lesser number of much larger companies use it extensively); (4) How companies approach the problem of risk analysis and what procedures/organization do they establish to make decisions under uncertainty; (5) What information systems do they set up to collect the data on currency exposures and how do they develop foreign exchange forecasts; and (6) How do companies cope with floating exchange rates and FASB 8. On the last three issues, their importance notwithstanding, despite an extensive literature search which includes doctoral dissertations and unpublished studies, this researcher could not uncover any sampling study which empirically addresses these questions. As to floating exchange rates, exceptions are Fieleke's studies, but they are limited by a narrower scope, conducted before floating exchange rates became generalized, did not provide a strategy-by-strategy comparison, and used mail questionnaires.[12] Jilling's study, on the other hand, only provides a static depiction of companies' practices in 1975, did not sufficiently address several important aspects of this subject matter, as pointed out in the literature review, and suffered some methodological problems by using mail questionnaires.[13]

By undertaking this study which investigates all of the above questions, it is hoped that the research will shed more light on them and provide a better understanding thereof. Hopefully, this will contribute to the building of more realistic theories and/or improving the realism of existing theories on foreign exchange management. In fact, this is one of the reasons which underlie the selection of Fortune 100 companies for investigation. It is hoped that because of their large size, available resources, and the scope of their operations, hence the magnitude of their foreign exchange problems, their experience will provide a state-of-the-art understanding of foreign exchange management practices, an indication of "What can be done in reality?" and can serve as a potential model for other firms to follow.

Furthermore, it is hoped that the results of this study will provide a better understanding of the implications of accounting rules on economic behavior. Regulatory agencies such as the Financial Accounting Standards Board can draw various policy implications from the study's findings for accounting rulemaking and regulating firms' public disclosure.

In addition, given a better understanding of the effects of alternative international monetary systems on multinational firms and vice versa, government and international monetary authorities can derive various policy implications for their international monetary management and reform work.

Methodology

The following discussion will lay out the research methodology and method of data collection.

Data

The data to be collected in the empirical research are:

1. the assets, liabilities, and transactions included in the computation of currency exposures; the reasons for such inclusion; the transactions which are not included in the currency exposures but are covered (hedged)
2. the foreign exchange management objectives expressed in qualitative or quantitative forms
3. the factors which constrain defensive strategies
4. the defensive strategies and changes in them
5. the data collected and how they are organized and used
6. the procedures to analyze, evaluate, and select defensive strategies;

the personnel involved; and the formal or work-related relationships among them

Item (4) needs some clarification. To investigate and analyze the changes in defensive strategies due to greater exchange rate uncertainty, it is necessary to determine which strategies had/had not been used in the fixed rate system, but were/were not used under floating exchange rates.[14] If a strategy has been used in both exchange rate regimes, the frequencies of its use in them are compared. As the frequency is measured by the four-category scale (always, usually, occasionally, never), in this case, if the frequency is increased by one scale (for example, from "occasionally" to "usually"), the increase is said to be "significant" and so classified. For comparison of changes in defensive strategies before and after FASB 8, the same classification scheme also prevails. Although this classification is not entirely unambiguous, the findings in these respects are compared with past studies, when available, so that some indication of the changes can be established.

Sources of Data

There are two sources of data: primary and secondary.

Primary sources
The primary sources are the companies subject to this study, that is, the population.

Population
The population is determined by firm size, firm activity, and scope of operations. The reason for using these criteria to define the population were explained in "Scope and Limitations."

Firm activity and scope of operations. The subjects of this study are large U.S. multinational manufacturing firms. "U.S. multinational manufacturing firms" are defined as those firms which are listed on "The 1977 Fortune Directory of the 500 Largest U.S. Industrial Corporations" (Fortune 500 List) providing they have manufacturing subsidiaries in at least six foreign countries. This definition was adopted in many of the recent studies on multinational firms.[15] In addition, manufacturing is defined loosely to include assembly plant, production and processing facilities, etc.

Firm size. A "large U.S. multinational manufacturing firm" is defined as a U.S. multinational manufacturing firm among the top 100 companies on the 1977 Fortune 500 List (the 1977 Fortune 100 List).

By examination of the list of 187 multinational firms compiled by Vaupel and Curhan,[16] and 10-K reports of 25 companies, 62 companies were found to be qualified as "large U.S. multinational manufacturing firms" for the purposes of this study. That is, the population of this study is one-third of Vaupel and Curham's list. Their total sales in 1976, however, slightly exceeded one-third of the 1976 total sales of the 1977 Fortune 500 companies (including the petroleum and nonmultinational firms).

Sample

Ten large U.S. multinational manufacturing firms were selected for inclusion in the sample. Hereafter, these firms are referred to as "the sampled companies." Of the sample companies, five belong to the upper half of the population and five to the lower half. In comparison to the 1977 Fortune 100 companies, the size of the sampled companies is indicated in Table 5.

Table 5
Size of the Sampled Companies

	First Quartile	Second Quartile	Third Quartile	Fourth Quartile	Total
Number in the sampled companies	1	4	3	2	10

In addition, the sampled companies were engaged in nine different industries—as defined in the 1977 Fortune 500 List—three of which are known to be capital intensive. Of these nine industry groupings, four required advanced technology in the manufacturing and engineering process. These sampled companies are also engaged in a variety of activities, from consumer products to capital goods marketed to both the private and public sector.

It was pointed out in the discussion of FASB 8 that a company's method of currency accounting before FASB 8, and the magnitude of the effects of FASB 8 on its reported earnings, could influence its behavior with respect to currency exposure measurement and defensive strategies in a number of ways. In order to study the effects of FASB 8 more objectively, the following groups of companies were included in the sample:

1. Those which used the monetary-nonmonetary method of translation (MNM companies) versus those which did not (Non-MNM companies).

2. Those which reported significant impact by FASB 8 on their reported earnings versus those which did not. (For the purposes of this study, "significant impact" is an impact of +5% or greater.)

In terms of currency accounting practices before FASB 8, the sample has the characteristics shown in Table 6.

Method of sample selection

Random sampling procedures are not used in this study because it appeared that the chance for companies which used the MNM method of translation, and for companies which reported significant FASB 8 impact on their 1975 earnings, would be at best 20 percent and 40 percent, respectively. An examination of 10-K reports of 25 companies yielded the results that seven companies had used the MNM method and four reported significant FASB 8 impact. The study by Rodriguez provided support for these estimates.[17] In other words, random sampling does not guarantee the inclusion of the MNM companies and those which reported significant FASB 8 impact. Another practical consideration is that random sampling does not guarantee accessibility to the would-be selected companies or that they would be willing to divulge the needed information. In addition, this study does not aim at testing hypotheses, but seeks to uncover the relevant variables and the relationships among them. For these reasons, quota sampling was used to generate the sample of companies to be interviewed. It goes without saying that this sampling procedure does not produce a representative sample in the strictly statistical sense of the word. This sample of companies, however, contains a cross-section of large U.S. multinational manufacturing firms subject to this study.

The sample size is limited to 16 percent of the population so that given the limited resources a larger quantity of in-depth data can be collected rather than to collect a lesser amount of data from a larger number of companies. This method of data collection is believed to be more appropriate for this kind of study, especially in view of the problems encountered in mail surveys. To verify the appropriateness of the sample size, past empirical studies were reviewed. It was found that this sample's size is greater than that of Jadwani's study,[18] comparable to the sample in Fieleke's mail survey,[19] and in some important respects would yield a higher response rate than that obtained in Jilling's mail questionnaire study.[20]

Other primary and secondary sources

In addition to personal interviews, another source of data were the sampled companies' internal reports/documents relating to their foreign exchange management activities, and their published quarterly, annual, and 10-K reports. To verify the reliability of the data collected from the sampled

Table 6
Currency Accounting Practices Before FASB 8

	Number of companies which used MNM method	Number of companies which reported significant FASB 8 impact[a]	Number of companies which did not use MNM methods and did not report significant FASB 8 impact
	% sample	% sample	% sample
This sample	20%	40%	40%
Pakkala[b]	18%	n/a	n/a
Rodriguez[c]	13% [d]	20%[e]	n/a

Source: 10-K reports of the companies.

[a] "significant FASB 8" means an impact on reported earnings of ± 5% or greater. The base year was 1975 for two companies; 1974 and 1976 respectively for the other two.

[b] Pakkala, "Foreign Exchange Accounting," Table 1, p. 35.

[c] Rodriguez, "FASB No. 8," Exhibit 5, p. 45.

[d] 13 companies of a 70-company sample.

[e] 3 out of 23 companies which reported some FASB 8 impact.

companies, five professionals active in foreign exchange advisory consulting and international banking were interviewed. Also, results from past empirical studies, such as the mail survey by the University of South Carolina are compared with the results of this study.

Method of Data Collection

It is obvious that the types of data required for this study can be collected only by survey methods. The personal interview is chosen instead of mail survey because of several important advantages.

Low percentage of returns. Low percentage of returns—or response rate—is the major disadvantage of mail surveys. This problem is especially serious in mail surveys of foreign exchange management practices. In the mail survey by Jilling and Folks,[21] the response rate was 27 percent—yet it can be considered large given the length and complexity of the questionnaire. However, the number of "no response" was uncomfortably high in many instances. For example, questions regarding "bases for division of responsibility" obtained 30 responses (28 percent of the sample);[22] "calculation of the dollar cost of a foreign currency loan," 73 responses (68 percent);[23] "comparison of the cost of forward contracts with the cost of reducing exposures by changing the 'natural' position of balance sheets," 71 responses (66 percent).[24] In the study by Fieleke of the float of the German mark, the response rate was less than 19 percent.[25]

Uniformity of meaning. An example of the problem in mail surveys is the phrase "minimize foreign exchange losses." As Rodriguez discovered, it has different meanings to different people.[26] The personal interview, however, helped overcome this problem by allowing for probing for clarification of the meanings of such phraseologies.

Flexibility and in-depth probing. In these respects, the personal interview definitely has an advantage over mail surveys.

Size of sample. In this respect, past mail surveys of foreign exchange management practices do not have an overwhelming advantage over the personal interview. In some instances, such as those indicated above, the personal interview is even more advantageous.

In this study, the technique of "focused interview" is combined with an interview schedule which consists of a series of "funnel sets" (i.e., a series of general questions each of which was followed by specific follow-up questions). (See Appendix A.) This technique is believed to be more advantageous than a purely structured or unstructured interview. It also helps to verify the reliability and internal consistency of the data.

It should be pointed out that this interview schedule was subjected to two different tests conducted in two separate pilot studies. In the first pilot study, the original version was used to interview four executives at three companies, two of which were qualified as "large U.S. multinational manufacturing firms" for the purposes of this study. (Actually, the other company was a multinational manufacturing firm on the 1976 Fortune 100 List. It was, however, dropped from the 1977 list.) The revised interview schedule then was subjected to another test in two interviews at another multinational manufacturing firm which was not qualified as a "large" company. Nevertheless, it was among the top 250 companies on the 1977 Fortune 500 List. From this second pilot study, further revisions were made on the interview schedule. The final version is shown in Appendix A.

The results reported in this dissertation are obtained from a series of interviews conducted in the Spring and Summer of 1978. Most of the interviews were with two financial officers in each of the 10 companies, one of whom had the title equivalent to "Foreign Exchange Manager" or "Manager of International Finance," and the other was an Assistant Treasurer, Treasurer, or Vice President. Except in one case, in single interviews, the interviewees had the rank of Assistant Treasurer or above. In addition to face-to-face interviewing, there were also numerous follow-up interviews over the telephone, and on several occasions, at lunches. In all of these meetings, these financial officers were very cooperative and willing to discuss the issues in great detail; in fact, they all showed an intense interest in this subject area, and in this study, in particular. Furthermore, the results from these interviews were discussed with five foreign exchange consultants/international bankers with a better-known foreign exchange consulting firm and four major multinational banks (without disclosing the identities of the interviewees and their companies). The purpose was to help verify the data and to obtain an overall perspective of the foreign exchange management process.

With respect to the interviewer's bias, it should be noted that the interviewees were upper-rank business executives of large multinational firms, with years of business experience and college (if not graduate) education. Furthermore, most of the data to be collected are financial data.

Use of control groups, personal interviews with professionals active in foreign exchange management consulting, and comparison of the collected data with past empirical findings help assure that the data are valid.

Method of Data Analysis

For the analysis of the data, the technique of content analysis will be used. This refers to the objective, systematic, and quantitative description of the information obtained from the interviews. It involves the definition, classification or categorization, quantification, and interpretation of the data.

The classification scheme employs both dichotomies and serials. The former refers to the presence or absence of the attribute or item under consideration. The latter seeks to rank order the categories. In this respect, the four-category scale (i.e., always, usually, occasionally, and never) will be used in addition to dichotomies in the analysis of the changes in defensive strategies due to greater exchange rate variations.

For the interpretation of the data, the behavior of the sampled companies will be compared. The findings then will be compared with those from past studies and those derived from the interviews with foreign management consultants and international bankers.

To derive the implications of the empirical findings, the actual behavior of the sampled companies will be compared with the measures prescribed in the literature, and the consistency of their behavior vis-à-vis their objectives and constraints will be examined.

Chapter III

Currency Exposure Measurement, Objectives, Defensive Strategies, and Constraints

According to economic theory, a company's currency exposure is the discounted present value of its future cash flows. From this point of view, an exchange rate change not only affects the value of its existing assets, but also, and more importantly, its future earnings, i.e., its profitability as an ongoing business operation. Thus a currency exposure is the difference between the discounted present values of the earnings and cost streams. The principle, however, still remains in the domain of economic theory for there is not yet any acceptable method to operationalize it for either reporting or foreign exchange management purposes.

From the standpoint of FASB 8, the solution to this problem is straightforward. It is the algebraic sum of the dollar values of monetary assets, monetary liabilities, plus net income and depreciation and amortization expenses. In other words, it is simply the statement of income and balance sheet items that are translated into U.S. dollars at the current exchange rate.

As it can be expected, the purely economic approach to currency exposure measurement could not be found in practice.[1] On the other hand, the purely FASB 8 measurement is not practiced by all companies. The purpose of this part of the research is to examine the methodologies whereby the sampled companies define their currency exposures. Specifically, answers are sought for the following subsidiary research questions:

1. What are the items included in the computation of currency exposures and the reasons for such inclusion?
2. What are the transactions covered?

With an understanding of the currency exposure measurement, the discussion will be focused on the objectives of foreign exchange management. The subsidiary research question is:

3. What are their foreign exchange management objectives?

Subsequently, empirical findings will be presented on the companies' defensive strategies and the factors constraining them:

4.   What are the defensive strategies employed to achieve these objectives?

5.   What are the factors which constrain their defensive strategies?

Currency Exposure Measurement

In the original conceptualization of the foreign exchange management process, certain discrepancies between the accounting and economic approaches to currency exposure measurement were discussed. Accordingly, it was suggested that a definition of currency exposures is a critical starting step in the management of foreign exchange. It is a manifestation of a company's objectives and a framework for its reporting system and defensive strategies. However, due to the unresolved issues regarding the concept of economic exposure and the recognition by economists as well as practitioners that the accounting approach does not fully capture the effects of exchange rate changes on a foreign operation, it would be expected that the measurement of currency exposures would vary among firms. Additionally, as it was pointed out by a banker/foreign exchange consultant participating in this study, these differences would be reinforced by the fact that some firms are more sensitive to cash flows, others to reported earnings, and still others to "economic" gains/losses. Nevertheless, the empirical findings indicate that in practice these differences involve one or more of the following components.

Transaction exposure. This exposure component includes all foreign currency monetary assets and liabilities which are receivable/payable within one year on the overseas subsidiary's books. It thus includes foreign currency cash holdings, receivables and payables, and short-term debts. Also it includes current maturities of foreign currency long-term debts (i.e., that portion due within one year). Since all of the sampled firms' foreign exchange management planning horizon is within one year, these exposed items involve the conversion of funds from one currency to another during the relevant planning period, hence the risk of realized exchange gains/losses. However, it should be pointed out that before these receivables/payables are actually paid off, adjustments on them remain unrealized.

Translation exposure. Included in this exposure component are all monetary items denominated in the local currency on the overseas subsidiary's books. It also includes the long-term portion (not due within one year) of foreign currency long-term debts. These long-term maturities do not require conversion of funds during the relevant planning horizon. Therefore, the recorded exchange gain or loss is an accounting entry, not an economic event. As to local currency monetary assets and liabilities, their inclusion in the translation exposure is derived from the theory that as long as a change in the local currency's exchange rate does not lead to a change in the local currency receivables and payables such that more/less home currency funds are required, such assets and liabilities are not economically exposed.

Exposed earnings. This exposure component consists of net income plus expenses related to assets/liabilities that are translated at the historical rates of exchange, e.g., depreciation expenses. Again, there are translation and transaction (local and foreign currency) elements in this component. For this reason, it is classified separately from the transaction exposure. Actually, to the extent that part of the flows of revenues and expenses is reflected in either the translation or transaction exposure, the exposed earnings component overstates the total exposures. To illustrate, suppose all sales and purchases are on credit, then the difference between receivables and payables is "exposed earnings." Since part of exposed earnings is captured in the receivable and payable accounts which exist at the balance sheet date, this portion overstates the total exposure.

Inventory. Economically, inventory is exposed if price increases are not possible. Such a distinction, for the purpose of currency exposure measurement, was not found in practice among the companies. Instead, for a company which includes inventory in its currency exposure, either the total inventory or a portion thereof is considered exposed. This portion is calculated based on the turnover rate of inventory or the supply source (local versus foreign). An extension of the latter method is to differentiate inventory by the markets where it is sold, in addition to the distinction between local versus foreign sources. To the extent that it can be documented, only one company does this extended analysis and calls it the purchase-production method. All these methods indicate the portion of inventory of which the acquisition cost is affected by exchange rate changes, hence the eventual necessity of price changes. However, they do not directly link inventory acquisition costs to pricing flexibility (or lack thereof). In other words, inventory is considered exposed if a change in the exchange rate leads to an increase in the cost of inventory acquisition whether or not price increases can be effected.

Off-balance sheet assets and liabilities. These items consist primarily of confirmed orders and purchase commitments for which deliveries are not yet made (therefore, related sales or costs, and receivables or payables are not recorded in the books). If any of these unbooked assets and liabilities are denominated in foreign currencies, they will eventually become part of the transaction exposure. If they are denominated in the local currency, they will be included in the translation exposure. It should be noted that dividend remittances are not reflected in the statement of income and usually not recorded in the balance sheet. Thus they may be considered a part of the off-balance sheet items. However, due to the visibility of these remittances, they are treated as a separate transaction by the sampled firms, hence another exposure component.

Remittances of dividends. Since these payments require conversion of funds, they are a part of the transaction exposure, though separate from it, regardless of the currency of denomination.

By now it is well known that FASB 8 requires the translation of monetary assets/liabilities and revenue and expense items (except those related to assets and liabilities that are translated at historical rates) at the current rate of exchange. For this reason, it would seem appropriate to classify the translation and transaction exposure components, exposed earnings, and remittances of dividends in a category called "FASB 8 exposure." However, for ease of exposition, in this study the term signifies only the sum of the translation and transaction exposure. Putting it differently, it is the balance sheet exposure after FASB 8. Its equivalent before FASB 8 is defined according to the translation method that was then used. It should be noted that only 1 of the 10 sampled companies formally includes exposed earnings in its currency exposure. Furthermore, when a company includes either exposed earnings, inventory, off-balance sheet items or a combination thereof in its currency exposure (that is, it goes beyond FASB 8), it means the company attempts to measure the economic effects of exchange rate fluctuations. In the remainder of this section, the discussion is focused on how the sampled companies define their economic exposure to foreign exchange risks. It is worthy in this connection to reiterate that economic theory defines a currency exposure in terms of future cash flows.

As mentioned earlier, the differences in currency exposure measurement among the sampled companies do not fall along the accounting versus economic lines. They differ only to the extent that one or more of the above exposure components are excluded from their currency exposures. Thus, for example, two companies in the sample have an overall strategy of maintaining a neutral exposed position (although, in actuality, their exposures are not necessarily zero). Toward this objective, they have employed a variety of defensive strategies. In the first company, in reaching this position, it includes inventory in the definition of currency exposures. However, inventory is excluded in the other. Table 7 shows the extent of difference among the companies: all of the 10 companies include the translation and transaction components but differ in the treatment of the others.

However, the exclusion of dividend remittances and the differences in accounting for the other exposure components are actually more apparent than real.

As to remittances of dividends and those off-balance sheet items that require conversion of funds, timing of fund transfers—for payments of dividends—and natural matching of flows to some extent reduce the exposed amounts. For example, one company has purchases denominated in Japanese yen which are largely offset by its licensing income denominated in the same currency. Another company has long-term purchase and sale contracts which significantly offset one another. To the extent that such natural matching does

Table 7
Currency Exposure Measurement

Exposure Component Included in Currency Exposure	Number of Companies
Translation exposure	10[a]
Transaction exposure	10
Exposed earnings	1
Inventory	5[b]
Off-balance sheet assets/liabilities	1
Remittances of dividends	0

[a] Six companies adjust this exposure component for income tax effects.

[b] Four companies move back and forth between the inclusion and exclusion of this exposure component.

not exist or is insufficient, or that timing of fund transfers is not possible because of tax considerations, they take out forward exchange contracts to cover
the exposed amounts. Table 8 shows the extent of forward contract hedging on
these off-balance sheet items.

Table 8
Use of Forward Exchange Contracts to Cover Off-Balance Sheet Items

	Frequency				Sample Size
	Never	Occasionally	Usually	Always	
Number of Companies	1	3	4	2	10

The exclusion of the exposed earnings component in most companies, on
the other hand, does not appear to be a serious distortion of the currency exposure. As pointed out earlier, to the extent that sales and purchases are reflected in the receivables and payables, this component tends to overstate the
exposure. Furthermore, since exposed earnings also include sales and purchases
denominated in foreign currencies (i.e., payments/receipts from import/export
transactions and off-balance sheet items), active hedging of these transactions,
as it is true in most companies (see "Defensive Strategies" of this chapter)
effectively eliminates that portion of exposed earnings denominated in foreign
currencies. Indeed, follow-up interviews with several of the executives indicated that, given the above, exposed earnings does not constitute a significant
part of their companies' overall exposure, although they agreed that technically
this component is exposed to currency fluctuations.[2]

With regard to inventory, the differences reflect the foreign exchange
management objectives of the companies, rather than their operating characteristics or theoretical justification. In other words, all of the 10 companies
consider inventory exposed. They differ, however, as to the amount of inventory
to be included in their currency exposure definition. Five companies account
for the total amount of inventory. The reason for this practice was well explained by one executive.

Analytically you may say that if your inventory fluctuates, only the volatile portion
of inventory would be exposed. Yet, in the case of [this company] you don't want
to do that because our inventory fluctuates pretty widely. So that kind of inventory,
it seems to me, is exposed. Now, of course, you do have FASB rules that if the product is of volatile price, then the inventory should be written off to the current price.

In which case, it is exposed. Furthermore, there is the ruling that if there is a large change in the exchange rate, then inventory is in effect exposed in the same way. As you know in accounting, if there is a small change in prices, you don't have to revalue your inventory. But if there is a large change in prices, you do. And now this is being applied also to the foreign exchange.

This situation is a result of the accounting treatment of inventory. According to FASB 8, inventory is translated at historical rates, therefore, no translation effects are recorded to recognize the changes of inventory values due to exchange rate movements. Thus, for a company which is concerned with translation adjustments, inventory is excluded from the currency exposure measurement. On the other hand, due to the "lower of cost or market" rule, inventory write-down is required when a devaluation occurs. In the opposite case, i.e., appreciation, inventory write-up is not allowed. Nevertheless, since cost of goods sold are computed on a historical basis and sales are translated at the current rate, gross margin is increased to the extent of the appreciation (assuming local currency prices are not changed); thus, the effects on inventory are passed through the statement of income over time, rather than recognized in the period when the rate change occurs. In other words, regardless of FASB 8's treatment of inventory, earnings are affected. Recognizing this problem, the above five companies include inventory in their currency exposures.

Of these five companies, only one has consistently managed its foreign exchange with inventory taken into account. In fact, it has "usually" taken out forward exchange contracts to hedge its FASB 8 exposure plus inventory. For the other four companies, most of the times, they managed their foreign exchange with inclusion of inventory. However, a neutral exposure strategy based on this definition would necessarily result in an FASB 8 exposure: (translated) earnings will fluctuate with exchange rate changes. For this reason, at times they have excluded inventory from their currency exposure measurement in an attempt to maintain stability of their reported earnings. In fact, three of these companies have "occasionally" used forward exchange contracts to hedge their FASB 8 exposure. The other company has not had to take this action (these four companies do not use forward exchange contracts to cover inventory), but its Treasurer indicated that it is possible, given the right circumstances, i.e., if its reported earnings are sufficiently impacted by exchange rate fluctuations.

Of the five remaining companies, one includes in its currency exposure that portion of inventory calculated on the basis of the turn-over rate. This practice is adopted because its auditors allow the translation of this portion of inventory at the current rate of exchange. This compromise thus enables the company to increase its exposed monetary assets. The other four companies exclude inventory but are well conscious of the effects of exchange rate changes on this component. In fact, three of them show inventory on their exposure reports as a memo item and calculate their exposure with and without inventory. However, since they have experienced significant adverse impact by FASB 8, they have been exclusively FASB 8 oriented in defining their balance sheet exposure in an attempt to stabilize the reported earnings.

In this connection, it is interesting to note the use of the strategy of "inventory level adjustment" in these companies. Table 9 shows the frequency in the use of this strategy by those companies which include inventory and those which do not.

Table 9
Adjustment of Inventory Level for Defensive Purposes

Type of Company	Never	Occasionally	Usually	Always	Total
		Frequency			
With inventory	3		2		5
With portion of inventory	1				1
Without inventory		3	1		4
Sample size					10

As to long-term debts, the companies believe that they are exposed to exchange rate fluctuations. It should be noted that if the Fisher Effect holds true, i.e., foreign exchange gains/losses are offset by more/less interest costs, one might argue that long-term debts are not exposed. A problem in making this distinction lies in the accounting of interest costs and foreign exchange adjustment on long-term debts; they are segregated. Furthermore, large exchange rate fluctuations can lead to volatility of reported earnings.

> . . . take the Canadian dollar issue. You would report 10 million losses in one year, 5 the next, a gain of 5 the next, and a loss of 10 the next year, etc. . . . Let's say the net effect over the life of the debt issue was a loss of 5 million. But over time there were reported gains and losses which have added to the volatility of your income. That can be a problem. I think you have to measure management performance over a significant amount of time.

The same reasoning is applied to the monetary assets and liabilities of the translation exposure:

> We have come around to the point of view that in reality the so-called translation losses are real losses over time and that if they continue they will, in effect, be translated into real losses. I think in the past year we have come around more and more to be more flexible to deal with our translation problems rather than letting them take care of themselves.

Interestingly enough, although all the sampled companies share this view of the local currency monetary assets and liabilities, they are reluctant to take out forward exchange contracts to cover this exposure. In fact, five companies have a policy of not using this defensive strategy for balance sheet hedging. A reason is the widely-held belief of the non-cash nature of the balance sheet exposure, i.e., cash flows are not affected when the exchange adjustments on the balance sheet accounts are recorded. Thus, the companies are not quite willing to risk cash losses on a forward exchange contract to avert a potential accounting loss. Such forward exchange losses could be substantial since there is always the possibility that the currency moves into the direction opposite to the forecast one. For example, if the pound sterling is forecast to appreciate from $1.80 to $1.90, and the forward rate is $1.85 but the spot rate at the maturity date turns out to $1.75, a pound sterling purchase contract will net a cash loss of $.10 on every pound, as opposed to a translation gain of $.05—for a company with a net liability in pound sterling. Of course, the before-tax cash loss is double if the tax effect—assuming a 50 percent tax rate[3]—is considered before engaging in the contract. (Six of the sampled companies adjust their exposures for such tax effects.) Further complicating the matter is that balance sheet hedging by forward exchange contracts could require a contract amount greater than the exposure—in this example, it would be twice as large, assuming the forecast is correct—to offset the expected translation loss. The contract amount so determined then would have to be further increased if tax effects are adjusted. In this case, the total contract amount would be four times as large as the translation exposure if after-tax forward exchange gain is to offset the $.10 translation loss. All of these adjustments which could result in substantial cash losses are necessary only to protect an accounting loss, hence a reluctance on the part of the companies to use forward exchange markets to hedge balance sheet exposure. In contrast, such complexities do not exist in the case of foreign currency transactions. Table 10 shows the frequency in the use of forward exchange contracts for balance sheet hedging by the sampled companies.

From the foregoing discussion, it is evident that the sampled companies go beyond the balance sheet to get at the overall effects of exchange rate

Table 10
Use of Forward Exchange Contracts for Balance Sheet Hedging

	Frequency				Sample Size
	Never	Occasionally	Usually	Always	
Number of Companies	4	5	1	0	10

changes. In this respect, there is almost complete agreement among the companies as to what items/transactions should be included in the currency exposure, notwithstanding the apparent differences in the formal definition. As noted, the exclusion of inventory in four companies stems from their concern for earnings fluctuations, not because they consider inventory not exposed. Another company includes a portion of its inventory (based on the turn-over rate) because its auditors allow such an interpretation of FASB 8's application in this regard. Thus, exactly half of the sample of companies follow FASB 8 to define their currency exposure insofar as the balance sheet is concerned. Interestingly, one consultant said that this distribution is just about what he would have guessed from the contacts with his bank's corporate clients.

Beyond the balance sheet, the companies attempt to get at the economic effects of exchange rate fluctuations by consideration for off-balance sheet items, such as confirmed orders. From the evidence of the use of forward exchange contracts for hedging on off-balance sheet items, it is concluded that 9 of the 10 companies use this approach for assessment of the economic effects.

The number of firms which adjust for their formal definition of currency exposure appears to be significantly larger than that obtained in Jilling's sample.[4] He reported that of the 107 respondents, 19.6 percent indicated that they always adjusted for their basic balance sheet exposure, while 28 percent sometimes did so. Since this author did not differentiate the company's size, it is not known how large companies acted in this regard. Furthermore, it is not known from Jilling's analysis as to what transactions most of these companies used to adjust the balance sheet for at least 71 percent of the respondents, and as much as 91.6 percent, did not answer some part of his question on the subject.

However, discussions with three foreign exchange consultants on this aspect of the research indicated that this measurement of currency exposure (balance sheet accounts plus off-balance sheet items) is prevalent among large multinational firms. One consultant specifically cited the example of another large multinational firm (not included in this sample) which follows this approach.

As it has been noted, this method of currency exposure measurement is divergent from economic theory. This situation can perhaps be best summed up by quoting one executive:

> I am not aware of the concept of economic exposure because nobody in my mind has ever defined what economic exposure is. I have heard many definitions. I am not a great believer in chopping the pie that way. I just really don't think that it makes all that much sense. We have to live with the fact that FASB 8 exists. I think that FASB 8 is not the ultimate wisdom. I think they should definitely change the inventory calculation and I also think that they will very well do that. But for the time being, that is the way it is, and that is the way we have to account for it. I think from a management point of view, you have to manage the company's financial affairs in such a way that substantial gains and losses should not arise because of FASB 8.

Foreign Exchange Management Objectives

As the preceding analysis of the method of currency exposure measurement might have suggested, all of the sampled companies are concerned to a large degree with the effects of currency fluctuations on their reported earnings. Therefore, not surprisingly, their objectives have been to minimize foreign exchange losses. This statement, however, is more applicable to translation effects than to gains/losses arising from foreign currency transactions. Also, it does not reveal the compromise that some companies have often had to make between economic versus accounting impacts.

Translation adjustments, a policy objective that is uniformly applicable to all of the companies, requires that these adjustments be kept at a minimum. More strongly and specifically, in this regard, the objective is to avoid losses and fluctuations of earnings due to exchange rate changes. One executive simply states that the objective of his company is "to avoid losses in foreign currency translation." More precisely,

> The overall objective is to make money. As far as the Treasury Department is concerned, specifically the foreign exchange management side of it, our directive is preservative and it is to avoid losing money. I think this applies specifically to the balance sheet exposure management side of things.

In a different fashion,

> Our objectives are to minimize losses to the corporation and to prevent any undue surprises, as the desire of management is to maintain very steady earnings.

However stated, clearly the companies' foreign exchange management objectives, at least as far as translation adjustments are concerned, are of a defensive nature. One company went as far as considering foreign exchange losses as another cost of doing business overseas. There are at least three reasons for this defensive posture. First is the desire to maintain stability. Since there is a belief that the stock market rewards companies having steadily increased earnings, it is not surprising that the companies are concerned with the effects of currency fluctuations on their reported profits. Second, translation adjustments are non cash gains/losses. As a result for this consideration, the companies are generally reluctant to use forward exchange contracts for balance sheet hedging. Third, it is difficult to adjust balance sheet structure for balance sheet hedging purposes. As it was repeatedly pointed out by several executives, "to change a balance sheet takes a lot of time."

The defensive posture is somewhat abated when it comes to transaction gains/losses. Generally, the companies will take advantage of opportunities for making a profit on foreign exchange transactions when they present themselves, but not to the extent of using high-risk strategies, such as commodity futures contracts. Actually, the terminology that was used by some executives to describe their companies' objective in this regard is to "come out ahead." Others used more specific phraseologies: one said "to make a profit in the foreign exchange transactions"; another described: "In the transaction exposure management, if we feel that we can improve our dollar return on a projected dividend, we can be a little more aggressive."

A reason for this more aggressive attitude is the cash nature of these transactions which justifies the use of forward exchange contracts to cover them. Additionally, it was explained, this defensive strategy is more flexible as compared to the others.

However, the overall objective of foreign exchange management in the companies is still minimization of foreign exchange losses. This objective is further strengthened by the belief that the companies are not in the foreign exchange trading business. One executive said:

> The people who are making money in this thing are traders trading where you can shift your position every hour and be in and out and play the market. There is no way we can even attempt to do that. That is not our business.

Yet, there is a conflict between the reported earnings (accounting) objective and economic performance. For the companies which have opted for the FASB 8 approach (five companies), or the one which chose to disregard FASB 8 altogether, the conflict is either manageable or nonexistent. For the other companies, the conflict is an ongoing phenomenon, and one which is difficult to solve and often attracts the involvement of the highest level of management, i.e., Chairman of the Board. One executive described this conflict as follows:

> One major objective is to keep a balanced position on an economic basis . . . but because we are a manufacturing company, we are generally long when we add back inventory. As a consequence, we are mindful of the exchange rate because of the short balance sheet position, although we are mindful that we are likely to earn back in subsequent quarters what we might lose on the balance sheet.

Even when a company is primarily FASB 8 oriented in its foreign exchange management, it is still conscious of the fact that there exists a concept of economic exposure—although there is disagreement as to its definition. The Assistant Treasurer in one such company, which is going through a reorganization in its foreign exchange management function, principally as a result of FASB 8, described the situation in the following way:

> The purpose would be to minimize losses. And I don't want to define the losses, because it could be economic losses or accounting losses; but to minimize losses, due to the fluctuations of foreign currencies against the U.S. dollar. You could drive about six trucks through that definition.

In another company, the conflict is partially resolved by its attempt to neutralize its FASB 8 exposure on an annual basis, rather than on a quarterly basis.

Further aggravating the problem is the absence of specific guidelines from top management. Where such policy guidelines exist—only 2 of the 10 companies have a formal, written foreign exchange management policy—they tend to be ambiguous, and therefore, depend on the interpretation from the treasury executives. In one company,

> A written policy exists. It is very short and states that the foreign exchange exposure management be geared toward the avoidance of unusual gains or losses. In practice, if there exist opportunities to come ahead on transactions, we would do it, but not to the extent of creating exposed positions that are not covered by real transactions.

In the other company, notwithstanding a formal policy of foreign exchange management on an economic basis, it occasionally takes out forward exchange contracts to cover its FASB 8 exposure. However, in one company, despite the absence of a formal policy, the mission objective seems to be clearly understood by the treasury department: "Our threshold, I would say, is one million dollars per year per currency. That applies to translation only." Such a clear, though not formally stated objective, nevertheless seems to be an exception rather than the rule. And perhaps it should not be so precisely stated. One executive explained the difficulty of fixing what he called the "pain threshold" in his company:

It is very, very subjective. We do not have a figure. At one time, I tried to get a figure and someone said two million dollars, but I never found out from him, whether he meant two million dollars per currency, or two millions dollars per annum, or what. I can tell you, at the present time, that the decision on a meaningful amount depends on many things, including what the overall earnings of the Company are for the quarter in question. If we foresee a very good quarter, we might be inclined to take, say, somewhat greater risks or to spend less on precautions on currency fluctuations, because if we take out forward contracts, you know you do run the risk of accepting a cash loss to protect an accounting gain. In our case, the amount that we would be prepared to lose, if necessary, would certainly run into several million dollars. But I couldn't be more precise than that.

Another executive said:

We don't feel comfortable at this point in time in trying to cast anything in concrete. Our situation is, between our manufacturing operations, licensing income, royalty income, quite different types of business, it's very difficult to put anything in writing that applies to everyone.

Nevertheless, the desire to have clear guidelines from top management remains, for this same executive later said:

We have no written, formalized policy in this area at all. I find it difficult at times. I have no problem whatsoever with having no written, formalized manual, but I would very much like to get a clear reading from top management as to what they would really like us to be going after.

A result is, as the interviewee at another company described, "a tough line to bridge. It has been a very, very political thing." He, of course, referred to the fine line between accounting and economic losses.

In this connection, it is worthy to note the analysis of a consultant. He distinguished four types of companies which tend to be more concerned with FASB 8's effects than others: (1) those companies which are sensitive to earnings per share being "their sole *raison d'être";* (2) those which have little earnings to be concerned about but large Euro-currency debt issues; (3) those which have strong earnings but large exposures; and (4) those which are "naive," accepting FASB 8 because their accountants say so. Partly supporting this analysis, an executive explained that his company defines its currency exposure in accordance with FASB 8 "to prevent any undue surprises as the desire of management is to maintain very steady earnings." Furthermore, the three other companies in the sample which follow FASB 8 have large amounts of Euro-currency long-term debts.

Thus, the empirical findings presented in this section confirm the overall defensive posture in the management of foreign exchange by multinational companies as reported by Jilling three years earlier,[5] but not so much insofar as transaction gains/losses are concerned. In fact, one company in Jilling's sample indicated that "moderate net gains" are preferred,[6] possibly because Jilling did not distinguish between translation versus transaction gains/losses. Or maybe,

> . . . since then,[7] expensive experiences in the forward exchange market appear to have moved the focus of exchange management from translation to transaction exposure.[8]

One thing, however, is certain: the foreign exchange management posture of the companies is not so defensive when it comes to foreign currency transactions.

With respect to the conflict between accounting and economic results which stem from a concern for reported earnings and simultaneously an awareness of economic data, it is useful to quote M. Joseph Lambert, Senior Vice President and Chief Financial Officer of Kraft, Inc. (ranked 37 on the 1977 Fortune 100 List):

> But for me the realistic starting point is—what is it that the stockholders expect of their management. I believe that they want a steadily growing stream of dividend income, which is reasonably within a management's control, and they want a steady appreciation of value in the stock market—and there's the rub. You probably have longer lists than I do of all the things that can impact stock market value—but as for currency fluctuations, I think management's responsibility to the stockholder is to avoid unpredictable fluctuations in earnings, especially unfavorable ones, insofar as reasonable in relation to the cost to avoid such fluctuations. I am coming down four square on the position that says that it's only the bottom line that counts; that explanations of variances are either unheard or not understood and that it doesn't matter much if it's a cash loss or an accounting loss. In the final analysis, the stock market says that it prefers a steady, predictable pattern of reported earnings, as opposed to an equal or better long run earnings picture, but with periodic fluctuations, even if they are explained fluctuations. The market *never* pays a premium for uncertainty, and I think management's obligation, second only to preserving the long range viability of the business, is to develop a steady and continually increasing stream of reported earnings.[9]

Obviously, Mr. Lambert does not endorse the proposition that the market is capable of filtering through accounting information to get at economic data. And his assessment is shared, in many instances, by most of the companies in this sample. On the other hand, they do not strictly adhere to this policy all the time; they move back and forth between the FASB 8 and economic definition of currency exposures.

Interviews with the foreign exchange consultants indicated that this state of affairs is prevalent among multinational firms. In fact, two of them felt that this behavior is desirable; they said, "I hope so," when the evidence in this regard was discussed with them. Another consultant provided a fairly detailed analysis of this situation:

> This is kind of a widespread thing . . . The biggest problem with the whole thing is the inability from the companies to come to some stated objective in terms of exposure management . . . And very often, you would come into some conflict of objectives.

This consultant explained how companies resolve this conflict:

> The other thing is, if you start to look to a definition of economics, anything other than FASB 8, what that means implicitly is, that if you're willing to live with increased fluctuations in the reported numbers and what happens is that companies are, very often, not aware of the opposition of those two. They say, well, we manage against the economic definition, and then once they do it for one or two quarters, when their economic definition is far enough away from their accounting definition, and they see those big numbers coming through in foreign exchange gains or losses, then they shift back again. Or they will say, we don't want to go that far, let's go half economics, half accounting. . . . So, what happens there is that they don't have any real policy. They think that they have a policy. They try it once and when they see some of the implications of that policy, they decide that this is not really the objective they want to go for; but they are never committed to another policy. So they sort of bounce back and forth between the parameters in order to, ultimately, keep a few people in the company happy.

It appears that the Bendix Corporation (ranked 70th on the *1977 Fortune 100 List*) has adopted a foreign exchange management policy which provides an excellent framework for such "bouncing back and forth." Consider the following.

> Bendix has not adopted an extreme position of hedging all balance sheet exposures or none of them; rather, it has adopted a moderately aggressive strategy which includes hedging selected exposures. The Bendix approach can be summarized by the following five statements:
>
> 1. We manage our international affairs so as to maximize the company's long-term net income expressed in dollars.
> 2. We emphasize annual predictability of earnings, but are also concerned with quarterly fluctuations. . . .
> 5. We are willing to consider forward contract hedging to reduce balance sheet exposure when:
>   a. The probability of recording a translation loss if we do not hedge is significantly greater than 50%, or
>   b. The potential unforecastable exchange gains or losses from the exposure are too large for management to tolerate.[10]

An assumption underlying this behavior is that investors are not able to filter through accounting data to get at economic values, and therefore, make investment decisions "naively."[11] Thus, to the extent that FASB 8 does not correctly measure the effects of exchange rate changes, such corporate practices and market reaction would have far-reaching implications on the efficient allocation of resources in the economy.

Defensive Strategies

Faced with currency fluctuations that erode profits and cause instability of reported earnings, the companies undertake a number of actions to protect themselves against foreign exchange risks. These strategies range from forward exchange contracts to price increases.

While most of these strategies are for short-term adjustment, some can be used for longer-term purposes, such as local/foreign currency borrowing or the strategy of specifying billing currency in import and export transactions. The use of the latter as a longer-term strategy reflects the concern for customer/ vendor relationships and the difficult in frequently changing the currency of billing for these outside parties are well aware that the risk of foreign exchange losses is being shifted to them. On the other hand, the management of short-term assets and liabilities for defensive purposes, primarily as a longer-term strategy in some companies, is an indication of the difficulty in quickly restructuring the balance sheet. The constraints on these and the other strategies are discussed in greater detail in this and the last section of this chapter.

Nevertheless, principally the defensive strategies are used for short-term adjustment. This short-term outlook is probably the most remarkable characteristic in the defensive strategies of these companies. Aside from their short-term nature, it is also reflected in the fact that none of the companies have a formal long-run foreign exchange management plan. Four of them however, do take into consideration the strength of a country's currency in their strategic planning. This is accomplished by projecting the currency's exchange rate beyond the one-year horizon. In one company, long-term forecasting of exchange rates is extended to seven years. This exercise, however, is far less elaborate and time-consuming than short-term forecasting, and it is an exception rather than the rule. Part of the reason is that the companies believe strategic planning for business expansion or contraction is more contingent on the local country's fundamental economic conditions, such as inflation rates, labor markets, etc., than on the exchange rate itself. Putting it differently, the exchange rate is believed to be the result of fundamental economic circumstances rather than the factor which produces them.

In all of the companies, short-term adjustment starts with the establishment of the business plan (exchange) rate. This is a ritual done before the beginning of a fiscal year in which the exchange rate of each currency—in which the company has operations—is established. While it is less elaborate than fore- casting for hedging purposes, it is designed to take into account the effects of exchange rate fluctuations on the company's operations and profits during the year. Although a currency fluctuates during this period, the business plan rate is maintained throughout the year. In this phase of the budgeting/planning process, translation and transaction gains/losses are also built into the overseas subsidiaries' financial statements. In this sense, there is a budget for foreign ex- change adjustments and an annual plan for the management of foreign exchange.

Under these circumstances, exposure management or hedging seems to be an attempt to correct any deviations of actual operating results from the annual plan or to reduce the effects of exchange rate changes by (conducting the opera- tions in accordance with) the plan. In fact, four of the companies indicated that the budget is a benchmark whereby they determine whether translation adjust- ments (as defined by FASB 8) are acceptable. Follow-up telephone conversa- tions with three other executives suggested that this method of assessing the acceptability of translation adjustments is quite prevalent among the companies.

One executive explained that the annual budgeting/planning process starts with the subsidiaries submitting their operating and profit plans for the fiscal year; these plans are expressed in U.S. dollars at the (business plan) rate furnished by the headquarter's treasury staff. Evaluation of these plans by top management which subsequently takes place may reveal that they do not meet the parent company's profit expectations or targets. At which time, the sub- sidiaries' management may have to revise their pricing and asset management strategies by providing for actions, such as price increases, faster collection of accounts receivable, or reduced investments in inventories. More often than not, the subsidiaries consult with the treasury staff to get their input on exchange rate movements. As such, the finalized plans/budgets have incorporated opera- ting strategies to meet top management's profit expectations and at the same time provide a protection against foreign exchange risks.

Additionally, the responsibility for the (operating defensive) strategies of price changes, credit policy, and adjustment of inventory levels, primarily falls on the overseas subsidiaries, although they are subject to approval—only at the planning/budgeting phase—by the headquarters. In contrast, considerably less leeway is accorded to the subsidiaries in the strategies of leading/lagging inter- company receivables/payables, borrowings, and forward exchange contracts. In fact, one company abandoned the strategy of inter-company accounts' adjust- ment because it feels that proper control was not maintained over this strategy. Uniformly, the subsidiaries must obtain prior approval from the headquarters before they can engage in the strategies of local/foreign currency borrowings and forward exchange contracts for defensive purposes.

With this perspective, combined with competitive pressure, it is easy to see why the operating strategies such as price changes, adjustment of inventory levels, and changes in credit terms are generally not used as frequently as those in the money and foreign exchange markets for short-term adjustment. In contrast, forward exchange contracts, borrowings, and inter-company accounts' adjustment are under control of the headquarter's treasury staff. As such, the sampled companies are quite active in using these strategies for short-term defensive purposes.

Earlier it was indicated that the foreign exchange management objectives of the companies are of a defensive nature. This is also reflected in the fact—and accomplished by it—that most of the companies undertake defensive strategies with the explicit overall objective of building up a neutral exposure in each of the individual currencies. While it is not necessarily that the individual exposures are zero, the tendency is to keep them as small as possible from a cost versus benefit point of view. Part of the reason is the desire to maintain a proper balance sheet structure for the overseas subsidiaries. In fact, all of the companies which have been negatively impacted by FASB 8 have a substantial amount of foreign currency long-term debts which are not adequately supported by cash flows generated by operations in those currencies. Another reason for the neutral exposure strategy is, as one executive put it: "If you want to manage balance sheet exposure, one way to do it is not to have balance sheet exposure and that is exactly what we try to do." Actually, those companies which adopt this strategy have maintained neutral exposure in accordance with their definition of currency exposure, i.e., economic or FASB 8, as may be the case. However, sometimes the latter reason seems to take precedence over the objective of maintaining a proper financial structure for the overseas subsidiaries, for it was found that local currency borrowings have been attempted, in lieu of dollar debts from the parent company, at the possible expense of reducing the credit worthiness of the subsidiaries.

The following is a discussion of the defensive strategies that have been undertaken by the companies. These strategies should be viewed, however, within the perspective of the foreign exchange management objectives and the overall strategy that has been discussed. They can be classified into the following major categories:

1. Forward exchange contracts
2. Pricing and inventory strategies
3. Leads and lags of third-party receivables/payables
4. Inter-company accounts' adjustment
5. Debt and working capital management
6. Netting

Forward Exchange Contracts

This is a foreign exchange market facility which enables a company to hedge or cover an exposed position in a foreign currency through the sale or purchase of a certain amount of that currency on a forward basis. That is, the foreign currency will be delivered on a future date agreed to by both parties at the date the contract is written. This future rate may be specified at the contract date. However, if the exact timing of the foreign currency receipt or payment is not known with certainty at the contract date, it is possible to negotiate an options contract. In this contract, a company can exercise the contract anytime within a certain time period, or at several alternative, but fixed dates in the future.

At the maturity or exercise date, the foreign currency amount will be delivered at the exchange rate which has been agreed on by both parties at the contract date, regardless of the then-prevailing spot rate. Thus, through the sale or purchase of a forward exchange contract, the proceeds from a foreign currency payment or receipt are locked in, therefore, are free from the risk that the foreign currency will appreciate or depreciate causing the proceeds to be more/less than expected. Such is the case for forward exchange contract hedging on foreign currency transactions.

Forward exchange contracts can also be used to hedge the balance sheet exposure. The purpose in this regard is to create an exposed position for gains which hopefully will offset, or reduce the expected translation loss. Since a balance sheet exposure does not involve any conversion/transfer of funds, the contracted foreign currency amount must be bought or sold in the spot exchange market on the maturity date before/after delivery of the foreign currency to fulfill the contract. And this is the fundamental difference between transaction and translation hedging in the foreign exchange market, because in the transaction case such spot sales or purchases of foreign currencies are not necessary.

The way it is under floating exchange rates, the currency may, say, appreciate rather than depreciate as expected. So, in this case, in lieu of an expected gain from the forward transaction, the company will suffer a loss. On the translation side, it will have to record a gain instead of a loss. In other words, in forward exchange contract hedging on the balance sheet exposure, the company is accepting one risk in the hope of offsetting another. Such is not the case with respect to transaction hedging. The example on page 61 shows the potential loss to which a company is exposed in balance sheet hedging via the forward exchange markets. A real life experience was reported in the press:

> ITT partly covered its balance sheet exposure in January, 1974, by selling $600 million worth of foreign currencies in the forward markets. If the dollar had strengthened, as most market watchers predicted it would, the company would have

reaped enough profit to offset unrealized loss on its foreign balance sheet translation. But the dollar's value fell, and ITT lost $48 million, including $10 million in fees for the forward contracts.[12]

In view of this potential outcome and the aspect of risk substitution, one might even suggest that balance sheet hedging in the forward exchange markets borders on speculation. Coupled with the fact that the forward exchange loss is cash, as opposed to the non-cash nature of the translation loss, it is not surprising that the sampled companies do not use this strategy on the balance sheet exposure as often as on foreign currency transactions. This is shown in Table 11. Consider the following statement from one Assistant Treasurer:

> We do not in principle, and that principle is pretty darn strong: we do not use forward exchange contracts for balance sheet hedging purposes. Which does not mean that we ignore balance sheet exposure positions but then we come back to balance sheet restructuring aspect which we talked about earlier. We are great believers, and we actively manage balance sheet exposure by restructuring the balance sheet.

One company, which is shown as using this defensive strategy "occasionally" for balance sheet hedging in Table 11, has recently abandoned this practice because, as the responding executive explained, "we feel we don't want to have the cash flow loss . . ." However, reinforcing the concern for fluctuations in reported earnings, this same executive later added:

> Our general corporate policy is not to have a coverage program [on the balance sheet exposure]. By that, I mean, we don't have a fixed program. It is flexible. It is subject to changes, just as the market is subject to change. We always reformulate our approach.

In this connection, one cannot help adding that this company has had some quite unpleasant experiences in the past from covering its balance sheet exposure in the forward exchange markets.

The concern for forward exchange cash losses, as opposed to accounting adjustments, and the awareness of the risk substitution aspect (which entails potentially large losses) in balance sheet hedging via forward exchange contracts pervade in all of the companies. These problems are noted by one executive:

> Generally speaking, our philosophy at this point in time, is that we do not cover translation positions. We basically try to do everything possible other than hedging a balance sheet position. Leading and lagging, changing terms, currency of invoicing, local borrowing, currency swaps—all those types of tools. Then, and only then, we would look at a balance sheet hedge, meaning a forward contract in the outside. But we don't particularly go for that because we really consider that a real risk to cash assets of the corporation. We really don't have a mandate from our management to

Table 11
Use of Forward Exchange Contracts
to Hedge Transaction and Translation Exposure

Exposure Components	Frequency				Sample Size
	Never	Occasionally	Usually	Always	
Payments/Receipts from Import/ Export Transactions	1	2	5	2	10
Off-Balance Sheet Items (Payments/Receipts not recorded in the books)	1	4	3	2	10
Net Exposed Balance Sheet Positions	4	5	1	0	10

Average frequency: Without net exposed balance sheet positions: 2.75 (This is the average number of companies which "usually" and "always" use a defensive strategy. Thus in this case (4 + 2 + 3 + 2) ÷ 4 = 2.75).
With net exposed balance sheet positions: 2.

risk a certain degree of cash or percentage of cash. This is what we would really consider as speculative hedging. It can go for you or against you. Our management is very control conscious and feels that this is not the way to utilize the resources of the company.

A less restrictive policy in another company is indicated by its Assistant Treasurer: "If we don't have to, we don't. Our preference is to manage the exposure with debt." Even for one company which "usually" uses this defensive strategy for balance sheet hedging, the concern for cash loss versus accounting gain is prevalent:

Everything that does not involve a dollar outflow from the Company is what we would do first providing the risk is not great. . . It's always the philosophy that we send the least dollars out.

This general reluctance in the use of forward exchange contracts is greatly diminished when it comes to foreign currency transactions. The main components of a transaction exposure that lend themselves to forward contract hedging are:

1. Payments and receipts arising from import and export transactions
2. Repayments of loan obligations
3. Payments of dividends, royalties, management, and licensing fees
4. Off-balance sheet items, such as confirmed sale orders and purchase commitments

Table 12 shows the companies which use forward exchange contracts to hedge these transactions. The results are quite as expected. Nine out of ten companies use this defensive strategy to protect the proceeds from import and export transactions. The same number of companies also use this facility to hedge on payments of management fees, etc. Forward exchange contract hedging is also used to the same extent to protect the gross margin on contractual sale and purchase agreements, although the goods in question are not yet delivered, and therefore, invoicing is not yet made. The policy of one company in the use of forward exchange contracts to hedge confirmed orders is worth noting:

Our philosophy is that as soon as the pricing and volume are established, the subsidiary should hedge it, although we will tamper with that if we feel that there is something that could ruin the market within a couple of days. If we have very strong reasons to justify that the forward market is not a good indicator of what we think is going to happen . . . we will play a little. Otherwise, as soon as that pricing is locked in, we lock in that margin. If it turns out that the cost of the forward exchange contract is terrible, that's fine. We really want the subsidiary to come to us before they start locking in price and volume.

Table 12

Use of Forward Exchange Contracts to Hedge Foreign Currency Transactions

Transactions	Number of Companies
Payments/Receipts from Import/ Export Transactions	9
Repayments of Loan Obligations	5
Payments of Dividends, etc.	9
Off-Balance Sheet Items	9
Sample Size	10

As to repayments of loan obligations, the question is relevant only for redemption of long-term issues. Underlying this situation is the fact that the choice of debt denomination hinges very heavily on the forecast that the currency in question will depreciate to the extent that upon maturity of the loan, the difference between the depreciation amount and the interest cost would be less than the effective costs of other financing alternatives. If the company then takes out a forward exchange contract to cover the foreign currency loan, *ex ante* the advantage would be eliminated. In other words, there is no inherent reason why a forward contract should be used for this purpose. It may be necessary, however, if the original exchange projections turn out to be wrong (on a forecast basis, but well after the financing decision has been made), such that the company wishes to rectify the situation by redeeming the loan and replace it with a loan denominated in another currency. To prevent the problem from further deteriorating, the company may wish to take out a forward exchange contract at the time the redemption decision is made, typically several months before the foreign currency is forecast to further appreciate. This is exactly what has happened.

Overall, as shown in Tables 11 and 12, forward exchange contracts are used frequently by the sampled companies to hedge foreign currency transactions, but not so much for balance sheet hedging.

Pricing and Inventory Strategies

A very effective strategy to reduce the effects of currency devaluations on earnings is to increase selling prices in the local as well as export markets.

The latter can be accomplished simply by keeping prices unchanged. From an exposure management point of view, strictly speaking, price increases do not reduce foreign exchange losses; only revenues, hence profits, would be protected from the devaluation effects.

While price increases do not entail any direct costs, indirect costs could be prohibitive. The latter costs may take the form of loss of market share with all of its implications on the very profitability of the foreign operation. Obviously, this potential outcome depends on the competitive strength as well as other market conditions, e.g., price elasticity of the product. In this regard, one company has found that in countries where devaluation is repetitive and price inflation is a way of life, threat of local competition and customer resistance are not overwhelming. In fact, one of its subsidiaries has the practice of charging credit costs to its local customers separately from selling prices. This practice has the additional advantage of keeping local receivables at a minimum level since it encourages payments by cash rather than credit. The Treasurer of another company indicated that his company does not have much problem with raising prices in developing countries, but has difficulty in doing so in developed markets. This case example appears to be indicative of the experience in the other companies. In other words, there seems to be a correlation between the amount of business in developing countries and the frequency in the use of price changes as a defensive strategy. Thus, a company which sells more to developing countries tends to use this defensive strategy more frequently than a company which sells more to developed countries.

Another factor which appears to account for the relatively less frequent use of price changes is the fact that pricing policy is established as part of profit planning in the annual budgeting process. Although the treasury staff is often consulted for their input on exchange rate movements and resultant effects on profitability, once prices are established, they are not subject to change, or at least not frequently. In addition, even if prices are to be changed as part of the exposure management activities, cooperation of operating managements is necessary.

In this connection, it is interesting to note an empirical finding on the relationship between price changes and exchange rate fluctuations. In a paper in 1970, Dunn used time series to study this relationship in six markets for goods traded in the U.S. and Canada.[13] His statistical analysis indicated that "there was not a close relationship in the exchange rate and relative prices in *any* of the markets, and only one market showed even a rough relationship."[14]

Table 13 shows the frequency in the use of pricing and inventory strategies for defensive purposes. As it is readily apparent, in most companies these strategies are only used "occasionally."

Used even less frequently than price changes is adjustment of inter-subsidiary transfer prices. When probed on the use of this strategy, most of the inter-

Table 13
Pricing and Inventory Strategies

Strategies	Frequency				Sample Size
	Never	Occasionally	Usually	Always	
Increase Export Prices		5	3	2	10
Increase Billing Prices to Local Customers		6	2	2	10
Increase/Decrease Inter-Subsidiary Transfer Prices	5	3	1	1	10
Increase/Decrease Local/Foreign Currency Inventory Levels	3	4	3		10

Average frequency: 2 (Without inter-subsidiary transfer pricing.)
                    1.75 (With inter-subsidiary transfer pricing.)

viewees were reluctant to concede that they have used transfer pricing for exposure management purposes, citing that tax regulations and local governments' scrutiny virtually rule out its use.

As to adjustment of inventory levels, its use is rather limited. A major reason is that inventory management is the responsibility of local subsidiaries and therefore is an operational matter which is best left to local management's judgment. There is also the corporate practice and policy of keeping inventory at the lowest possible level which will help minimize local financing—an exposed item.

Leads and Lags

The purpose of leading and lagging receivables and payables with third parties (non-affiliated customers/vendors) is to shift the exposure into the direction consistent with exchange rate movements. Thus, when a currency is expected to depreciate, this defensive strategy would be used to reduce the levels of accounts receivable denominated in that currency and at the same time increasing accounts payable in the same currency. Several techniques can be used to accomplish this objective.

For one, a company can accelerate the collection of accounts receivable and delay the payment of accounts payable. To effect the leading of trade receivables, the company can offer a discount for prompt payments and levy a late charge on past due accounts, or simply change the credit terms extended to its customers. These practices can entail considerable costs.[15] Available empirical studies then point to this cost consideration as a major factor in the relatively infrequent use of this defensive strategy for exposure management purposes.[16] The evidence collected in this research indicates, however, that the cost consideration does not enter into the decision-making process for the selection of leading trade receivables as a defensive strategy as explicitly and formally as these studies implied. In fact, the cited studies did not empirically demonstrate that the companies in their samples explicitly considered for the associated factor.

The results from this study indicate that the relatively infrequent use of leading/lagging receivables stems from a conscious effort, or more accurately, from a policy of keeping accounts receivable at the lowest possible level. This level of receivables is determined at the budgeting/planning phase. Presumably, in this phase of the decision-making process, the cost factor is considered. However, several of the interviewees pointed out that they do whatever they can in view of the competitive situation, rather than because of the cost of leading trade receivables is advantageous or not advantageous as compared to the other defensive strategies. Inspection of Table 14, which shows the frequency in the use of leads/lags, indicates that this reason seems to provide a better explanation

Table 14
Leads and Lags of Third-Party Receivables/Payables

Strategies	Never	Occasionally	Usually	Always	Sample Size
Leads/Lags Local/ Foreign Currency Receivables from/ Payables to Third Parties	2	5	1	2	10
Specify Currency of Billing	1	4	4	1	10
Extend/Receive More/Less Credit Terms	1	6	3		10

Average frequency: 1.83 (all).

for the fact that a couple of companies use this defensive strategy more frequently than the others. This policy also discourages the building up of accounts receivable in anticipation of a currency appreciation. To quote one executive:

> We collect as fast as we can. We think it is good management to collect promptly. As to the overwhelming importance of that, I can't visualize today that for exposure management purposes we would start to slow down on our collections due to billed assets anyway.

If indeed cost comparison is a factor in the selection of leading/lagging receivables as a defensive strategy, *a priori,* building up accounts receivable should not be ruled out.

The situation is somewhat different with respect to accounts payable, for a company has more latitude by taking prompt payment discounts or simply making prepayments on deliveries in anticipation of an appreciation. Conversely, it can forego prompt payment discounts or simply delay the payments after the due dates if it anticipates a weakening of the currency in question. The executive quoted above said, "We, of course, play a little bit with that [i.e., leading/lagging payables]." On the other hand, "as far as payables go, we try to maintain a good image in the market which means that you pay your bills"; this indicates a conscious consideration for relationships with vendors in the use of this defensive strategy.

The consideration for relationships with vendors and resistance from customers, i.e., competitive strength, also play an important role in changing sale and credit terms. In addition, under floating exchange rates, currency fluctuations occur continuously. In order to carry out leads/lags (by using this technique) accordingly, a company would have to change its credit terms quite often. Such a policy would lead to confusion bordering on poor business practice. For this reason, some companies have standard practices in billing, such as 60-day terms. However, one area where changing credit terms is not very difficult is in long-term sale and purchase contracts in which various aspects of the sale/purchase can be negotiated on a contract-by-contract basis. Two companies indicated that they have often been able to take advantage of this situation.

Specification of the billing currency also faces the same obstacles. In this strategy, a company would effectively shift the foreign exchange risk to the other party. In view of the relative sophistication of participants in international trade, especially those in European countries, this is not always possible. However, the competitive strength of a company may help it overcome any customer resistance. For example, one company has been able to specify that the billing currency be in U.S. dollars in its long-term contracts of capital equipment sale and construction in developing countries.

A final consideration is the fact that, like adjustment of inventory levels, leads/lags strategies are within the purview of local managements, although they are subject to the parent company's limitations and guidelines established during the planning/budgeting phase. For this reason, the treasury staff at the headquarters are not involved in this level of decision-making unless consulted by the operating managements of the overseas subsidiaries. This limited involvement of the treasury personnel is further reduced in those companies which staff most of their overseas subsidiaries by local nationals. (There are two such companies in the sample.) As a result, unless initiated by local managements, faced with a "hedge-versus-no-hedge" decision, the treasury staff do not even consider these alternatives (in comparison with other options, such as forward exchange contracts). A possible exception is in one company which has a routine procedure of holding monthly meetings between the treasury staff and the divisional managements for discussion of exposure management strategies for the upcoming period. And even in this case, the results of such meetings provide only guidelines for operating managements rather than any directives of unchangeable value. This is not to say that this sort of dialogue between the staff and operating personnel does not exist in the other companies. It does, but only on an "as needed" basis. Another illustration of the influence of the organizational structure on the frequency in the use of leads/lags is the case of two manufacturers of capital goods sold in the industrial market. In one company, the emphasis has been on the translation exposure which is managed primarily by debt and forward exchange contracts. As a result, its overseas subsidiaries are not actively engaged in leads/lags strategies. In the other company, the reliance, however, is placed on price increases, leads/lags, and inter-company accounts' adjustment. It seems that the company is able to do this, thanks to a relatively large exposure management staff and the resources of a formal foreign exchange management committee.

Finally, leads/lags can be used often only if the company has significant amounts of cross-border transactions. In fact, one interviewee characterized his company as "an aggregation of domestic corporations with little cross-border business." He then lamented that this is unfortunate because of a lack of opportunities to engage in leads/lags strategies. In another company which derives about 20 percent of its sales from international operations, a large part of its overseas business is strictly local. Of the remainder, a sizeable amount is billed in U.S. dollars. Whatever is left consists mostly of inter-company transactions, and in fact, "to a large degree, these transactions represent almost the total amount of our cross-bordering."

Thus it appears that the use of leads/lags strategies depends heavily on the organizational structure of a company, its operating philosophy, and foremost of all, the availability of cross-border business with unaffiliated customers. If the cost factor is a consideration, it does not enter into the decision-making explicitly and formally. Under the circumstances, it is not surprising that leads/

lags strategies have not been used very extensively in some of the sampled companies. In fact, two of the companies do not use leads/lags of trade receivables and payables at all; in one company, this is simply because it feels it has not instituted the kind of control procedures that it deems necessary. (This will be discussed in greater detail in the following section on inter-company accounts' adjustment.) Table 14 shows the extent that leads/lags strategies have been used for exposure management purposes in the sampled companies.

Inter-Company Accounts' Adjustment

Like leads/lags with third parties, inter-company accounts' adjustment is directed toward shifting the exposure in one currency into a direction consistent with exchange rate forecasts. But, this strategy involves the receivables/payables of one subsidiary with its sister company(ies). It thus ultimately leads to the shifting of the exposure from one currency to another. To the extent that excess cash, or shortage of funds, then occurs in one or more of the subsidiaries, a decision has to be made on the use of the cash or, as it may be the case, how to finance the operations of the affected subsidiaries.

In contrast to leads/lags with third parties, the sampled companies have used relatively more extensively the strategy of inter-company accounts' adjustment in their exposure management. The reason is simply because this strategy involves little direct costs. The little cost that does arise reflects the extent that the subsidiary from which cash is drained has to borrow to finance its working capital. However, this interest cost is partly offset by the return on short-term investments made by the subsidiary to which excess cash is channeled.

As the experiences of the sampled companies indicate, there are three basic difficulties with this defensive strategy. First, there must exist sufficient amounts of inter-company transactions. Obviously, if there is little of this type of transaction, inter-company accounts' adjustment cannot be effectively deployed. Second, like leads/lags, the companies must conform with local rules and regulations on payment terms, although this constraint is not very serious. Third, inter-company accounts' adjustment must be properly controlled, otherwise, as one executive put it, "it could be very messy." For this reason, his company has abandoned the strategies of leads/lags and inter-company accounts' adjustment altogether. However, recognizing their effectiveness, this company is planning their re-institution with proper control procedures.

The need for proper control stems from the fact that inter-company transactions affect the transaction and translation exposure, as well as a subsidiary's financing needs. To illustrate, consider an inter-company receivable of 100 Deutsche marks on the books of a German subsidiary with a French affiliate; the French company shows a payable on its books. Suppose that at time t = 0, FF = DM.50 = U.S.$.25 and at time t = 1, FF = DM.45 = U.S.$.2475. At t = 1, upon consolidation into U.S. dollars, translating the DM receivable into dollars will give rise to a translation gain of U.S. $5.00 and translating the DM payable into FF then into U.S. dollars (as required by FASB 8) will result in a translation loss of U.S. $5.00. However, if at t = 1, the French subsidiary pays off its DM payable, it will incur a cash loss of FF22.00 (= U.S. $5.00), whereas, the gain on the DM receivable (which is now converted into cash on the German subsidiary's books) is a translation gain. When tax effects are taken into account, the corporation as a whole will show a gain. This is the difference between the translation gain on the cash of DM100 and the transaction loss of FF22 less the French tax liability. On the other hand, if the DM payable is not paid off at t = 1, so as consolidated earnings are not affected by the French devaluation, the German subsidiary may need to borrow to finance the receivable of DM100, whereas the French subsidiary may need to find an investment for its funds. The question then arises as to in which currencies the borrowing and investment should be denominated. It is noteworthy that in four of the sampled companies, the tax effects are not considered; therefore, this after-tax impact is overlooked. In one of these companies, inter-company transactions are considered offsetting, as it is primarily translation-oriented.

The thrust of inter-company accounts' adjustment is to shift exposures from one currency to another. The direction of these adjustments depends on the exposed positions of the subsidiaries concerned, as well as the strength of their currencies. As noted in the above example, this position adjustment can be effected through leading/lagging inter-company accounts receivables and payables and borrowings.

By leading/lagging, i.e., accelerating or delaying settlements of inter-company receivables and payables, the exposed position of a subsidiary in a depreciating currency will be reduced as some of its exposure is shifted to a subsidiary in a stronger currency. This shift may result in the elimination of both transaction and translation losses. In the above illustration, if the DM100 receivable is settled before t = 1, the subsequent complications of the French franc's depreciation will be eliminated. If the French subsidiary does not have sufficient cash on hand, it can borrow locally to finance the payment of the receivable. Upon translation of the franc debt of FF200, the group will record a translation gain of U.S. $5.00, in addition to the gain of the same amount on the DM receivable which is now converted into cash. The group can further increase the translation gains by borrowing more French francs to pre-pay deliveries from the German subsidiary, which in turn, can use the funds for short-term investments in Deutsche marks. This scenario is, however, unlikely since the companies indicated that they do not create an exposed position to take advantage of currency movements. Generally, the companies seem to be reluctant to create an exposure, unless such exposures are supported by the subsidiary's underlying assets and liabilities as it may be the case. Again, this goes back to the overall strategy of neutral exposure at the individual currencies' level and the defensive posture in exposure management.

Thus, when internal conditions permit, i.e., there are sufficient inter-company transactions and the subsidiaries' exposures are in a position to support these adjustments, the sampled companies will take advantage of the inter-company flows to shift their exposures among the overseas subsidiaries. However, with respect to remittances of dividends, there is an additional constraint which is income tax. Thus, for example, in one company, dividends are not re-mitted from England for tax purposes, but there is a large degree of dividend taking from Germany. In this strategy, a company can accelerate/delay the payments of dividends or vary the dividend amounts. In this regard, the practice is different among several of the companies. Three companies in the sample resort to the timing of dividend remittances more often than variation in the dividend amounts. In three other companies, the practice is reversed. This is revealed by inspection of the frequency in the use of "accelerate/delay dividend remittances" and "adjust the flows of dividend remittances" strategies, as shown in Table 15.

Table 15 shows the extent of the use of inter-company accounts' adjustment in the sampled companies. As it can be readily seen, the use of this defensive strategy is rather extensive and more widespread and frequent than leads and lags of receivables and payables with third parties.

Debt and Working Capital Management

These strategies involve the management of the debt and working capital structure of the individual subsidiaries to arrive at a desirable mix of external obligations in terms of the amounts and currency denominations. Several alternatives are available for this purpose. Foremost is to borrow locally and/or in foreign money/capital markets. Subsequent restructuring of the debt components may involve pre-payment of the borrowings before the maturity dates and replacement of these debts with dollar loans from the parent company or simply borrowing again, but in a different currency. As the experiences of the sampled companies indicate, this restructuring can be accomplished by both short- and long-term loans. Obviously, short-term debts are subject to more flexible manipulation than long-term issues. Short-term issues can also be used in connection with inter-company accounts' adjustment and dividend remittances. For example, in one company, before the recent French prime-minis-terial election, during which time the French franc was under heavy pressure to depreciate, the French subsidiary prepaid "quite a bit"—leading—its inter-company payables to build up inventory. In Germany, its dividend payments are equalized by inter-company borrowings. Loans with short-term maturities are also easier to be pre-paid, although some companies do pre-pay their long-term

Table 15
Use of Inter-Company Accounts' Adjustment

Strategies	Frequency				Sample Size
	Never	Occasionally	Usually	Always	
Leads/Lags Intersubsidiary Receivables/ Payables	2	2	4	2	10
Accelerate/Delay Dividend Remittances to Parent Company		4	5	1	10
Adjust the Flows of Dividend Remittances to Parent Company	1	3	4	2	10

Average frequency: 3 (all).

obligations. Finally, there remains the possibility of managing short-term assets and liabilities consistent with the direction of the currency movements. The sampled companies are also active in this practice.

The use of local and foreign currency borrowings for exposure management purposes is quite widespread among the sampled companies. In fact, all of the 10 companies have used this defensive strategy to some extent. As shown in Table 16, eight companies either "usually" or "always" borrow locally for defensive purposes, whereas six companies engage in foreign currency borrowings with the same degree of frequency. The frequent use of local and foreign currency borrowings seems to indicate that although a borrowing by and in itself may be a result of a financing need, the choice of a currency denomination is highly influenced by considerations for foreign exchange risks. However, as several interviewees pointed out, borrowing in the local currency has been in many instances a result of exposure management considerations, i.e., no financing needs exist. The case of the Mexican peso was cited several times in the interviews. The Canadian dollar is another example. In Europe, the French franc and the pound sterling have been used in this regard. Furthermore, it was pointed out in some of the interviews that local currency borrowings are often used in conjunction with inter-company accounts' adjustment (of receivables and payables). Sometimes, such borrowings are used to swap cash assets (i.e., making deposits in appreciating currencies) among subsidiaries. Although this strategy has not been used often in most companies, because it creates an exposure in the currency of the investment, a couple of companies are quite active in this regard.

As to the mix between local and foreign currencies, most companies borrow locally as often as in foreign money and capital markets. However, three companies "usually" engage in local currency borrowings while they only "occasionally" do so in the foreign currency markets. Yet, in one other company, the practice is exactly reverse.

Table 17 shows the maturities of the loans. Four of the sampled companies borrow both short- and long-term locally for defensive purposes. Two companies restrict themselves to long-term local currency borrowings, whereas four other companies engage in this practice only on a short-term basis. The situation is somewhat different with respect to foreign currency borrowings. Five companies borrow both short- and long-term in the foreign currency markets. Three companies enter the foreign capital markets for long-term capital, while two companies resort to the foreign currency money markets only for short-term funds.

In connection with this discussion of short versus long-term borrowings, it should be pointed out, as one executive explained, that although a company restricts itself to short-term borrowings, it can always renew the loan at the maturity date, thus effectively treating it as a long-term loan. Obviously, an

Table 16
Use of Debt and Working Capital Management Strategies

Strategies	Frequency				Sample Size
	Never	Occasionally	Usually	Always	
Local Currency Borrowings		2	6	2	10
Foreign Currency Borrowings		4	4	2	10
Pre-payment of Bank Borrowings and like Commitments to Third Parties	2	5	3		10
Adjust Parent Company's Planned Dollar Investments	1	5	2	2	10
Adjust Local/ Foreign Currency Long-term Debts	2	3	3	2	10
Reduce Short-term Assets and Increase Short-term Liabilities		3	5	2	10
Negotiate Foreign Currency and/or Credit Swaps	3	5	1	1	10

Average frequency: 2.57 (all)

3.50 (Local/foreign currency borrowings and short-term assets/liabilities management)

Table 17
Debt and Working Capital Management: Short- Versus Long-Term

Strategies	Primarily Short-term	Primarily Long-term	Short- and Long-term	Sample Size
Local Currency Borrowings	4	2	4	10
Foreign Currency Borrowings	2	3	5	10
Pre-payment of Bank Borrowings and like Commitments to Third Parties	3	1	4	10[a]
Adjust Parent Company's Planned Dollar Investments	3	5	1	10[b]
Adjust Local/ Foreign Currency Long-term Debts		8		10[c]
Reduce Short-term Assets and Increase Short-term Liabilities	5	3	2	10
Negotiate Foreign Currency and/or Credit Swaps	2	3	2	10[d]

[a] Two companies do not use this strategy.

[b] One company does not use this strategy.

[c] Two companies do not use this strategy.

[d] Three companies do not use this strategy.

advantage of this practice is flexibility. In contrast, foreign currency long-term debts may expose the company to severely adverse impact by exchange rate fluctuations. In this regard, the experience of one company—and by no means unique—is worthy of note:

> We had over the years taken certain long-term views on the relative values of currencies, and we had deliberately . . . borrowed in certain currencies in excess of our assets in those currencies where it was possible to do so under exchange control regulations and other government regulations, with the idea and expectations that over a period of time the very often higher interest rates that we would pay for borrowing those currencies would be more than offset by the benefit that we would get from the devaluation of the debt which we incurred in those currencies. And in fact, we were right. When FASB 8 came along, like in every other company, our top management's attention was drawn to the fact that these exchange gains that we had expected to realize over a period of years as the long-term debt in weak currencies which we had incurred came to maturity that those gains were realized all of a sudden all in one year. And it then became apparent that what was realized in one year could quickly be reversed in the second year. That we had instead of a small amount of exposed assets and liabilities, we had very large amounts, and of course, like many other companies in our position, had moved very heavily to a negative exposure on the majority of foreign currencies.

(The effects of FASB 8 on the sampled companies will be discussed in full detail in Chapter V.)

As the experience of this company suggests, borrowing is both a financing, as well as exposure decision, and especially so with respect to long-term debts. (Short-term borrowing, purely for defensive purposes, is an exposure and investment decision.) Once the financing need is established, a company would take into account interest as well as exchange rates to determine the costs of the alternative financing vehicles. However, as one foreign exchange consultant pointed out, this logical analysis was often overlooked in a number of large multinational firms before FASB 8 was issued. As the choice of a currency denomination has effects on the translation exposure, a company which resorts to foreign currency capital markets for its long-term needs may find itself open to earnings fluctuations due to exchange rate changes. The reason is that under FASB 8, translation adjustments on long-term debts must be recognized as part of current income. Six of the ten companies have found themselves in this situation, albeit in varying degrees. In this connection, it is worthy to note the borrowing policy of another company in the sample. When asked whether or not his company borrows locally, specifically for the purpose of hedging, the Assistant Treasurer-International Finance responded:

> Based on our concept of an appropriate local balance sheet, we will borrow locally to the extent that that fits into the appropriate local financial profile. If it is too expensive, we may decide that we are better off borrowing elsewhere. But the basic

concept is that each operating subsidiary is a sustained financial unit in the market. Normal borrowing and working financial needs are met in the local market and to the extent that there is a need for and an ability to fund long-term borrowing needs, it is done in that market as well. Borrowing as a hedging tool is approaching the same question from another direction. The overall balance sheet structuring program is a hedging tool as such, in which borrowing is a portion.

The theme of balance sheet structuring and borrowing locally only if there are sufficient underlying supporting assets, pervades the interview with this executive. To the extent that floating exchange rates and FASB 8 have led companies to be more active in this financial policy, and there is evidence that they do, the implications for international capital markets are enormous. These issues will be analyzed in Chapter VI.

To counter these earnings fluctuations, a company can borrow short-term in a weak currency to offset the translation adjustments on its foreign currency long-term debts. This has happened in at least three of the sampled companies. Alternatively, it can pre-pay the strong currency debt and refinance it in a weak currency or in U.S. dollars. As shown in Table 16, four companies "usually" engage in this practice, while four others do so "occasionally." Although it seems that it is easier to pre-pay short- than long-term debts, five companies practice pre-payment on both short- as well as long-term debts, whereas three companies only pre-pay short-term debts. On the other hand, one company restricts itself to long-term debts, while two others have not used this strategy.

The replacing dollar debt may come from the parent company. Alternatively, the dollar debt from the parent company may be replaced by local currency borrowings. For example, one company facing a substantial long position in the Canadian dollar when this currency was depreciating, felt that it needed to balance the exposure in that currency. To accomplish this, in Spring, 1978, it decided to increase commercial paper issues in Canadian dollars, and at the same time, pay down U.S. dollar debts in the United States. Although it had to pay premium interest to borrow in Canada, "it has worked out fairly well in the past couple of months." Of course, a company can always replace the dollar or local currency debt by another issue denominated in a foreign currency. However, the experiences of the companies which have had foreign exchange problems with their local/foreign currency long-term debts suggest limited choices as to the refinancing currency. That is, the refinancing currency will be the U.S. dollar or a local currency if the original debt is denominated in a foreign currency. (Actually, given the scope of operations of these companies, the distinction between local and foreign currencies is somewhat academic. Therefore, in this context, a foreign currency should be understood to be one in which insufficient underlying supporting assets are denominated.) Conversely, if the original debt is denominated in U.S. dollars, the refinancing currency will be in the currency of the subsidiary of which the operations were financed by the dollar debt, and vice versa. This situation exists because these companies have long-term debt finan-cing in those currencies in which it had not sufficient amounts of offsetting cash flows. Therefore, the refinancing currency depends on the exposure that already exists.

Table 17 shows the extent of adjusting dollar debts from the parent com-pany. Again, the strategy is widely used by the sampled companies. In this regard, five companies engage in this practice only on a long-term basis, whereas three companies restrict themselves to short-term obligations. One company does both.

The above long-term debt strategies will ultimately lead to a restructuring of the currency denominations on long-term borrowings. Confirming this, Table 17 shows that 8 of the 10 companies engage in the practice of adjusting long-term debt denominations, the same companies which pre-pay their borrowings.

The management of short-term assets and liabilities of a subsidiary can also make a significant contribution to the reduction of its exposure. However, once strategies such as leads/lags, inter-company accounts' adjustment, and borrowings have been exhausted, there is little else that a company can do ex-cept in the area of cash and short-term investments. In this regard, the com-panies have used these cash management techniques for exposure management purposes rather extensively, except in those which delegate this responsibility to their subsidiaries. In other words, there seems to be a strong correlation between the extent that these techniques are used and the degree of centraliza-tion of control over them. Table 18 shows the differences among the sampled companies in this respect.

Table 18
Degree of Centralization and the Use of Cash Management
Techniques for Exposure Management Purposes

Degree of Centralization	Frequency			
	Never	Occasionally	Usually	Always
Responsible by Parent			4	2
Responsible by Subsidiary		3		
Responsible by Parent and Subsidiary			1	

Sample Size: 10 companies

As shown in Table 18, the two companies which centralize control over cash are quite active in using cash management techniques for exposure management purposes; they "always" use this strategy. In one company, the policy is to drain cash from the overseas subsidiaries so that "we don't leave them much cash to play with." In the other company,

> We have watched the market in the last few weeks and at times when the premium of the Swiss franc over the German mark has contracted, we have moved from German marks to Swiss francs. We use seven percent as a cut-off level. Whenever the Swiss franc drops below a seven percent premium, we use German marks. This week we moved 10 million dollars from German marks to Swiss francs.

Finally, there is the "swap" facility which enables a parent company to lend its subsidiaries in hard currencies, or U.S. dollars at reduced exchange risks. Swap transactions may or may not involve a forward exchange contract.[17] In a foreign currency swap, the parent company uses the foreign currency funds available to buy the subsidiary's local currency in the spot exchange market and simultaneously engage in a forward exchange contract to sell the local currency amount. It thus is guaranteed of the foreign currency amount when the local currency loan is repaid. Of course, this technique cannot be used if there is no forward exchange market for the local currency in question. In such a case, the parent company can arrange for the subsidiary to enter a credit swap. In this transaction, a local bank (in the country where the subsidiary is located) will make the loan to the affiliate with interest charge, and is in turn, granted a free hard currency loan outside the country. This arrangement may be very attractive to the lending bank if there is a shortage of the hard currency in question. But then it must assume the foreign exchange risk. As shown in Table 16, most of the sampled companies either do not use these swap transactions or only use them "occasionally."

Exposure Netting

Netting can be accomplished among a multiple of currencies or within a single currency. The former is inter-currency netting. The latter is intra-currency netting.

Inter-currency netting

Inter-currency netting is not so much a strategy of exposure reduction as a willingness to accept an open position in one or more currencies in anticipation that the resultant gains/losses will be offset by the adjustments in the exposures denominated in other currencies. Therefore, a company adopting this strategy will not cover, as an example, a Deutsche mark exposure if it anticipates an offsetting gain from its Dutch guilder exposure. This illustration can be extended to include a larger number of currencies.

Thus, inter-currency netting is a strategy of diversification of foreign exchange risks across a multiple of currencies. Consistent with this approach, the management of foreign exchange would be directed toward the elimination/ reduction of foreign exchange losses in all currencies combined, rather than those in individual currencies. While most of the companies have used this strategy to some extent to manage their economic exposure, and sometimes their transaction exposure as well, it has been used, as it was repeatedly pointed out by the interviewees, strictly with regard to those currencies which have exhibited a high degree of correlation in their exchange rate movements, such as those in the "snake" group. Conversely, inter-currency netting generally is not used in currencies which move independently or exhibit a low degree of correlation, such as the Deutsche mark and the Brazilian cruzeiro. This is, of course, a stricter requirement than the theoretical feasibility of inter-currency netting. Two considerations underlie this requirement.

(1) The companies are generally averse to creating exposed positions and believe that by leaving an open position unhedged, they would engage in speculation.

(2) For the above consideration to be relaxed, the companies will have to have greater confidence in their exchange rate forecasts. Otherwise, the unhedged positions would result in foreign exchange losses which are not offset by gains in the other currencies, hence the requirement of correlation. That is, if the exchange rate forecasts do not materialize, the gains/losses from the exposures in the correlated currencies would still largely offset, even though the individual gains/losses will be different from the forecast amounts.

However, it appears that the difficulty with exchange rate forecasting is a more important consideration. In one way or another, it seems that the companies are more concerned with the consequences of being wrong in their forecasts than being averse to creating open positions. For example, one executive lamented that violent fluctuations of exchange rates make it very difficult to create positions to counter the effects of FASB 8. One executive, in commenting on the example about inter-currency netting involving the exposures in two currencies in two perfectly uncorrelated currencies, said: "If I have the certainty that my net results would be zero, I probably wouldn't do anything." Consider in addition the following statement:

> Earlier this year, we had a net liability position in the Dutch guilders, and we had a net asset position in Deutsche marks, and we decided that for purposes of measuring our translation exposure against the dollar, we would regard those two currencies as being the same currency. Therefore, we deducted the Deutsche mark asset position from the Dutch guilder liability position and that turns out to have been a correct decision because they did continue to move together. I cannot think offhand of any other similar decisions that we have taken, but certainly we would do so if it were appropriate in the future.

This conclusion is further supported by the fact that the companies are willing to accept open positions to effect inter-currency netting as long as the currencies move together.

This discussion leads to the inherent riskiness of inter-currency netting. On this aspect, one executive said: "It is a risky technique, in my opinion. Because it is not always guaranteed that they'll move together. There's always the possibility that they'll move out of line." This assessment was found in all of the interviews and was echoed in conversations with the foreign exchange consultants with whom this technique was discussed. Approaching the same question from another direction is to say that in order for inter-currency netting to be used extensively, the user must be confident of his exchange rate forecasts. One consultant observed:

> Ultimately, it comes down to the question of currency forecasting. The accuracy of your ability to forecast the currencies . . . and on that point, I have yet to be convinced that anyone can do it accurately and consistently.

This consultant's observation on the difficulty of exchange rate forecasting under floating exchange rates was readily shared by the interviewed executives. (This consequence of floating exchange rates will be discussed in greater detail in Chapter V, in connection with the effects of floating exchange rates on the companies' use of defensive strategies. Given this difficulty in exchange rate forecasting, the same consultant cautioned:

> I would be very wary of extensive use of the cross-currency netting type of scheme. I can see it with fairly narrow parameters, not if the amounts are significant. It is a dangerous type of thing to do because of the difficulty in forecasting. If you were held to narrow bounds, it is not so bad. But, if you are going to cover significant exposures, I would be very reluctant to take that approach.

Notwithstanding the above reservations with inter-currency netting, 9 of the 10 companies have engaged in this practice to some extent. Two companies indicated that they "always" engage in inter-currency netting, while four companies "usually" use this strategy, and three "occasionally" use it. In this regard, the remarks of two executives are worthy of note. One said:

> Theoretically, we do it constantly. It is one of the building blocks of exposure management as it is done here. There is even talk of an inter-company settlement procedure model which would merely do what you are discussing taking into consideration even more variables.

The other said, in commenting on the frequency that his company has used inter-currency netting:

It would be a primary operational type of action. We have had that situation over the year. We have had that policy to cover ourselves in the Dutch guilder. We do not have situations which involve currencies which move in opposite directions.

(Incidentally, the above company uses inter-currency netting only "occasionally," while the other "usually" uses it.)

Lest these remarks suggest a contradiction between the problems with inter-currency netting and the frequency in the use of this strategy, it should be noted, to quote one executive, that "when the overall risk is low, you tend to leave things the way they are." This points to a fundamental principle in exposure management, as suggested from the experiences of the sampled companies, which is that after all feasible defensive strategies have been used, if exposed positions remain, the resultant foreign exchange gains/losses are simply accepted. This ultimately is inter-currency netting, albeit at a lower level of risk. The question then is, what is this level of risk acceptance? The process of solving this problem is discussed in full detail in Chapter IV.

Intra-currency netting

This strategy involves the netting out of transactions denominated in the same currency, leaving the residual to be hedged in the forward exchange markets. In theory, it can be used for inter-company transactions, as well as those with third parties.[18] However, of the 10 companies in the sample, only 6 have set up arrangements to effect netting on transactions between sister subsidiaries.

To net out transactions with third parties, there is a mechanism called "internal hedge." This situation arises when an overseas subsidiary wishes to take out a forward exchange contract to cover a transaction which it feels is necessary to be protected. The parent company may decline the subsidiary's request for reasons, such as that there exists another transaction in the same currency, but is exposed in the opposite direction. However, in order that the subsidiary can protect its own profits, the parent company will agree to engage in an internal forward exchange contract with the subsidiary in question. This forward exchange contract has all the characteristics of such a contract with third parties, except that it involves two affiliated corporations. Engaging in this contract, the parent will have to eventually record a gain or loss, as the case may be, to protect the subsidiary's profits. This gain or loss is, however, purely a book entry, for it does not in any way have a cash or earnings effect on the consolidated financial statements.

Thus, from the foregoing analysis, it is clear that the sampled companies have used extensively the mentioned defensive strategies for foreign exchange risk protection purposes. In terms of the average frequency, these strategies can be ranked as follows, in declining order:

1. Debt and working capital management techniques
2. Inter-company accounts' adjustment and inter-currency netting
3. Forward exchange contracts
4. Pricing and inventory strategies
5. Leads and lags of third-party receivables and payables
6. Internal hedge

Of the defensive strategies, those used most frequently appear to be local/foreign currency borrowings. Next comes leads/lags of inter-subsidiary receivables/payables and forward exchange contracts on foreign currency transactions.

These results are comparable to the findings by Jilling, although the respondent companies in his study ranked the defensive strategies in terms of their usefulness.[19] Apparently there is a direct correlation between the usefulness of a strategy and the frequency of its use. On the other hand, certain methodological differences should be noted: (1) on the average, about one-third of his sample of companies did not respond to some part of his question; (2) his list of strategies is not comparable to the above on a strategy-by-strategy basis; (3) his analysis did not include a distinction between the behavior of large versus that of smaller firms; (4) his investigation took place in the summer of 1975, before FASB 8 was issued. On this last point, his results showed that a greater number of companies considered "local currency borrowing" to be more useful than "intracompany cash flows." The evidence presented in Chapter V of this study indicates that the emergence of floating exchange rates does not give rise to a significant increase in the use of local/foreign currency borrowings. However, after FASB 8, most of the companies in this sample have significantly increased the use of debt and working capital management techniques for defensive purposes.

Constraints

Whereas the sampled companies engage to some extent in various defensive strategies to protect themselves against foreign exchange risks, the use of these strategies is subject to a host of constraints. These constraints may be inherent in their operating mode or in parts of their external environment. How these constraints limit the companies' ability to act, and how the companies cope with them, is addressed elsewhere—as far as the empirical evidence can document—most notably in the preceding sections and Chapter V. This section seeks to categorize them and discuss some additional constraints of which the relationships with specific defensive strategies can only be discussed in a general manner.

External Constraints

These are the constraints external to the firm which it can conceivably devise ways to bypass but cannot remove. Most discussed in recent years are the introduction of generalized floating exchange rates and FASB 8. Their effects on exposure management activities of the sampled firms are analyzed in Chapter V. More traditional and familiar to firms doing business overseas are host and home country (1) laws and regulations and (2) business customs/practices.

Of the first type, controls on foreign exchange market operations and pricing flexibility, and tax laws stand out. The effects of these external constraints on international corporate finance have been discussed in great detail in the literature.[20] More directly applicable to this discussion is the fact that certain government controls effectively remove the feasibility in the use of some defensive strategies. Thus, forward exchange contract hedging of the balance sheet exposure is not possible in some developed countries, such as France and England. Even hedging of *bona fide* commercial transactions (in the forward exchange markets) is not feasible in many developing countries, simply because this facility does not exist. On the other hand, one executive pointed out that exchange controls are generally reduced since the advent of floating exchange rates:

> Under fixed exchange rates, there were a lot of controls in many countries, and you had to devote a lot of time to that. So in terms of resources expended, you have a trade-off there.

Whereas price controls presumably have a direct effect on pricing flexibility, the extent of this effect on the use of price changes as a defensive strategy cannot be readily established; although it can be suggested that where price controls are strong, price changes simply are not possible. However, nowhere in the interviews is this reason advanced to explain the relatively lesser use of price changes for defensive purposes.

In contrast, tax laws are often cited as a major obstacle to using remittances of dividends as a defensive strategy. Likewise, transfer pricing is not very favored by the sampled companies for fear of local tax authorities' scrutiny. However, income tax considerations affect forward exchange contract hedging in a different way: in order to hedge the entire amount of a balance sheet exposure, generally it is necessary to cover twice that amount if a 50 percent tax rate is assumed, thereby doubling the risk of this type of coverage. The reason is that usually unrealized exchange losses are not tax deductible, whereas the gain from the forward exchange contract is taxable at the effective tax rate.

Another type of controls which are directly relevant to exposure management are limits on leads/lags and netting of import and export payments.

However, inspection of a recent report by Business International reveals that leads/lags regulations imposed by most developed countries do not appear to be seriously restrictive, as they allow, on the average, between four to six months to effect leads and lags.[21] Denmark is an exception, imposing a 30-day limit on import leads and export lags; however, there are no limits on export leads and import lags. On the other hand, netting is more difficult. For example, Italy and Japan do not permit netting; France requires permission, but it is difficult to obtain.

Concerning business customs and practices, noteworthy are the so-called "good citizenship" consideration and concern for relationships with the local banking community. Whereas past research indicates that multinational corporations actually refrain from engaging in practices that contribute to the further detriment of a currency under pressure,[22] the results of this study do not uncover any such evidence, even after much probing. Most of the interviewed executives expressed the feeling that their companies' defensive actions do not have much impact on the foreign exchange market of any currency. One executive explained that if he feels his trading activities have any impact, in lieu of selling or buying large amounts of foreign currencies in a single day, he will spread the trading out over two to three days. Alternatively, he will engage in trading in several markets, instead of concentrating in, say, New York. The Treasurer in another company gave almost exactly the same explanation when the issue was raised in the interview. Another executive responded to the question with the answer, "Absolutely none." (The reader may refer to the questionnaire in Appendix A for the exact questions on these two issues.)

When the "good citizenship" consideration does enter into the decision-making process, it does not seem to result in much restraint. An Assistant Treasurer indicated that while he does consider this aspect, he is only concerned for developing countries "with ill-developed financial markets where we would try to avoid being disruptive in our actions." For developed countries, such as Switzerland, they "are perfectly able to manage their own affairs." Another Assistant Treasurer said:

> I am not convinced that actions in the forward market have any short-term effect on the spot price. Therefore, about forward market transactions, I would not allow myself to be concerned about that.

Similar responses were obtained when the issue of relationships with the local banking community was raised. This question arises when a company heavily engages in local currency borrowing if the currency is depreciating and usually abstains from this source of funds in the reverse case. The result is that when a currency is under pressure in either way, demand for local credit would exceed or fall short of the level that would otherwise prevail. On a macro level, this may have a destabilizing effect on the trend of the currency's exchange rate movements. From the viewpoint of a local banker, the effect might also be detrimental if his corporate clients' borrowing practices lead to insufficient funds to meet the demand when his country's currency is depreciating, but idle funds when the currency is appreciating. Although somewhat extreme, this hypothetical situation is not so far-fetched; an Assistant Treasurer acknowledged that his company had a difficult time finding a Mexican banker to lend the Mexican pesos it needed to cope with the then pending—eventually substantial—peso devaluation. Therefore, potentially active local currency borrowing—or lack thereof—may jeopardize the relationships with the local banking community.

Although one executive indicated that his company is sensitive to this sort of situation, the others did not feel either that the local banker knows the real purpose of the borrowings or that their companies' actions have much impact. As one executive said, "We would only say that we need funds." Whereas this explanation is standard, another interviewee recognized that the local banker may be able to find out the real purpose of the loan.

Since the "good citizenship" consideration was documented to be widespread in past studies and the responses obtained in this research—including those on the relationships with the local banking community—are quite similar, it is difficult to suggest that any of the findings are invalid. However, this research does not seek an explanation for this discrepancy. One possible hypothesis is that, as a result of floating exchange rates and FASB 8, potentially large foreign exchange losses have forced companies to abandon the luxury of letting themselves be constrained by these considerations.

The third type of external constraints relates to the very business of the firm which defines the specific laws and regulations applicable to it; the competitive conditions; the relationships with customers and suppliers; and the geographical distribution of its international operations. All of these factors, either directly or indirectly, have a bearing on its freedom to act for exposure management purposes. In this regard, at least one company seems to be more willing to accept foreign exchange losses than the others, as it would not seek to overminimize exposures by undertaking hedging actions that could be misinterpreted as speculation for fear of adverse publicity.

Internal Constraints

These are the constraints which relate to the internal operating mode of the firm and which characterize the ways it does business. The effects of several of these constraints on exposure management defensive strategies have been discussed in the preceding sections and will be further expanded in the next chapter:

1. The amounts of cross-border transactions with third parties and sister subsidiaries
2. Division of responsibility between overseas subsidiaries and the headquarters, and between the operating managements and the treasury/exposure management staff
3. Financial policy and plans/budgets

As found in the empirical research, there is another internal constraint that might place some limitation on the headquarter's staff to act for exposure management purposes. It is what might be called the local currency perspective of the overseas subsidiaries. Basically, this problem refers to the difficulty of communicating to overseas subsidiaries the U.S. dollar results of their profit performance which, under floating exchange rates, should usually be different from the local currency profits and losses. From a somewhat different viewpoint, this is the problem of how to evaluate subsidiary performance. To illustrate how exposure management is affected by this factor, consider the approach adopted by a company in the sample.

This company holds the headquarter's staff responsible for foreign exchange losses arising from translation of subsidiaries' statements and the cost of inventory adjustment. Since it is more difficult for the local subsidiary to manage the translation loss, it seems logical to measure its performance without consideration for this currency effect. On the other hand, inventory management is an operating responsibility as it is related to the ability to increase prices; it appears, therefore, that any currency effects on inventory should be the subsidiary's responsibility. If exempted from this responsibility, the subsidiary will not be penalized for failure to keep prices current with higher inventory costs, thereby jeopardizing the gross margin and profitability. And yet, the headquarter's staff cannot effectively correct this situation since it does not have control over pricing decisions. As a result, either higher hedging costs will have to be incurred or currency effects on inventory are not adquately dealt with.

The difficulty in communicating U.S. dollar results with the local subsidiary is further increased if it is staffed mostly by local nationals. It is mentioned on several occasions in the interviews that a lot of persuasion is required so that such local subsidiaries cooperate with the headquarter's staff to undertake defensive strategies which might be perceived detrimental to the host country.

Overall, the multinational firm operating in different areas of the world generally faces a great number of constraints, both internal as well as external. Therefore, the above discussion is not meant to be a complete list of the factors limiting a firm's ability to act. It merely reports those constraints that have some direct relevance to exposure management activities as they are found in this empirical research. The following quotation from an Assistant Treasurer illustrates how an exposure management action can have an implication beyond the financial area:

> If it becomes general knowledge that your subsidiary in a particular country is reducing its assets, how would that affect your competitive strength?

Summary and Conclusion

This chapter is devoted to the discussion of the methodologies of currency exposure measurement in the sampled companies, their foreign exchange management objectives, and the defensive strategies and constraints.

On currency exposure measurement, the empirical findings indicate that the companies do not follow the concept of future cash flows to define their currency exposures. However, they do go beyond the balance sheet to get at the overall effects of exchange rate changes. In this respect, there is complete agreement among the companies on a conceptual level about the transactions/ items that should be included in the currency exposure. In practice, certain differences exist.

All of the sampled companies include the translation and transaction components in their formal exposure definition. The reason for the inclusion of the transaction component is straightforward: it consists of items that require the conversion of funds from one currency to another, hence are exposed to the risk of cash losses from changes in the relative value of currencies. The translation component is included because, under FASB 8, adjustments on them are required to be recognized as current income, although at the time of recognition cash flows are not affected. Putting it differently, whether or not cash losses are at risk, reported earnings are affected due to adjustments on these exposure components.

The companies also consider inventory an exposed item. Their practices in this regard, however, differ because of concern for earnings fluctuations. This is a result of FASB 8's treatment of inventory and the "lower of cost or market" rule. Thus, four of the sampled companies exclude this component from their currency exposure measurement because they are quite concerned with the translation effects on their earnings. Those companies which include inventory, however, do not follow the economic distinction between inventories which are subject to price controls or otherwise pricing inflexibility and those which are not. They either include all inventories or that portion calculated based on the turn-over rate. Of these (six) companies, again, because of concern for earnings fluctuations, four have moved back and forth between the inclusion and exclusion of this exposure component.

Off-balance sheet items (including dividend remittances) are also considered exposed because eventually they will become part of the translation and/

or transaction exposure, although most companies do not include them in the formal exposure definition. Nine out of ten companies, however, do take out forward exchange contracts to hedge these items. With respect to exposed earnings, the analysis suggests that the exclusion of this exposure component does not constitute a significant distortion of the currency exposure. Actually, its inclusion tends to overstate the exposure amount to the extent that part of revenue and expenses are reflected in the translation and transaction exposures.

With the currency defined as such, the overall objective of the sampled companies is to minimize foreign exchange losses. From the standpoint of translation losses—as defined by FASB 8—the primary objective is to keep these losses at a minimum. This defensive posture, however, is somewhat abated when it comes to foreign currency transactions. In fact, on transaction gains/losses, the companies seek to make profit when opportunities arise, but not to the extent of engaging in speculation or creating exposures to take advantage of currency movements. Yet, often there is a conflict between the reported earnings (accounting) objective and economic performance, a conflict which is difficult to solve and frequently involves top management in the exposure management activities. As a result, four of the companies which choose to define their currency exposures differently from FASB 8—insofar as the balance sheet accounts are concerned—have found themselves moving back and forth between the "FASB 8" and "FASB 8 plus inventory" approaches. This conflict is further aggravated by the absence of definitive policy guidelines from top management. This is not to say that this conflict of objectives does not exist in the other companies. It simply means that the conflict does not result in any shift in the currency exposure definition.

Toward these objectives, the companies engage extensively in defensive actions. They range from forward exchange market operations to price increases. Following is a ranking of the defensive strategies in terms of the frequency of their usage:

1. Debt and working capital management techniques
2. Inter-company accounts' adjustment and inter-currency netting
3. Forward exchange contracts
4. Pricing and inventory strategies
5. Leads and lags of third-party receivables and payables
6. Internal hedge

Within these groups, the most frequently used strategies appear to be local/foreign currency borrowings and short-term asset/liability management, followed by leads and lags of inter-subsidiary receivables and payables, and forward exchange contract hedging of foreign currency transactions.

The use of these strategies is subject to a number of constraints, both internal and external to the firm. These constraints not only serve as limitations on the feasibility of certain defensive actions; in some instances, they also rule out the use of some strategies. Examples are availability of cross-border transactions or absence of the foreign exchange market facility.

Of the internal constraints, directly relevant to the defensive strategies are:

1. The amounts of cross-border transactions with third parties and sister subsidiaries
2. Division of responsibility between overseas subsidiaries and the headquarters, and between the operating managements and the treasury/exposure management staff
3. Financial policy and plans/budgets
4. The local currency perspective of the overseas subsidiaries
5. The nationality of the overseas subsidiaries' managements

The external constraints can be classified into two broad categories: (1) laws and regulations, and (2) business customs and practices. Of the first type, controls on foreign exchange market operations and tax laws stand out. For example, forward exchange contract hedging is not possible in many countries. Or, tax laws are often cited as major obstacles to using dividend remittances or transfer pricing for defensive purposes. Another type of controls which are directly relevant to exposure management are limits on leads/lags and netting of import and export payments. Of the second type, noteworthy is the weak influence of the so-called "good citizenship" consideration and the concern for relationships with the local banking community on the sampled companies' exposure management activities.

Overall, the multinational firms with worldwide operations are subject to a broad array of constraints; all serve either directly or indirectly to limit their ability or freedom to act. Nevertheless, the sampled companies have extensively used the defensive strategies available to them for protection against foreign exchange risks, and more so in the face of greater uncertainty under floating exchange rates and the constraints of FASB 8's provisions. These aspects are discussed in Chapter V.

Chapter IV

Information Systems, Risk Analysis, and Selection of Defensive Strategies

The previous chapter presented the empirical findings on corporate practices in the methodology of currency exposure measurement, foreign exchange management objectives, defensive strategies, and the factors which constrain these strategies. This chapter presents the evidence on two elements which link the above chain of events in the foreign exchange management process, i.e., information system and risk analysis. The first half of the chapter is devoted to a discussion of the systems whereby the sampled companies collect the data necessary for their exposure management activities. It provides an answer to the following research question: What information systems collect the data on future exchange rates, currency exposures, and risk/cost consequences of the defensive strategies? In the second half, the discussion will be focused on the process whereby the companies analyze the risk-return trade-offs of the defensive strategies and select those consistent with this risk analysis and the foreign exchange management objectives. Answers are sought for the following research question: What are the procedures and/or organization used to analyze, evaluate, and select defensive strategies with consideration for their risk-return trade-offs?

Information System

Within the context of foreign exchange management, the role of an information system is to provide the decision-maker with a set of data on the operations and/or assets and liabilities being exposed to foreign exchange risks, as well as the risk/cost consequences of any defensive strategies taken to achieve the objectives, implicitly or explicitly stated. On the currency exposure, the data must be organized to provide numerical measurement of the amounts exposed on a currency-by-currency, as well as global basis. Another set of data that must be provided by the system is that of future exchange rates.

The importance of the information system cannot be overemphasized. As one executive put it, it is the very "backbone" of any exposure management system. And this refers more to the exposed positions than exchange rate forecasting. Some executives were even willing to suggest that reporting of currency exposures takes precedence over forecasting of exchange rate movements. Consider some of the statements made by the interviewees in this regard in response to the following question: We have discussed division of responsibility, reporting systems, exchange rate forecasting, planning, and defensive strategies. These activities can be be viewed as separate, but interrelated parts of an overall foreign exchange management strategy. What would you consider is/are the most important element(s) of your foreign exchange management strategy?

One response was: "The reporting system at this junction is the key to it all."

Another response was:

> I really think the backbone is knowing your risks. You have to know your exposure. If you don't know, you can't do anything. That's knowing what your exposures are; reporting; by control over things. To protect the company, you have to know what is going on. It takes a lot of discipline to yank out of the woodwork. The reason why I think it is the most important thing is that the job function here isn't projecting exchange rates. That doesn't earn a bit of money for the company. We aren't traders, we aren't selling forecasts. That isn't our function. Our function is minimizing risks of currencies that can affect our balance sheet or our earnings. The most fundamental thing is to know what your risks are. Then, once you know what they are, you are in a position to assign costs; what is an acceptable risk.

One executive answered,

> The reporting system is crucial. It tell us what to do. Without knowing, you're lost. If you don't know what your exposures are, you can't do anything. This is the first thing. Forecasting is something that comes after. But you're talking about the backbone; the most crucial thing is reporting the figures.

Another executive said,

> I would be hard pressed to really view those as separate functions. I think they are all integral portions. I can't see that forecasting without an adequate reporting system is going to be of any use to the company in determining their position. I would say that this Company, as of late, has recognized the importance of reporting. The reporting up to now has been limited to basically the three reports that I have mentioned to you. I think what has happened is the recognition has come that, in order to do a more effective job, the reporting structure itself is going to have to be expanded. We are going to need forecasts. By this, I am talking about forecasts of balance sheets. They are going to require information regarding inventories, sources of supply, price controls, elasticity, etc. But that has only evolved as we have become more knowledgeable of what the function is.

Although exchange rate forecasting is procedurally—and perhaps in terms of its contribution to the overall foreign exchange management effort—secondary to reporting, it has attracted great attention since the emergence of floating exchange rates. An Assistant Treasurer said,

So we had to institute around 1973, some very time consuming and terribly sophisticated systems of forecasting exchange rates to allow the controller function in the company to forecast to top management what the dollar value of foreign currency earnings and revenues were going to be.

That exchange rate forecasting under floating exchange rates is important is hardly surprising. What might be surprising is the emphasis on the reporting system in the overall foreign exchange management strategy. The evidence uncovered in this research suggests that this phenomenon is a direct result of FASB 8. (This will be discussed in greater detail in Chapter V.) Perhaps for this reason, here was hardly, if any, discussion on this aspect of the foreign exchange management function before 1976. Even "the first comprehensive study of how corporations actually are attempting to manage the exchange risk"[1] initiated in mid-1975, failed to include even a passage on this subject area.

In this section, the discussion will be focused on the process whereby the sampled companies attempt to generate the data necessary to determine their exposures and the risk/cost consequences of their actions.

Currency Exposure

Consistent with the emphasis on those defensive strategies which are available in the money/capital and foreign exchange markets, the focus of exposure management on reported earnings, and the division of exposure management activities between the overseas subsidiaries and the headquarter's treasury/ exposure management staff, the data base and reports on currency exposure are oriented toward the balance sheet. In other words, such data as local competitive conditions and other operating factors which may have effects on the currency exposure are not part of the companies' foreign exchange management information systems. On the cost side, the emphasis is on exchange rate movements.

Data base

The reports sent from the subsidiaries provided the treasury/exposure management staff at the parent headquarters with two sets of data: translation and transaction exposure—these terminologies are defined in Chapter III. These reports seek to project the present—actually, as they exist at the end of the immediately preceding reporting period, i.e., month—and future short-term effects of currency fluctuations, i.e., one year or less, rather than their longer term effects. They are also oriented toward reported earnings (which include accrued items), rather than cash flow effects. In this regard, only two companies indicated that they integrate their cash flow and cash forecast reports into their exposure management information systems.

Typically, the reports of exposed positions on a balance sheet basis are sent from the overseas subsidiaries to the parent headquarters on a monthly basis. In one company, the exposure management group further refine the information by making up estimates for the interim exposure data by currency every 15 days. As these statistics provide only fixed, as opposed to anticipated, exposures, provisions are made for the subsidiaries to forecast their exposed positions, mostly up to 12 months. These forecasts are particularly important, for exchange rate fluctuations affect future positions, not those existing at the previous reporting date. They are even more so for companies which have significant changes in their natural exposures, i.e., due to operating circumstances, not as a result of exposure management activities which seek to change them.

It should be pointed out that forecasts for exposure management purposes are different from those for planning. For the latter, the forecasts only need to be expressed in dollars with inter-company flows not identified as such. On the other hand, for exposure management, the data have to be broken down by currencies and inter-company transactions need to be specifically identified, also by currency.

One company does not feel that it is necessary to obtain forecast exposed positions, i.e., it relies on past data, because there is little change from quarter to quarter. Another company does not have access to forecast positions but plans to do so. The Assistant Treasurer, however, feels reluctant to ask for projected data beyond a six-month period, for he is concerned about the integrity of the data on a longer forecasting horizon. An additional reason lies in the accounts receivable financing method of its largest operating division. This division finances its sales by the financing lease method. The Assistant Treasurer explained:

> The result of them being on the financing lease method is that what you are abrogating in one year is five years' worth of receivables. Albeit, you are going to have a profit running through, but you also do have an exposed receivable that represents five years of monthly collections. So, we can have wild fluctuations in our exposure depending on the time that a lease is signed, the equipment is sold and operational. It becomes very difficult to go beyond the six-month period of time, and sometimes it becomes very difficult to deal within the confines of a specific month. We may very well find that what we are going to have to rely on is quarterly information as monthly becomes too finite.

Another reason is the scarcity of the required skilled personnel at the subsidiary level. The Assistant Treasurer-International Finance at another company said:

> It is the nature of the people involved. It requires a certain financial expertise which we don't have in general. There are certain of the larger operating subsidiaries that could do it.

Consequently, this company refrains from asking its overseas subsidiaries to provide the headquarters with forecasts on balance sheet data for exposure management purposes. However, recognizing the importance of these forecasts, this weakness is complemented by three-month projections on cash holdings and debt balances, as well as yearly budget data, although the latter are not directly useful for exposure management activities. The Assistant Treasurer-International Finance explained:

> We do use the financial planning data as a management tool to take a longer range look at the foreign exchange management aspects. Financial planning is a very important part of our overall management. Consequently, the numbers there are pretty good, and local managements tend to stick to them. But of course, they are not provided in a way that would make them directly usable. Specifically, they are provided in foreign currencies which do not take into account third currency assets and liabilities. It is really used as an additional tool for strategic planning for the foreign exchange management effort.

Under the circumstances, cash and debt forecasts are particularly useful, as the company's inventories remain relatively stable, since they can largely indicate the swings in the balance sheet exposure.

The forecasts are performed on all the components of the currency exposure, as these companies define them. In this connection, it is interesting to note that whether or not a company includes inventory in its exposure definition, inventory is still considered an exposed asset, and therefore found on the exposure reports sent in from the overseas subsidiaries. If the exposure definition does not include inventory, this item is treated as a memo item on the exposure report.

The exposed items which are related to the balance sheet may be broken into separate components or lumped together to yield net figures. From the viewpoint of exposure management, this refinement is not particularly important, except that it indicates those components which most contribute to the exposure. Seven of the companies require this breakdown from their subsidiaries. Additionally, five of the companies require the reporting of the balance sheet items—other than inventory—which are translated at historical rates, i.e., fixed assets, capital accounts, and retained earnings. This fine-tuning is to insure that assets equal liabilities.

Since all of the companies adjust their balance sheet exposure for outstanding forward exchange contracts, these data are also presented. The information on these transactions consists of the currency denominations of the contracts, the amounts bought and sold, the maturity dates of the contracts, and the contracted or forward rates.

Another exposure component consists of inter-company receivables and payables. These items are then netted out at the parent headquarters to yield the amounts of the external exposures. One company does not require this information, since it has very little inter-company transactions.

All of the exposure components are broken down on a currency-by-currency basis on the exposure reports. In this regard, the practice of the companies slightly differ. There are three varieties in this respect. At one company, only the local currency of the reporting unit is reported, i.e., the subsidiary's third currency transactions are not segregated. The justification for this practice is that it does not have a significant amount of cross-border transactions. At two other companies, the local currency items are segregated from third currency components. The latter are lumped together and expressed in U.S. dollars. In one of these two companies, those foreign currency amounts greater than U.S.$500,000 are detailed by currency and amount. At this point, a comment is in order. When the exposure components are not broken down on a currency-by-currency basis, the reporting would be reduced to a country-by-country format. However, if cross-border transactions are negligible, this distortion would not be material. For the other companies, the exposure components are broken down into individual currency denominations.

Whether or not foreign currency items are segregated, the reports from the overseas subsidiaries would then be consolidated to yield a company-wide exposure by currency. The global exposure would then be adjusted for individual countries' tax effects. Four of the companies, however, indicated that they do not adjust their exposures for tax effects. The reason, they claimed, is that they do not take out foreign exchange contracts on a regular basis, or sometimes not at all. One of the remaining six companies adjusts for tax effects only when balance sheet hedging in the forward exchange market is undertaken. In this connection, it is useful to recall the previous discussion on the effects of income taxes on inter-company transactions: On an after-tax basis, inter-company transactions do not offset, as some companies believe.

For the one company which formally includes exposed earnings in its exposure definition, this exposure component is also broken down by currencies. The future positions on this component are then provided by the subsidiaries, as in the case of the other exposed items.

Data configuration

The data on the exposure components remitted from the overseas subsidiaries can be compiled in different formats and are included in several different forms. This section discusses the reports which are sent from the subsidiaries and constitute the currency exposure measurement part of the foreign exchange management information system, as found in the sampled companies.

As found in the field research, the first approach is a full-blown balance sheet by currency. This balance sheet report presents all the balance sheet items, as well as provides for a computation of the currency exposures in individual currencies. One such combined balance sheet and exposure report is shown in Figure 4. With some minor deviations from the report format shown in Figure 4, the overseas subsidiaries' combined balance sheet and exposure reports include all standard balance sheet items broken down by currency. By blocking out the relevant spaces, adding all the balance sheet items that are translated at current rates, will give the amounts of the individual currencies' exposures.

A presentation alternative is shown in Figure 5. Instead of following the conventional balance sheet format, in this format, all the items to be translated at current rates, are shown in the upper half of the report, whereas the items to be translated at applicable historical rates are shown in the lower half. It is obvious that there is no meaningful difference between the format illustrated in Figure 4 and that in Figure 5, except that the latter seems easier to read.

A third alternative is to delete all balance sheet items that are translated at historical rates. This is shown in Figure 6 and labeled "exposure report." In order to assess the effects on inventories and inter-company transactions, these items are included as "memo items" at the bottom of the report. The disadvantage of this format is that some exposed items may be unintentionally left out of the exposure computation. This error occurs most probably on the "prepaid expense" and "other noncurrent assets" categories because some part of these items may be translated at current rates, and the remaining items at historical rates. However, due to the relatively insignificant share of these items in the total assets, the distortion should not be material.

A fourth alternative is to net out exposed assets from exposed liabilities, as shown in Figure 7. To help reconcile the accounts, the items to be translated at historical rates are also added. This format also has the weakness of that shown in Figure 6. Additionally, it conceals the maneuverability of the individual exposed. In other words, the breakdown of the individual exposed items would help direct attention to the items of which the contributions to the overall exposure are either inordinate or most reduceable.

Since all of the companies consider inventory exposed, although not all of them undertake hedging on it, an analysis of inventory is also provided to segregate the portion which is imported from that which is locally acquired/produced. This inventory analysis is shown in Figure 8. Usually, this analysis is included in the exposure report or the combined balance sheet and currency exposure report. However, when this approach is used, the inventory components are not broken down. An alternative to this procedure is to have the overseas subsidiary assess the impact of currency fluctuations on inventory on a flow through basis, i.e., that portion of inventory which is sold, and therefore reported under the category of "Costs of Goods Sold." This inventory analysis is shown in Figure 9. This alternative is equivalent to calculating that portion of inventory which is exposed to exchange rate fluctuations. Thus, if the inventory turn-over rate is less than 12, which is the case for manufacturing companies—

Foreign Exchange Management in Multinational Firms

Figure 4
Balance Sheet and Currency Exposure Report (I), Period Ended ———

	Local Currency	Foreign Currency	U.S. Dollar Equivalent
Assets:			
Current Assets:			
Cash			
Accounts Receivable			
Less: Reserve for Bad Debts		XXXXXX	
Inter-company Receivables			
Miscellaneous Receivables			
Inventory			
Prepaid Expenses			
Total Current Assets			
Long-term Receivables			
Property and Equipment	XXXXXX	XXXXXX	
Other Noncurrent Assets	XXXXXX	XXXXXX	
Total Assets			
Liabilities:			
Current Liabilities:			
Notes Payable			
Accounts Payable			
Accrued Expenses			
Current Portion of Long-term Debt			
Income Tax Payable		XXXXXX	
Inter-company Payable			
Total Current Liabilities			
Long-term Debt			
Deferred Income Tax	XXXXXX	XXXXXX	
Stockholders' Equity	XXXXXX	XXXXXX	
Total Liabilities			
Exposure			XXXXXX

Figure 5
Balance Sheet and Currency Exposure Report (II), Period Ended ———

	Local Currency	Foreign Currency	U.S. Dollar Equivalent
Translated at Current Rates			
Assets:			
Cash			
Accounts Receivable			
Less: Reserve For			
Bad Debts			
Miscellaneous Receivables			
Prepaid Expenses			
Other Noncurrent Assets			
Total Assets			
Liabilities			
Notes Payable			
Accounts Payable			
Accrued Expenses			
Current Portion of			
Long-term Debt			
Income Tax Payable			
Long-term Debt			
Noncurrent			
Total Liabilities			
Translated at Historical Rates			
Assets:			
Inventory			
Prepaid Expenses			
Other Noncurrent Assets			
Total Assets			
Liabilities:			
Deferred Income Tax			
Stockholders' Equity			
Total Liabilities			
TOTAL	-0-	-0-	-0-

Figure 6
Currency Exposure Report (I), Period Ended ———

	Local Currency	Foreign Currency	U.S. Dollar Equivalent
Cash			
Short-term Receivables			
Long-term Receivables			
Total Monetary Assets			
Notes Payable			
Income Tax Payable			
Other Current Liabilities			
Long-term Debt			
Total Monetary Liabilities			
Memo Items:			
Inventory			
Inter-Company:			
Receivables			
Payables			

Figure 7
Currency Exposure Report (II), Period Ended ———

	Local Currency	Foreign Currency	U.S. Dollar Equivalent
Accounts Translated at Current Rate:			
Long (Short)			
Accounts Translated at Historical Rate:			
Inventory			
Property and Equipment			
Other Assets/Liabilities			
Total			

and for the sampled companies—this would reduce the share of inventory in the exposure computation. In other words, if the turn-over rate is three (i.e., four months worth of sales is in the inventory), approximately one-fourth of inventory (assuming imported and local inventories are evenly divided) is included in the exposure. When the measurement period is quarterly, the inventory share in the exposure is three-fourths.

Included in the report shown in Figure 9 are the effects of currency fluctuations on the statement of income. This includes, in addition to those on costs of goods sold, all the revenues and expense items. These effects are derived by adding back to profit-after-tax, those expenses which are translated at historical rates, e.g., depreciation expenses. From a balance sheet point of view, the net effect of this procedure is to add a portion of retained earnings into the currency exposure computation.

Besides the balance sheet and statement of income, there are also two other exposure components that the companies take into consideration in computing the earnings effects of exchange rate fluctuations. The first category includes off-balance sheet items which consist primarily of confirmed orders and unbooked liabilities. They are exposed to currency fluctuations by virtue of the fact that the local/foreign currency amounts cannot be changed. This report is illustrated in Figure 10. The next item is the forward exchange contract hedge which all of the sampled companies uniformly adjust for earnings effects. The report for this item is rather simple, as shown in Figure 11. It includes the currency denomination of the contract, the amount, the forward rate, and the maturity date.

Exchange Rates and Risk-Return Trade-Off

This section presents the empirical findings on the process that generates exchange rate forecasts and the risks and costs/benefits of the defensive strategies. Combined with the data on currency exposures, they constitute the data base for the exposure management function. This section also discusses the form of the data that are generated in this process.

Exchange rates

From the findings, a remarkable feature of the forecasting procedure as it was found in the sampled companies emerges: the critical role of the treasury/exposure management staff in the generation of exchange rate forecasts necessary for planning as well as hedging purposes. This is true whether or not a company has the in-house capability to produce the initial forecasts. Furthermore, while one individual, e.g., the Foreign Exchange Manager, may be charged with the task of monitoring exchange rate movements, the final forecasts to be used for decision-making are the result of group effort.

Figure 8
Inventory Analysis, Month Ended ———

	Local Currency	Foreign Currency	U.S. Dollar Equivalent
Finished Goods			
Raw Materials:			
x_1			
x_2			
*			
*			
*			
x_n			
Total			

Figure 9
Statement of Income and Flow-Through Effects of Currency Fluctuations, Period Ended ———

	Local Currency	Foreign Currency	U.S. Dollar Equivalent
Profit after Tax			
Add:			
Depreciation		XXXXXX	
Costs of Goods Sold		XXXXXX	
Other Items at Historical Rate		XXXXXX	
Net Revenue (Expenses) at Current Rate			
Effects on Costs of Goods Sold of 1% change in Exchange Rate at Month-end of Current Month			
Effects on Costs of Goods Sold of 1% change in Exchange Rate at Month-end of the following Month			

Figure 10
Off-Balance Sheet Items

	Local Currency	Foreign Currency	U.S. Dollar Equivalent
Confirmed Orders:			
Quarter ended			
*			
*			
*			
*			
Unbooked liabilities:			
Quarter ended			
*			
*			
*			
*			
Net			

Figure 11
Forward Exchange Contracts

Currency	Amount	Maturity Rate	Contract Rate
Currency 1			
Currency 2			
*			
*			
*			
Currency n			

The process of exchange rate forecasting can be divided into two phases which are quite distinct: technical analysis and decision-making.

In the first phase, exchange rate forecasts are obtained from all sources, including internal economists. However, only 3 of the 10 companies who have economists in their employ participate in the process of developing the forecasts. Of these three, two companies use formal mathematical modeling to assist the effort. In one company, the technical analysis starts with an analysis of balance of payments data to determine a country's foreign exchange reserve levels. It is then moved on to an econometric model which is based on the regression method. Thus, for example, the Deutsche mark/U.S. dollar exchange rate is regressed to the German and U.S. current account balances, the ratio between the levels of the German and U.S. interest rate and the Euromark/Eurodollar rate. For the Canadian dollar, the model is modified to take into account the fact that a lot of Canada's foreign exchange earnings come from exports of raw materials which are less responsive to exchange rate changes than to domestic price levels. The other company relies exclusively on interest differentials. But the purpose of the forecasts so generated is to verify the forecasts produced by the treasury department; these model-based forecasts are generated in the Controller's office. The third company does not use a model—or at least not identified as such.

For most companies, the bulk of the information comes from two sources: foreign exchange consultants and banks. Six of the companies subscribe to foreign exchange consulting services for this purpose—but not for it alone. Of these six companies, three also use the resources of their internal economists for exchange rate forecasting. Another company, although it does not subscribe to outside consulting services, actually has access to the services of a consulting firm, by virtue of the fact that the head of its economics group is an officer of this firm. At any rate, whether or not outside forecasting services are available, input from banks are used very extensively in the forecasting process. All of the companies claim that they frequently contact their banks—as often as daily—for the latest developments in the foreign exchange markets as well as the bankers' projections of future rates. Bank services in this regard encompass both short- and long-term forecasting.

On the other hand, one company which does not have an internal economics group (for exchange rate forecasting) or subscribe to an outside consulting service finds that country visits—in countries where it has subsidiaries—provide very useful input for developing medium-term forecasts as well as the business plan rates to be used in the fiscal year.

In sum, the principal sources of exchange rate forecasts external of the treasury/exposure management staff are, in declining order: banks, foreign exchange consultants, in-house economists, and mathematical models. Table 19 indicates the number of companies which subscribe to each of these sources.

Wherever the companies obtain the forecasting input, the treasury/exposure management staff play a major role in the development of the final forecasts for both planning as well as hedging purposes. This is the decision-making phase. Although in this phase of the forecasting process the procedures are not structured and formalized, they do not take place in a vacuum. As indicated, typically, the forecasting starts with the input from sources outside the company. These sources range from in-house mathematical models to banks' advice. Subsequently, the staff attempt to consolidate the external input into a consolidated forecast by going through a process which one interviewee described as "scratching our head." It nevertheless has two distinct features: evaluation of the external input by the staff using, among other factors, fundamental economic indicators and intuition, and group discussion.

Table 19
Sources of Exchange Rate Forecasts

Source	Companies
Banks	10
Foreign Exchange Consultants	6
Internal Economists	3
Mathematical Models	2

Evaluation of the external input is considered a very important phase in the forecasting process. The reason is two-fold. On the one hand, as it was explained in the interviews, exchange rate forecasting under floating exchange rates has been a quite difficult task. As fixed par values and narrow margins were removed, currencies can fluctuate in any direction and often in large swings. As one executive described this environment, "I cannot think of any other market that is subject to this kind of gyrations—commodity futures or whatever." Combined with the market sensitivity to psychological factors, these fluctuations reduce the usefulness of any analysis of exchange rate movements based on fundamental economic forces, such as interest differentials or balance of payments data. Since most, if not all, forecasting services provide forecasts based on economic indicators, which may or may not be tempered by the forecasters' judgment of the factors that produce them, a re-evaluation of these factors must be made by the corporate users. Additionally, as it was often said in the interviews, banks tend to be very short-term oriented while economists' orientation is in the long-run. Therefore, the gap must be filled by the corporate users of the forecasts produced from these sources.

Another reason for a corporate review of the external input is a recognition shared by the corporate users and the foreign exchange consultants: No single source can produce forecasts consistently in the right direction, much less chance that they are correct consistently in the magnitude of the changes; hence, the necessity of a multiple of forecasting sources which require a consolidation to derive a set of final forecasts.

For the evaluation of the initial forecasts, they are filtered through what may be called the treasury staff's perception of the factors, and their relative importance, which determine the exchange rate movements. While a host of factors may affect this perception—including the individual's professional training and background, the depth of his exposure to forecasting problems, and even personality—the following factors can be identified as to have a direct contribution to this filtering process:

1. Feedback from subsidiaries
2. Financial publications
3. Fundamental economic indicators, e.g., interest differentials
4. Contacts with the markets, e.g., banks
5. Individual intuition and judgment

Of course, the relative importance of the above factors does not necessarily follow the order that they appear. One executive said that he relies mostly on bank contacts, while another principally on country visits and the forward rate. An Assistant Treasurer said: "On an overall basis and longer term basis, I have a tendency to rely on the purchasing parity concept more than anything else." It thus seems that how these factors and to what extent these factors contribute in the filtering process depend on the individual.

In this connection, it is informative to cite a survey result on the relative usefulness of different forecasting sources. According to this survey, slightly over 80 per cent of the respondents felt that financial publications are an important source of their forecasts, second only to banking institutions; of tertiary importance is feedback from subsidiaries.[2] Since the survey did not distinguish between technical analysis and decision-making, the results are not directly comparable to the findings in this research. However, the fact that these sources were cited as most important seems to confirm the finding that the decision-making phase is considered most important in the forecasting process at the sampled companies, and that the individual evaluator's perception plays a critical role in this phase. This conclusion is based on the observation that financial publications by themselves do not provide forecasts, whereas banks and subsidiaries supply the forecasts as well as their sentiments about the strength or weakness of a currency.

Once the forecasts from all available sources have been consolidated and evaluated at the staff level, they are subject to further evaluation by going through what may be called "group discussion." In this final phase of the forecasting process, the consolidated forecasts are subject to scrutiny by a group of which the members include the highest level of the treasury's organizational hierarchy. In one company, even the Financial Vice President is involved. In another, the forecasts are submitted to the President on a routine basis. In yet another company, there exists an even more formalized approach to this group discussion. In this company, the Controller's office maintains a historical charting of interest differentials using 1973 as the base. These interest differentials would be used to determine the future movements of a particular currency against the U.S. dollar as if they were the only influence. The treasury department's forecasts must be compared with the forecasts generated from the Controller's office. Any significant discrepancies then will have to be reconciled by the two departments.

The results of the group discussion are a set of exchange rate forecasts which are accepted as official for distribution and used for decision-making purposes. Because of this use of forecasts generated by this process, the final phase of the forecasting process is characterized as the decision-making phase, as opposed to the preceding steps which are basically data gathering and data evaluation.

Risk and cost

At the outset of this empirical research, it was conceptualized that risk is a critical decision variable in the foreign exchange management decision-making process. It was then suggested that the measurement of risk should recognize the central tendency measure and some measure of dispersion such as variance. (For ease of exposition, hereafter the measure of dispersion is assumed to be the variance.) In the context of exposure management, this risk measurement requires the specification of the expected value (or mean) of the currency's exchange rate forecasts and the variance about the mean.

The field research indicates that risk is indeed recognized in practice as a critical decision variable in the decision-making process. The executives who are involved in this process are quite conscious of it and attempt to deal with it, and very seriously so. However, mathematical modeling such as the risk-return framework suggested in the original conceptual model does not play a very important role in this process, or at least not so in the final phases when a decision is about to be made. In this phase, the basis of a decision is derived from what some executives called "subjective judgment." In some companies, there exists a more formalized approach in the form of an organization called the "foreign exchange management committee." For the purpose of this discussion, this phase is termed the "decision-making phase." Preceding it is what may be called the "technical analysis phase." It is in this phase of technical analysis that some form of probability estimation is attempted to measure the risk. This analysis, however, is not structured and formalized, and the depth of it depends on the individual performing the analysis. This non-mathematical approach to risk analysis, which will be detailed in the second half of this chapter, is reflected clearly in the presentation of exchange rate forecasts.

Part of the reason for the little use of probabilistic statements for presentation of exchange rate forecasts lies in the erratic movements of exchange rates, not due to any question on the validity of probabilities. In fact, 3 of the 10 companies in the sample had at one time attempted to present their forecasts in terms of probabilities, or in such a way that either probabilities or even variance can be derived. This effort, however, was quickly abandoned. The Treasurer of one company said that probabilities are not useful in the environment of floating exchange rates. The Assistant Treasurer of another explained.

> We have tried that and found that it does not work. . . . We don't say that there is 30 per cent chance, 70 per cent chance or even more than 50 per cent chance or less than 50 per cent chance. We don't give a range. We tried to do all those things and our Controller's office said they understood how difficult it is to forecast exchange rates. We understand that you would like to give it in terms of probabilities. But in fact, our computer does not understand probabilities. You have to say that the Japanese yen will be 210, or it will be 220 or 185. There is no good telling us that there will be a 55 per cent chance, etc. . . . That doesn't work.

The third company had used range estimation, but quickly dropped this practice for it found that this level of fine-tuning was "not that useful." Furthermore, "probably management would not understand it."

Consequently, all three companies, like the others in the sample, now present their exchange rate forecasts in terms of point estimates. Underlying this practice is the large variability of exchange rate movements in the present floating rate regime. This is not to say that these corporate officers believe that exchange rate movements follow random walk. An implication of the random walk hypothesis is that in a market where prices fluctuate randomly, i.e., in speculative markets (and indeed some writers have suggested that the foreign exchange markets do possess some, if not all, characteristics of a speculative market) [3] forecasting is profitable (in other words, the forecaster can do better than the market) only if he meets one or more of the following conditions:

> (1) he has a superior model, known only to himself (and in a competitive market, nobody can keep a secret); (2) he has consistent access to information before others in the market can get it (and this is a rarity in the highly-informed international network of banks; (3) he is an in-and-out trader who exploits small, temporary deviations from equilibrium (and these actions in themselves serve to bring rates to reflect the new information); (4) he is able to predict the ways in which the government will intervene in the foreign exchange markets. [4]

One might suggest that from the viewpoint of corporate users of exchange rate forecasts, the above is a moot point if they do not seek from their own forecasts to outperform the market. At least as far as the sampled companies are concerned, the objective seems to be just to predict market trends, just to do as well as the market. In the words of one Assistant Treasurer: "We are not a trading room; this is not a foreign exchange trading office."

This observation probably better explains the proliferation of exchange rate forecasting services and the need by corporate users for a multiple of forecasting sources. It might also better explain the efforts of the consulting firms to broaden their client base. Indeed, as an extension of this observation, if the efficient market hypothesis is realistically descriptive of the foreign exchange markets, the greater the number of people using these forecasts and acting accordingly, the more self-fulfilling these forecasts become.

More relevant to this discussion, if indeed companies only aim at predicting market trends when making exchange rate forecasts, they would rely on balance sheet re-structuring strategies such as inter-company accounts' adjustment in their exposure management effort. The fact that the sampled companies do use these strategies extensively suggests that their exchange rate forecasting is of a defensive nature.

On the other hand, under the conditions of an efficient market, to be consistent with this forecasting objective companies should not be concerned with the currency denominations of their debts. The reason is, from the standpoint of cost, when interest and exchange rate are both taken into consideration, the effective costs of debts denominated in different currencies are the same (except to the extent of small deviations from the theoretical Fisher Effect). Companies should especially avoid engaging in forward exchange contracts, and more particularly, should avoid hedging translation exposures. The fact that the sampled companies do use these strategies extensively (infrequently to hedge translation exposure in the foreign exchange markets) suggests that they do seek profits from exchange rate forecasting.

Apparently conflicting, this dual objective nevertheless is consistent with the finding that the sampled companies manage their translation exposures defensively while seeking moderate gains from foreign currency transactions. For those companies which hedge their translation exposures in the foreign exchange markets, this profit-seeking motive is stronger and broader, even only to protect their earning fluctuations.

Theoretically, while profit-making from forecasting is difficult under conditions of efficient foreign exchange markets, it is more achievable if exchange rate movements do not follow a random walk. On this point, several executives to whom this question was addressed do not endorse the proposition that the random walk hypothesis is realistically descriptive of the foreign exchange markets. Nevertheless, like the other interviewees, they agree that forecasting exchange rates has become a difficult task since the emergence of the floating rate regime. One executive exclaimed:

> A problem right now with the markets the way they are, particularly this first quarter [of 1978], is the volatility. It is so great that things can jump any way. For example, the pound sterling; it's like a horse race.

Under these circumstances, for defensive purposes, all of the 10 companies are content with spot rates and directional or trend forecasting. These spots rates represent either end-of-period rates or the periods' average rates. Four of the ten companies make their forecasts in terms of quarterly averages, and three in terms of end-of-quarter spot rates. Only three companies in the sample attempt to forecast on a monthly basis. Sine the exchange rate forecasts are filtered through the treasury/exposure management staff's evaluation and group discussion, spot rates are more in the nature of expected values.

Lest these specific rates lead one to believe that these companies aim at a minute level of precision, it should be pointed out that the real purpose here is to detect the trend of a currency's movements. One company has a convenient rule called the "three per cent rule." As long as a currency moves within three percentage points, no action on the translation exposure is required. One interviewee at another company, in making a point, suggests that he is willing to contract out the foreign exchange management function to anyone who can guarantee a foreign exchange loss not greater than three per cent of his company's net income. This executive observes that the forecasts from outside sources (banks and a foreign exchange consultant) usually vary within five percentage points from which he would "simply" average out and put down a number.

The horizon of these spot rate forecasts is limited to the current fiscal year with the exception of one company which produces forecasts up to only two quarters. Within this forecasting horizon, 3 companies produce monthly forecasts 12 months ahead whereas the other companies are interested only in quarterly forecasts.

Almost as a rule, these forecasts are updated monthly. In addition to the obvious benefit of incorporating updated information into the beginning-of-the-year forecasts, these revisions also serve an additional purpose: To provide management with an estimated impact of exchange rate changes on end-of-period earnings. It is interesting to note that in making these revisions, one company relies primarily on forward rates. However, 1 of the 10 companies does not routinely revise its forecasts; these revisions are made on an "as-needed" basis.

For contemplation of forward exchange contract hedging, these directional forecasts are used to provide an extended outlook of the movements of the currencies in question, hence, an indication of the specifït periods in which a company should enter the forward exchange markets. For this type of decision, the companies frequently monitor the exchange rate movements primarily by contacts with the trading departments of their banks. This sort of "market update," to use the terminology of one executive, is done as frequently as daily and also depends on the overall atmosphere in the markets. At any rate, the information is quite readily available if desired. This monitoring, in turn, helps the revision of monthly or quarterly trend forecasts.

Uniformly, these event-based forecasts rarely go beyond the specific time periods in which a company contemplates entering the forward exchange markets. On the other hand, several rates are obtained for this purpose from which some expected value is derived. Again, these forecasts are not presented in terms of probabilistic statements.

For budgeting and planning purposes, the exchange rate forecasts lack the details of the forecasts developed for defensive or hedging purposes. First, the development of these business plan rates are much less elaborate and correspondingly less time-consuming. Second, once a business plan rate is established, it will not be changed during the fiscal year. In this regard, 3 of the 10 companies in the sample provide forecasts beyond the fiscal year. One company provides forecasts up to three years ahead. In another, this type of forecasting is extended to seven years.

Thus, at the exchange rate forecasting stage, the forecasts are not presented (for distribution) in such a way—e.g., range or probabilities—that some measure of dispersion can be derived. An exception is that when forward exchange contract hedging is contemplated, several rates expected to be prevailing at a specific date are obtained. In this situation, conceivably probabilities can be derived from the forecasts but they are not presented in these terms.

On the cost side, the relevant data are forward discounts/premia and interest rates.

In theory, the cost of a forward contract is the spread between the forward rate and the spot rate at the contract maturity date. This is the opportunity cost. It seems that this opportunity cost is the only acceptable measure of the cost of a forward contract, especially when balance sheet hedging is under consideration. The reason is straightforward. In this type of hedging, i.e., balance sheet, a company does not have foreign currencies on hand to deliver to the purchaser on the contract maturity date; it must buy them in the spot exchange market at the spot rate then prevailing. Thus the actual cost is the difference between the forward rate and the spot rate at maturity. For transaction hedging, the same argument applies.

In practice, however, the spot rate at maturity is not known until the contract comes due. In addition, for transaction hedging in which the contract is self-liquidating, i.e., the company does not have to purchase foreign currencies for delivery, the opportunity cost is not visible. That is, no opportunity gain or loss will be recorded in the books. Thus, as explained by the executives to whom this question was addressed, for forward contract hedging on transactions, the practical and relevant measure of the cost of a forward exchange contract is the spread between the present spot rate and the forward rate. In this regard, it is interesting to note a theorist's viewpoint:

> I understand the logic of Mr. Bradford's opportunity cost argument for determining the cost of forward covers,[5] but I nevertheless agree with Mr. Pelli that when the currency is sold forward the transaction is completed and the subsequent spot rate is of no consequence except in the case where the corporate treasurer enjoys bemoaning his lost profit opportunities or pointing to the sequence of losses he has avoided.[6]

On the other hand, as two executives explained, in contract negotiations for sale and purchase of goods, the contract price is pegged to forecast exchange rates—in the case of long-term contracts—or forward rates—in the case of shorter-term contracts. Invariably, when a long-term sale or purchase contract is under consideration, these companies try to insert a price escalation clause. Presumably, the provision would protect the companies against price inflation and exchange rate changes. In these situations, it can be said that the opportunity costs of forward contracts have been figured in the selling/purchase price.

With respect to balance sheet hedging, the companies decide to enter into forward exchange contracts—if this strategy is allowed by company policy—only if the exchange rate forecasts are such that the potential translation losses are unacceptable. If the forward rate is more favorable than the forecast spot rate, the decision would be to enter the contract. An example would clarify the point. At time t_0, the spot rate is e_0, and the forward rate for the relevant time period is e_f. It is forecast that at time t_1, the spot rate will be $\tilde{e}_1$. To the extent that $\tilde{e}_1$ is less than e_0 and e_f, the company will sell forward to cover its long position. At t_1, the actual spot rate is e_1. For each unit of the foreign currency, the books will show a translation loss equal to $(e_1 - e_0)$ and a transaction gain of $(e_f - e_1)$. These gains and losses are visibly reflected in the financial statements. The point of this illustration is that the decision variable for balance sheet hedging is the difference between the forecast spot rate and the forward rate whereas the measure of the cost of forward cover on foreign currency transactions is the spread between the forward rate and the present spot rate, i.e., forward discount/premium.

With respect to the interest rate, interest costs on existing credit facilities are generally remitted to the parent company along with the information on the subsidiaries' available credit lines, outstanding loans both with third parties and sister subsidiaries. In some companies, this report is called the "credit/liquidity report." In two companies, this report does not seem to exist. Nevertheless, costs of borrowings are available in some other form, primarily through monitoring the money markets at a regional office, in one company, or at the parent company's headquarters, in the other. In addition, they both have cash holding and cash flow reports as part of their exposure management information systems.

The credit/liquidity report typically includes cash balances at the subsidiary, bank lines available and balances outstanding, the applicable interest rates, and in the case of inter-company loans, the maturity dates of the loans. Figure 12 illustrates a credit/liquidity report.

Risk Analysis and Selection of Defensive Strategies

In the initial conceptualization of the foreign exchange management process, it was suggested that the process leading to the selection of a particular defensive strategy, or a combination thereof, consists of two distinct steps: (1) identification and evaluation, and (2) selection. In the first step, facing with an exposed position, the decision-maker would identify all the alternative defensive strategies from which the feasible ones—those which are not ruled out by constraints such as local rules and regulations or company policy—will be evaluated. The evaluation consists of the specificiation of the cost or (negative) return and risk of each decision alternative. Risk was defined as the variance of the probability distribution of the forecast spot exchange rate. Subsequently, the feasible alternatives are ranked in terms of their return and risk. As a result of this ranking, there remains a set of (feasible) defensive strategies compared to any one of which there is no other alternative which either has: (1) a lower level of risk for the same expected return; or (2) a higher expected return for the same level of risk. These alternatives are said to constitute an efficient set of defensive strategies. In the selection phase, it remains to choose among the efficient set of strategies the one which is consistent with the risk acceptance level.*

While the empirical research indicates that the identification-evaluation-acceptance cycle found in practice largely follows this model, there are sufficient exceptions to warrant a revision of the hypothesis to obtain a better insight into the process of foreign exchange management decision-making. These exceptions are discussed under the headings "Identification," "Risk-Return Trade-Off," and "Risk Acceptance."

Identification

In the initial modeling, it was hypothesized that, facing an exposed position, the decision-maker would identify the feasible defensive alternatives that could reduce the exposure to an acceptable level, that is, consistent with the level of risk tolerance.In actual practice, the identification is performed at the staff level by an individual whose title is equivalent to "Foreign Exchange Manager," "Manager—International Finance" or "Specialist." The difference in

Figure 12
Credit and Liquidity Report As of –––

I.   Outside Loans

Financial Institution	Cash Balance		Short-term Debt			Long-term Debt	
	Local	Foreign (Specify)	Credit Line	Balance O/S	Interest Rate	Balance	Interest
Total							

II.   Inter-Company Loans

From/To Company	Local	Foreign (Specify)	Interest Rate	Maturity Date	Loan Date
1. From:					
Total From					
2. To:					
Total To					
Net:					

the title stems from the fact some companies have a fairly large exposure management staff. In one company, the staff is an individual specialist. In any event, this individual is at least one rank below the Assistant Treasurer level. The identification is further carried on to a corporate financial officer whose title is Assistant Treasurer. Only in two companies—to the extent that it can be documented—does this officer have the authority to make final decisions on exposure management defensive strategies, but then only if it involves clearcut cases or the decision does not expose the company to a substantial amount of losses.

Furthermore, the identification process does not take place in an orderly fashion that the model implies. Though the alternatives are identified, they emerge in a less formalized and structured manner. Part of the reason is that this process takes place under a lot of time pressure and that a number of alternatives are foreclosed rather quickly. One executive explained:

> What you are really getting at is: Do you cost out your different strategies and choose an alternative which is most cost advantageous? We really don't take the types of risk that I think you are talking about. When we run into such a situation, a lot of the costing-out analysis is rather quick and dirty. We don't formalize the process particularly well. We do consider leads and lags, inter-company accounts, etc. . . . But that is sort of a gut feel. And also there's a lot of time pressure. The approach is certainly not as formalized as your question would like to have for an answer; but it is done. But it isn't done in quite a structured fashion that you are questioning me. I would have to say that to a large degree a lot of the options are foreclosed rather quickly and the key on that are tax considerations.

Needless to say, the above approach is not applied across the board in all exposure management problems. There are at least three types of exposure management decisions which require different levels of formalized identification.

The first type involves the reduction of currency exposures by strategies other than those available in the money and foreign exchange markets. Such defensive strategies are those which do not result in a direct cash outlay to a third party. They are leads/lags, inter-company accounts' adjustment, and their variations. As one executive pointed out: "It's always the philosophy that we send the least dollars out." The result is that the companies would first attempt to undertake whatever actions possible, other than forward exchange contracts and borrowings, to reduce their currency exposures to an acceptable level. For these strategies, cost is rarely a major consideration, at least not explicitly in day-to-day exposure management. Of greater importance is their feasibility.

The feasibility question comes into play in two respects. For those companies which do not have significant amounts of imports and exports to third parties and inter-company flows between the subsidiaries, leads and lags either with third parties or among sister subsidiaries do not constitute a significant defensive strategy. This is not to mention the fact that these companies have a policy and practice of draining cash from their subsidiaries beyond the level required for working capital needs, thereby leaving little room, if any, for manipulation of cash holdings at the local subsidiaries for exposure management purposes. (Note: This should be distinguished from the parent company's investments of excess cash in short-term market instruments.) From this policy, the companies attempt to collect all accounts receivable as fast as possible. One executive pointed out:

> It is difficult to imagine a situation where we defer cash receipts for exposure management purposes. We collect all the cash we can get.

"We don't leave much cash for them (the subsidiaries) to play with anyway," another executive added. This leaves dividend remittances. In this respect, however, there is the overwhelming consideration for tax effects.

Notwithstanding these constraints, as mentioned earlier, these defensive strategies are used whenever possible. But then, they become extinct rather quickly because of the very nature of exposure management under floating exchange rates. This is the second aspect of the feasibility question. Under floating exchange rates, exposure management takes place continuously in response to constant currency fluctuations. Then came FASB 8 which has added an additional motivation for the companies to continuously monitor their balance sheet exposures to achieve a neutral position through the use of leads/lags and its variations. Thus, when an exposed position is identified, the strategies of balance re-structuring have largely been exhausted, leaving room for forward exchange contracts and/or further local/foreign currency borrowings.

In addition, there is the aspect of the responsibility over different defensive strategies between the headquarter's staff and the local subsidiaries. Although related to the feasibility question, for the purpose of this discussion, it should be separated. Typically, leads/lags and related strategies are within the purview of local managements, though subject to control by the parent company. Since these strategies have profound ramifications over the competitive strength of the local subsidiary, consultation between the headquarters and the local management is necessary. This communication problem and the time needed to implement them materially restrict their use in short-term exposure adjustment situations.

Thus, for the above reason, in day-to-day exposure management, the real defensive alternatives that remain open to the headquarters' treasury/exposure management staff are forward exchange contracts and borrowings.

The second type of exposure management decisions involves the use of borrowings. The principal alternatives in this type of defensive strategy are the currency denominations of the loans and their respective interest costs. The third type of decision has only two alternatives: hedge or no-hedge in the forward exchange markets. As will be discussed in the next section, the companies perform elaborate analysis for these types of exposure management decisions.

Risk-Return Trade-Off

It has been demonstrated that the companies have in place a fairly complex information system to collect the data on potential foreign exchange losses and the costs of the alternative defensive strategies. Due to the difficulty in forecasting exchange rates, risk—in the sense defined in the conceptual model—is not an item which is systematically collected and provided for by the information system. The actual analysis of risk-return trade-off reflects this difficulty. Risk is nevertheless taken into consideration in the form of probabilistic analysis and a qualitative entity called "flexibility." However, the emphasis on the technicalities of the analysis seems to decline as the decision problem is moved up the organizational hierarchy. The depth of the analysis also seems to depend on the individual performing the analysis and varies with type of decision problems.

On the one hand are those decisions which involve leads/lags and its variations. As noted earlier, for these decisions, feasibility is the major consideration. On the other are those decisions which involve forward exchange contracts and borrowings.

The evaluation of forward exchange contract hedging can be rather formalized and structured. At one company, there is a written, formal presentation by a staff of analysts. The presentation can be best described by a direct quote from the Assistant Treasurer of the company:

> Let us say that this date is the end of the fiscal year. Then we generate a forecast of the exchange rate against the U.S. dollar of that currency would be at the same date. Then we produce a table which shows on the left hand column a series of possible exchange rates including today's spot rate, the forward rate of today for the end of the period we are looking at, our forecast of what the rate will be at the end of the period, and a couple of rates at the upper and lower sides. Then applying those exchange rates to the forecast exposure, we show what our profit and loss would be in the balance sheet, which is, of course, a pre-tax and after-tax profit and loss since it is not a tax-affected figure. We show what our profit and loss would be, or our gain or loss would be, if each of those exchange rates are the actual spot rate at the future date. Then we say that we assume a 50% tax rate . . . We then show how we can eliminate that gain or loss by taking forward exchange contracts for twice the amount of exposure. The last column is the net and the net is always the same for any value of the currency. Then we have a discussion. Let us say sterling. Today's sterling is 181. If sterling falls to 170, we shall have gains of X million if we do nothing. If sterling rises to 192, we shall have losses of X million because we have a net liability in sterling. Next, we show how many millions of pounds we would have to buy forward to cover that net liability position.

This procedure is more or less structured in the same fashion in all the companies as evidenced in the interviews. The degree of elaborateness, however, varies among companies, and it tends to correlate with the size of the staff of analysts assigned to the management of foreign exchange. In the company of which the Assistant Treasurer is quoted above, the analysis is carried one step further: the analysis performed by the exposure management group in the treasury department is discussed with the specialists in the Controller's office before the recommendations are submitted for review by the Financial Vice President. At another company, the formal presentation takes the form of expected values, although the aspect of probabilistic evaluation does emerge in subsequent discussions. It also depends on the individual performing the analysis. The Assistant Treasurer of yet another company explained:

> I am always dealing with an indifference level to begin with. I will then run through a series of alternatives so that if my decision is based upon a 10% revaluation, and I can support my judgment to take whatever actions based on that . . . I will further sensitize it and present a 0% revaluation and a 20% revaluation or a 30%, depending on the environment I am working in. I would probably go back and start indicating subjective probabilities and perhaps come up with an expected value.

However, this analytical approach may be useful and informative, it may not always be a productive exercise under floating exchange rates. Another Assistant Treasurer explained:

> The other thing that one often does is to sit down and quantify one's perceptions of the markets. Because sometimes when you do your conclusion may be a little different. You put down rates and assign probabilities and multiply them and see what it comes out to be. It was either higher or lower than if someone has just asked what you thought. It sometimes comes out differently. Then you have a chance to say "Well, if you don't like the end rate, then let's look at what I just assigned and go through that." And in a fine-tuning sense, you can multiply that through. But the more the market becomes erratic, determined by psychological factors and so on, a lot of that analysis is pie-in-the-sky.

For borrowings, the analysis is almost always elaborate and formal, except when the financing is primarily for local working capital needs. For a company which has a policy "Always borrow locally to finance working capital," needless to say this decision rule eliminates a substantial amount of analysis and, in a sense, reduces the decision problems to one of establishing the financing need. It nevertheless should be pointed out that whatever the financing is for, a borrowing necessarily has an impact on the currency exposure. Accordingly, a certain amount of analysis of the foreign exchange risk implications must be performed. To quote one executive,

> We are going to look at what we think. What the interest rates are. What are the fore-
> cast exchange rate movements of the currency. We'll be looking at what it's being
> used for. We'll look at the whole thing and decide which is best. The over-riding thing
> is that you're looking at your exposure, the exposure before and after the financing.

If the problem is to refinance existing debts in order to restructure the balance sheet for exposure management purposes, i.e., the loan proceeds would be invested in money market instruments denominated in another currency or pre-pay existing debts, the analysis as well as the decision-making can range from being informal to very time-consuming and painstaking. In one of the six companies which have had to deal with the debt refinancing problem as they attempt to work out strategies to counter FASB 8's effects on their earnings, the issue has not yet been resolved. In the meantime, it continues to use forward exchange contracts to cover its net liability position created by the hard currency debts denominated in such currencies as the Swiss franc and the Deutsche mark. However, once a strategy to deal with FASB 8 has been established, the cost/benefit analysis of the debt refinancing alternatives becomes fairly routine. One executive at another company explained how he approached the debt refinancing problem:

> When the market situation alters as it did in the case of the Canadian dollar a few
> months ago, I came up with a proposal to begin to alter our exposure which had a
> substantial long position in the Canadian dollar on a balance sheet basis. I explored
> different alternatives for reducing that exposure and determining the best ways to
> increase our commercial issuance in Canada.

Along the lines of the variability concept, the Manager of International Finance at another company explained how risk-return trade-off is analyzed in borrowing decisions:

> Clearly the volatility of those currencies would be a factor in our decision. For
> example, suppose you know of a currency that was going to appreciate at a rate
> of 2% per year and not vary from that. Suppose there was another one which was
> not going to appreciate at all but would swing plus or minus 10% over the course of
> a year. You might opt to take the slowly appreciating currency simply because
> there was less variability.

However rudimentary or elaborate, informal or painstaking this risk-return analysis may be, the emphasis on the technical aspects seems to decline as the problem moves up the organizational ladder. In this phase of the analysis, what seems to be more important is the judgment and experience of the evaluator, or in the words of an Assistant Treasurer, "The probabilistic analysis is really a formal procedure; for in the final analysis, it is a subjective decision." An important criterion in this phase of the analytical process is "flexibility." This criterion is related to the ability to undo a particular decision. Given the nature of "brick and mortar investment" of a manufacturing company, the volatility of exchange rate movements, and other constraints such as loan covenants restricting debt prepayments, exchange controls, etc., it is easy to see why flexibility is an important evaluation criterion in exposure management decisions. In a sense, it has all the characteristics of a qualitative entity substituting for variance of probability distribution of return as a measure of risk. The following quote illustrates the role of flexibility in decision-making under risk:

> I think perhaps the most important element in what we are looking at is flexibility. So if we were to do something, could we undo it? How quickly could we undo it? If we were going into local currency borrowings, would we have the flexibility of prepayment? If we were going into a forward coverage, could we unwind it? I would say that the aspect of flexibility is probably the most important, after assessing the cost. In other words, if you take a look at the cost of a hedging vehicle and you come up with the ranking, the ranking would further be sensitized for "Could what you have done be undone?" Of course, you would have to pay additional costs for this flexibility.

Another executive explained:

> The clearest thing that I found the most useful is to ask oneself if you can afford to be wrong. You look at a risk and you are working with a budget and there is a decision process that is involved, you have to ask whether (in) a course of action . . . you can afford to go wrong the other way. Because in this world, there's a very high probability that one's analysis does not hold up . . . You don't stick your neck out.

Along the same lines, another Assistant Treasurer pointed out:

> I would say that one consideration we would have if we were taking a very large position, we would consider to what extent it might be difficult to get out of that position or reverse it in a hurry, especially if the markets were in a state of confusion at the time. So if we go into a position, we do not try to get into such a big position that we could not reverse it in a reasonable period of time.

From the foregoing discussion, it is evident that the criteria for evaluation of risk are: Feasibility, Probabilities, and Flexibility. The companies, however, do not use any modeling such as the mean-variance framework to aid their risk analysis and decision-making. On the other hand, the analytical process appears to be more involved and broad-based in view of the fact that in most cases the decision problem and feasible alternative actions are deferred for further review by a committee.

At the time of the interviews, only two companies in the sample have a formal foreign exchange committee. In one company, this committee consists of the Treasurer, the Director of International Finance, and the Manager of European Operations whose sole function at the time is devoted to exposure management. This committee basically serves in an advisory capacity for any policy exposure decisions must be approved by the Vice President of Finance who is not a member of this committee. The actual workings of this committee start with the exposure reports sent in from the overseas subsidiaries. The two interviewees in this company explained the subsequent events that actually take place. One interviewee said,

> The information is sent from the foreign subsidiaries and it is aggregated here . . . The analysts will take the range of possibilities . . . and sensitize it for whatever they do know as to where the assets are likely to be moving in the course of time. It is then discussed at a weekly meeting . . . The findings of that will be presented to the Chief Financial Officer and pretty much his decision will count.

The other said,

> The Treasurer gets this exposure report every month as it comes out and we discuss continually. I do a report to our Financial Vice President once every two weeks explaining what our positions are, what we are doing to alter them, and what our outlook is for the exchange rate and what problems we foresee and how we will deal with them. If the Financial Vice President disagrees, he'll let us know. When it comes to undertaking a new type of transaction, we go to him and show to him the proposal and get his general policy guidelines. But he does not approve every individual action after that. He does approve the type of activities that we do as a policy.

From an exposure management point of view, similar to this foreign exchange committee is the international finance committee at a larger company. The latter, however, is charged with a broader scope of responsibilities and has a more diversified membership. It consists of the representatives from the Controller's Office, the Treasurer's and legal departments, and an international tax expert. Its activities include all matters relating to capitalization, inter-company financing, dividends, parent company guarantees, and naturally, exposure management. Again, it serves more or less in an advisory capacity—or, in the words of the Assistant Treasurer—International Finance, a "sounding board"— for all major decisions in the area of international finance. The Assistant Treasurer—International Finance who reports to this committee on a monthly basis on balance sheet exposures, transaction exposure actions that have been taken, and those being contemplated, explained how this committee works.

> Once a month, this international finance committee meets, and as one of its agenda items, has a corporate foreign exchange exposure summary. This report is on a currency-by-currency basis which goes out every six months, and includes foreign exchange projections, and splits out transaction exposures. The committee then discusses the potential risks on the horizon and what our attitudes should be. I give them indications on where I think actions should be taken or not be taken, clearly in

numbers what the risk-reward is which is all written down in front of them. During the next four weeks, decisions are made, always in consultation with the operating divisions involved. Then I consult on a spot basis with the Manager of Foreign Exchange and come up with the recommendations and in 99 of 100 cases, I'll touch base with the Treasurer and see if he has any problem with it, and if he doesn't, give the go-ahead and do it.

The remaining companies in the sample presently do not have a formal foreign exchange committee. One, however, is considering establishing such a committee. Notwithstanding the lack of a formal organization, the exposure management decision-making process in this company does not appear to be much less structured than that at the two other companies, at least in substance. Its Assistant Treasurer explains how decisions are reached within the framework of this *ad hoc* committee.

We in the treasury function generate recommendations as to what should be done using forecasts which we generate ourselves and the forecasts of exposures which we obtain from the Controller's Office. When we decide what our recommendations ought to be, we then discuss them with the specialists in the Controller's Office and get their agreement and then we all go and talk to the Vice President of Finance and he takes, as a rule, the ultimate decision on whether or not we should take some precautions. If the amounts are very large, he may decide to discuss the question with his superiors before he makes the final decision.

Basically, the same decision-making process abounds in the other companies which do not have a formal foreign exchange committee, although in these companies the discussion tends to be somewhat less structured. There are two other exceptions. One is related to the frequency and amount of consultation. As it might be expected, this depends on the magnitude of the currency exposures. Secondly, the membership of such *ad hoc* committees tend to be more fluid, simply because the membership is not formally defined. From the evidence, two extremes can be identified.

In the first group belong four companies which have a "committee" but its membership is somewhat restricted to those executives who are directly involved in exposure management on a day-to-day basis. At two of these companies, the committee membership consists of the Treasurer, an individual who has the title equivalent to "Manager of International Finance," and an analyst. In the third company, the membership is limited to the Assistant Treasurer, the Vice President in charge of business planning and forecasting, and an analyst. It must be pointed out that regardless of the composition of these so-called committees, there are instances where the amounts of exposures are quite large; the highest levels of management, including the chairman of the board, are also involved in the discussion.

In the second group are four companies in which the dialogue not only flows among the treasury staff but also between the treasury staff and the higher levels of management, including the president and/or the chairman of the board of directors. As an example, in one company, this process takes places when the foreign exchange manager does not find sufficient support for his position among his immediate superiors, i.e., the assistant treasurer and the treasurer, and feels that the situation warrants a broader discussion.

The point of this discussion is that the process of risk analysis in practice is much more involved and broad-based than any degree of quantification can provide. In this process, the insight and perspective of different levels of management and functions are injected into the final decisions. It would be difficult, if not impossible, to quantify all of these judgments in a hard and fast number.

Risk Acceptance

From the foregoing discussion, it is evident that the decision-making process involves a group of executives, whether or not they constitute a formal committee. In most companies, these executives are from the treasury department. When the recommendations of the group members are not controversial, the decision problem is resolved in this group, though subject to a formal approach. Conversely, when the group cannot reach a consensus, the matter would be deferred to a higher level of management. One executive stated: "Sometimes the meetings can get quite lively . . . When they can't agree, they will speak to the Treasurer of the Company." From this experience and some other similar situations found in the interviews, it appears that this analytical process in group meetings not only leads to the establishment of a set of efficient defensive alternatives—to use the terminology suggested in the conceptual model—but also to a decision which is consistent with the corporate risk acceptance level. In this eventuality, the approval from a higher authority appears to be only a formality.

However, it is generally not possible to determine quantitatively from the interviews the amount of additional return that is required to compensate for increased risk. One executive mentioned a ratio of three-to-two. Another said that a ratio of four-to-one is considered satisfactory. Both, however, pointed out that these are not hard and fast numbers. On the other hand, it seems clear that the plan/budget provides a powerful guide in determining whether a translation loss is acceptable. In other words, in deciding whether or not the effects of exchange rate fluctuations on earnings are acceptable, the executives would look at the planned profit for guidance to determine the level of risk that is acceptable to the company. In the words of one assistant treasurer: "If we foresee a very good quarter, we might be inclined to take somewhat greater risks or to spend less on precautions on currency fluctuations . . ."

In the event that a decision cannot be reached at group meetings, the problem is moved up to a higher level. For large exposures, especially when translation hedging is contemplated, the involvement of the highest level of management is required. However, exactly where the demarcation lines are, they generally cannot be determined from the interviews. In one company, the board of directors provide specific authorizations—not unlike spending limits in capital budgeting decisions—for how much a corporate officer can commit the company. Yet, these numbers are not disclosed. In the other companies, these specific authorizations simply do not exist. Nevertheless, the executives involved in exposure management, including such senior officers as the treasurer, seem to have a fairly clear idea as what these limits are. In one of these companies, the interviewee indicated a figure of five million dollars of exposure beyond which the Treasurer would go to his superiors for guidance/ decision. But, again, this is not a hard and fast number. In another company, there was one instance when the decision was actually made by the Chairman of the Board. In this instance, the amount of potential loss exceeded 10 million dollars. From these examples and others found in the interviews, it seems clear that the exposure management problems, depending on the magnitude, can involve an authority as high as the chairman of the board.

Inasmuch as the management of foreign exchange receives attention from the very top level of a company's management, the exposure management activities of the subsidiaries are also centrally controlled at the parent company's headquarters. The degree of central control can be looked at from two different viewpoints: (1) the control over the balance sheet and transaction exposure, and (2) the kinds of defensive strategies that must be approved by the headquarters.

As to balance sheet versus transaction, without exception balance sheet exposure is the responsibility of the treasury department at the parent company. With respect to transactions, the companies differ only in the matter of degree of how much this control is exercised, not in "whether or not" it will be exercised. The reason lies in the fact that whereas balance sheet and transaction exposures are different in concept, in actual operations they cannot be separated.

The differences in the degree of control over the transaction exposure can be looked at from the viewpoint of reporting requirements. From this standpoint, the parent company seems to have complete knowledge of the transaction exposures at the individual subsidiaries and how their transactions affect the balance sheet exposure.

The actions of the subsidiaries are further restricted by the annual plans/ budgets to which they are committed at the beginning of each fiscal year. It is in the annual plan that pricing and inventory strategies as well as borrowing requirements are established. Barring the incompetence of local managements and/or adverse market conditions, these plans tend to be self-fulfilling, thus providing a mechanism whereby the parent company can exercise control over the transaction exposures of its subsidiaries.

Between plans, the parent company can also exercise control over the transaction exposure via a formal communication system whereby it issues exposure management guidelines to the subsidiaries. Only 2 of the 10 companies have such a formal structure. One of these companies still manages its international operations under an "international division" umbrella. The other company holds a monthly meeting between the subsidiaries' management (at the divisional level) and the Corporate Finance Department in which the strategies on the management of transaction exposures are established. These strategies are then communicated to the individual subsidiaries of each division. These guidelines, however, are not viewed as instructions to hedge or not to hedge, but as directives to operate within certain limitations. In the other companies, such a formal structure does not exist. However, as pointed out by the interviewees, there exist frequent two-way communication flows between operating managements at the subsidiary level and the treasury staff at the headquarters. Although such staff consultation does not constitute a directive which local managements are obligated to follow, as one executive pointed out, staff advice can be very forceful and borders on being a directive to local managements, especially when the contemplated action has a material impact on the balance sheet exposure.

With regard to defensive strategies, the local subsidiaries will not adjust the levels of their exposures via local/foreign currency borrowings unless so directed from the headquarters. However, local subsidiaries have greater latitude in the use of leads/lags with third parties, and inventory and pricing strategies. These strategies are nevertheless restricted by plan guidelines. As to inter-company accounts adjustment, 6 of the 10 companies have a netting system which gives the parent company substantial control over inter-company flows. One of the remaining companies will institute such a system in 1979. Regarding forward exchange contracts on transactions, local subsidiaries can take out such contracts but they must first obtain consent from the parent company. However, it appears that the subsidiaries seldom exercise this authority. One company even has the policy of requiring its subsidiaries to cover sale and purchase agreements by forward exchange contracts to protect the gross margin.

Summary and Conclusion

This chapter was devoted to a discussion of the information system that the sampled companies have set up to collect the data necessary for their exposure management activities and the process whereby they analyze the risk-return trade-offs of the defensive strategies.

On the information systems, the findings indicate that the sampled companies design their reporting systems to collect the data relevant to the currency exposure around the subsidiaries' financial statements, consistent with their currency exposure definitions. In other words, the data are taken directly from the subsidiaries' balance sheets and profit and loss statements, which give a breakdown of the translation and transaction exposure components. They are also detailed currency-by-currency unless the cross-border transactions are negligible. These reports are sent monthly from overseas to the parent company's headquarters where they are consolidated worldwide, again, to give a currency-by-currency break-down. Since exchange rates affect only future exposures, provisions are made for forecasts of future exposures by either the subsidiaries or the headquarters' staff. These projections are performed on all of the exposure components in accordance with the companies' definitions. "Typical" reports constituting the reporting systems were also presented to show how the relevant data are configurated to produce the necessary exposure data. Basically, they consist of the currency exposure report, inventory analysis, statement of income and flow-through effects report, off-balance sheet items, report of outstanding forward exchange contracts, and credit and liquidity report.

On development of exchange rates forecasts, it was shown that whereas the companies obtain the forecasting input from a variety of outside sources, most notably, banking institutions and foreign exchange consulting services, the treasury/exposure management staff play a critical role in finalizing, evaluating, and consolidating these outside forecasts. In this respect, although an individual may be charged with the task of monitoring exchange rate movements, the forecasts used for decision-making are actually the result of a group effort.

Typically, the forecasting process consists of two distinct phases: technical analysis and decision-making. In the first phase, the forecasting input is obtained from all available sources. Most notable are banking institutions, foreign exchange consulting firms, external economists, and mathematical modeling. In the decision-making phase, the input is evaluated by the exposure management staff to determine the relevant economic factors and their relative contribution to the exchange rate movements. Subsequently, the consolidated forecasts are scrutinized by other individuals in the treasury department. In this final phase, representatives from the controller function and/or higher authorities in the treasury department, e.g., the treasurer, may also be involved. The result of this group discussion is a set of final forecasts ready for distribution and used for decision-making purposes.

This involved forecasting procedure is used to compensate for the difficulty in making forecasts under floating exchange rates. Furthermore, this forecasting effort is not directed to a minute level of precision but is aimed at detecting the trend or direction of currency movements. Therefore, presently, the companies do not make any attempt to present the forecasts in terms of probabilistic statements, even when hedging decisions in the forward exchange markets are contemplated, though several rates are obtained for this purpose.

However, risk is well recognized and dealt with, and very seriously so. As it was shown in the second half of this chapter, the process of risk analysis and selection of defensive strategies largely follows the conceptual model formulated at the outset of this research. However, in lieu of relying on mathematical modeling such as the mean-variance framework, the companies have set up rather elaborate organizational procedures to deal with the risk factor in the decision-making—like in the development of exchange rate forecasts, this process consists of two distinct phases; technical and analysis decision-making.

In the first phase, the exposure management staff attempt to identify the available defensive alternatives. In this respect, operating strategies such as leads/lags or third-party receivables/payables and pricing and inventory strategies do not emerge in a formalized and structured manner. Instead, the companies undertake these defensive strategies wherever possible. For these strategies, cost is rarely a major consideration. Of greater importance is feasibility which is related to such constraints as the availability of cross-border transactions, division of responsibility between the headquarters' staff and local subsidiaries, and the speed that these strategies can be implemented.

With regard to forward exchange contracts, the identification is limited to hedge-versus-no-hedge. In this respect, the analysis can be quite formal and elaborate as it may include probabilistic estimates. In any event, the depth of the analysis varies with the individual performing it. As to borrowing, the alternatives involve, among other things, the choice of currency denominations and the purpose of the loan. Almost always the analysis of debt alternatives is formal and elaborate and may involve considerations for the variability of exchange rate movements. However, rudimentary or elaborate technicalities decline in importance as the decision problem moves up the organizational ladder. At higher levels of the hierarchy, subjective judgment becomes dominant and the criterion of "flexibility" which is related to the ability to undo a decision gains great importance.

Although this procedure may appear rather informal, in fact, the decision-making process leading to a decision is more broad-based than any mathematical modeling can provide. Evidence is the fact that once the decision alternatives are identified and analyzed, they are further evaluated in either formal or *ad hoc* foreign exchange committees. The membership of such a committee may include only the personnel of the treasury department or representatives of higher levels of management, e.g., the treasurer or from the controller function and the legal department. This organizational procedure thus brings the expertise and experience of various executives from different disciplines to bear on the exposure problems. It is this "consensus of opinion" approach that seems to substitute for an explicit measure of risk.

Inasmuch as the final decision is reached on the basis of the analysis of the risk and return trade-off of the defensive alternatives, and after careful consideration, or at least involvement of more than one individual, this procedure is very akin to the risk-return framework outlined at the outset of this research, except that it benefits from insight and experience of the various levels and disciplines of management.

Depending on the type of the exposure problem, a decision may or may not be made at the committee level. When the committee cannot reach a concensus, the matter would be deferred to a higher level of management for resolution. This higher authority may be the treasurer, but it may go as far as the chairman of the board. The involvement of this officer, however, is infrequent and required only if the exposure is very large or it involves large translation losses.

However, it is generally not possible to determine either the dollar amounts beyond which a senior officer like the financial Vice President will make the decision or the additional amount of return that is required to compensate for the incremental risk. It appears, nevertheless that the plan/budget provides powerful guidelines to determine when a trans-loss is unacceptable.

In any event, it is clear from the evidence that top management is quite involved in the foreign exchange management decision-making process. Furthermore, the exposure management activities of the overseas subsidiaries are centrally controlled at the parent company's headquarters. Not only the translation exposure is a responsibility of the headquarters' staff, the transaction exposure is controlled via reporting requirements, plan/budget guidelines, and frequent consultation between the staff and subsidiaries' management. On defensive strategies, the overseas subsidiaries must obtain prior consent from the parent company before engaging in forward exchange contract hedging, borrowing or changing inter-company settlement terms. On the operating strategies, e.g., pricing and inventory adjustment, they have greater latitude, but again are subject to plan/budget guidelines.

From the foregoing analysis, it is concluded that the decision-making and risk analysis as found in practice largely follow the risk-return model depicted at the outset of this research, but more involved and broad-based than any mathematical modeling. It is also closely controlled by top management and centrally located within the parent company.

Chapter V

Floating Exchange Rates and FASB 8

Characteristics of the present regime of floating exchange rates are large movements in exchange rate relationships. As it has been demonstrated, unlike the environment of the fixed rate system, these fluctuations can take place within very short periods and have been sustained for extended lengths of time. Under these circumstances, many companies have suffered large losses due to currency fluctuations. Expectedly, they have stepped up their efforts and increased the use of certain defensive strategies for reduction of currency effects on their earnings.

However, for many other companies, from the standpoint of reported earnings, before FASB 8 the negative effects of exchange rate fluctuations were less intolerable thanks to a variety of accounting techniques. These accounting treatments enabled a company to avoid recognition of currency effects on some balance sheet items; offset these effects by defining their currency exposures such that the exposures were close to being neutral; or simply not to recognize some part of the currency losses on current periods' earnings. In some companies, a combination of these techniques was so imaginatively employed,[1] such that it became quite difficult for an investor to assess the year-to-year currency effects on their earnings, much less how much they were economically affected.

Amid this state of confusion, the Financial Accounting Standards Board stepped in and issued FASB 8 at the end of 1975. For most companies, this ruling represents a drastic departure from the methods they used to recognize the earnings effects of currency swings. Not surprisingly, many of them saw their earnings fluctuate with exchange rate changes, and as a result, have taken measures to dampen these earnings fluctuations.

The purpose of this part of the research is to examine the defensive strategies that the companies in the sample have taken to deal with these two major changes in the environment of international corporate finance. Specifically, in the first half of this chapter, the analysis of the empirical findings seeks to answer the following main research question: What are the changes in their defensive strategies due to greater exchange rate variations?

The two subsidiary questions are: (1) What are the defensive strategies which had/had not been used in the fixed exchange rate system but were/were not under floating exchange rates; and (2) What are the defensive strategies which had been used in the fixed exchange rate system and also used under floating exchange rates but more/less frequently?

The second half of this chapter seeks to provide an analysis of the effects of FASB 8 on some aspects of exposure management: What are the effects of FASB 8 on their currency exposure measurement and defensive strategies? Stated more specifically, this question can read: What are the items that were/were not included in the computation of currency exposures and the defensive strategies that were/were not used but now are/are not as a result of FASB 8?

Floating Exchange Rates

As exchange rates exhibit wider fluctuations, it has become more difficult to forecast rate changes. When an executive says, "It's hell on wheels; it is a very bad situation," his view is readily shared by the financial officers and consultants participating in this study. These interviewees attributed this situation to the lack of predictability in the intervention policies of central banks in the foreign exchange markets of their respective currencies and the influence of non-economic factors, e.g., psychology of the market participants in the determination of currencies' prices. One executive said,

> It was much easier under fixed exchange rates . . . simply because in part you only had to decide whether the currency would be devalued or not. Now, you don't know whether it's going to be devalued or revalued. Another factor is that under the Bretton Woods system, central banks tried to support their currencies' exchange rates. Under floating exchange rates, they still want to support their currencies. But what they are going to do . . . is much more unpredictable.

Of the leading industrialized countries, foreign exchange policies have been found to differ in both the aggressiveness and the frequency of intervention.[2] All have attempted to resist or moderate pressures on their currencies at one time or another. But some have operated predominantly against appreciations, others against depreciations, sometimes more actively in one direction than the other, and with different degrees of intensity. Also the degree of intervention of each country has changed over time. Their motives of exchange management policies have differed and so has the mix of techniques. Although these countries generally contended that they have followed the guidelines of "disorderly market conditions" and "fundamental market trends," these terms have never been officially defined and have been very flexibly interpreted. Furthermore, with few exceptions, such as the United States—which has a very passive policy as compared to that of the other industrialized countries—published statistical data on official foreign exchange operations are scarce. When available, the data are usually presented in net rather than gross form which at times gives a misleading picture of the amount of intervention during the period in question.

This scarcity of data on intervention operations of central banks only adds more difficulty to a better understanding of foreign exchange policies for exchange rate forecasting purposes.

As central banks' intervention in foreign exchange markets becomes more limited and less predictable, the role of private transactions in the determination of exchange rates gains greater importance. As a result, economic fundamentals are often overshadowed by psychological factors in rate determination, making some currencies such as the Swiss franc, as one better-known forecasting service has advised its corporate clients, become unforecastable on the basis of economic analysis. Even for some currencies of which the exchange rate movements are more responsive to underlying economic forces, at times political and psychological factors have predominated. This situation is well recognized by observers of the foreign exchange markets and the interviewed executives of the sampled multinational firms.

The combined effect of less intervention by central banks and increased importance of private transactions in foreign exchange markets has produced a situation where it becomes much more difficult to predict the direction of rate changes, much less the magnitude of the changes. Referring to this problem, an Assistant Treasurer commented:

> I think it is more difficult. . . . [In the fixed rate system,] it wasn't really that important how accurate you were as to the extent of the change as long as you were guessing in the right direction and had the time more or less right. Right now, with this floating market, it is very messy. The problem is that rates can go up or down. In the past, you knew that they were only going to go in one way. In this day and age, that isn't the case anymore. I think that this makes it much more difficult.

Under these circumstances, it is not surprising that companies have increased the use of defensive strategies to protect losses due to exchange rate fluctuations.

It was suggested at the outset of this research that due to greater uncertainty in exchange rate movements, companies would increase hedging of their currency exposures. To the extent that greater demand for hedging leads to higher hedging costs, companies would increase the use of those defensive strategies which incur less direct costs. The implication was that forward exchange contracts would lose dominance as a defensive strategy. In terms of the data to be generated from the research, it would mean that the number of companies which would increase the use of forward exchange contracts for hedging would be less than those increasing the use of the other defensive strategies. This would be especially true for forward contract hedging of the balance sheet exposure. For balance sheet hedging, companies would resort more frequently to such strategies as inter-company accounts' adjustment and decrease forward buying and selling of foreign currencies because the former do not involve any outflow of funds to third parties—although conceivably the subsidiary from which cash is drained may have to borrow at a higher cost than the return realized from short-term investments made from the funds it has released.

Admittedly, the size of the sample is not large enough to draw a statistically testable conclusion for the above hypothesis. Nevertheless, for the purposes of this study, it appears that large multinational firms have increased hedging of their currency exposures. It is certainly true for most of the companies in the sample. As to forward exchange contracts, it seems to be true only with respect to balance sheet hedging. Indeed the increase in the use of leads/lags of inter-company accounts seems to be more widespread than the increase in the use of forward exchange contracts to hedge balance sheet exposures. This is certainly true as to the absolute frequency that each type of defensive strategy is used. This is demonstrated in Chapter III. As to hedging on foreign currency transactions, it appears that forward exchange contracts continue to predominate over such strategies as price increases or specification of billing currencies. This should have been expected given the constraint of competitive pressures on pricing policies.

Overall, most of the sampled companies have "significantly"[3] increased the use of various defensive strategies to hedge their currency exposures. Most widespread appears to be the increase in the use of forward exchange contracts to hedge foreign currency transactions. Following is a ranking of the defensive strategies in terms of the number of companies which have increased their usage due to greater uncertainty in exchange rate movements:

1. Forward exchange contract hedging of foreign currency transactions
2. Inter-company accounts' adjustment and working capital management
3. Leads/lags third party receivables/payables
4. Price changes
5. Debt management

Also under floating exchange rates, there exist two defensive strategies that had not been used in the fixed rate system:

1. Inter-currency netting;
2. Internal hedge.

"New" Defensive Strategies

Under this heading will be discussed those defensive strategies which have been used under floating exchange rates but were not in the fixed rate system. As mentioned, two of these are inter-currency netting and internal hedge. They are discussed in detail in Chapter III.

Additionally, there are two companies which have now used certain "traditional" defensive strategies which they did not have in the fixed rate system. These strategies fall into the broad classifications of leads/lags and inter-company accounts' adjustment.

Specifically, one company which had never used the strategy of leading and lagging remittances to the parent company has "occasionally" resorted to this facility under floating exchange rates for better timing of fund flows from the subsidiaries to the parent company. This company also increased the use of U.S. dollar investments by the parent company in substitution for local currency borrowings. Whereas it had never used this defensive strategy in the fixed rate system for exposure management purposes, with the advent of floating exchange rates, this strategy has been used "occasionally" to alter the working capital structure of the subsidiaries. "Occasionally," it has also engaged in currency swaps, a strategy that had never been used before. Cumulatively, the combined effects of the increased use of these strategies represent an increase of U.S. dollar investments by the parent company in its overseas subsidiaries. This can be easily seen in the context of the declining strength of the U.S. dollar and the fact that it has little inter-company transactions for the movement of exposures from one currency to another and that it has some sizeable amount of debts denominated in Euro-currencies, especially the Swiss franc and the Deutsche mark.

Another company that had not used changes in credit terms as a defensive strategy has begun using it under floating exchange rates, but only on an occasional basis.

Table 20 summarizes the defensive strategies that had not been used in the fixed rate system but have been increasingly practiced since the emergence of floating exchange rates. Whereas only two companies have adopted these "new" strategies, nine companies in the sample have used inter-currency netting and two have used internal hedge under floating exchange rates, though these netting schemes had not been used during the fixed rate period.

"Old" Defensive Strategies

As it was expected, the environment of greater uncertainty since the emergence of floating exchange rates has created necessary conditions for some of the sampled companies to react with intensified hedging activities. This heightened level of hedging has encompassed the use of forward exchange contracts as well as the other traditional defensive strategies.

One company, however, is excluded from this discussion because it has emerged only recently as a multinational company. Prior to the period being studied (1975), it was basically a domestic corporation. Another company is only included in the discussion on forward exchange contract hedging of foreign

Table 20
Defensive Strategies Under Floating Exchange Rates That Had Not
Been Used in the Fixed Rate System

Strategies	Number of Companies Significant Increase
Extend/Receive More/Less Generous Credit Terms	1
Accelerate/Delay Remittances to Parent Company	1
Adjust Planned Parent Company's Dollar Investments	1
Negotiate Foreign Currency and/or Credit Swaps	1
Inter-Currency Netting	9
Internal Hedge	2
Sample Size:	10

currency transactions. Although the international operations of this company have been sufficiently extensive to qualify it for being a large multinational manufacturing firm for the purposes of this study, the data on the other defensive strategies are such that they are incomparable. They are simply poor. This is due to the inadequate reporting system that it had in place before FASB 8 was issued:

> Our information flows before the advent of FASB 8 were so bad that it was totally haphazard. We have evidence, as a case in point, where decisions were made that were 180 degrees wrong. They hedged in the wrong direction based on what they thought were their exposures because the information they were receiving at that time was so poor that on further detailed analysis they should have been hedging in the other direction.

Thus for the analysis of the effects of floating exchange rates on "old" defensive strategies, the sample is effectively reduced to eight companies, except that on forward exchange contract hedging of foreign currency transactions, the sample consists of nine companies. Of these nine companies, all have been affected to some extent by floating exchange rates.

Forward Exchange Contracts

All of the nine companies in the sample have experienced some increase in the frequency of forward exchange contract hedging. In some companies, the increase has been quite significant while in the others, the impact of floating exchange rates in this regard has been negligible. Six companies reported that they have significantly increased the use of forward exchange contracts to hedge foreign currency transactions. Five have done so for off-balance sheet items. On the other hand, none of the companies indicated that they have stepped up the use of this foreign exchange market facility to hedge the balance sheet exposure. One company actually reduced the use of this strategy and has recently abandoned this practice after some unpleasant experiences in the market. Table 21 shows the number of companies that have significantly increased the use of forward exchange contracts in the face of greater uncertainty in exchange rate movements.

While it is remarkable that so many companies, relatively speaking, have increased the use of forward exchange contracts to hedge foreign currency transactions, it is less surprising when cost is taken into consideration. Referring to the cost of forward cover in the fixed rate system and under floating exchange rates, Kohlhagen suggested that at least as a whole, forward discounts or premiums have not been greater with floating rates.[4] He then noted in another paper that in the case of Germany and Switzerland, "the forward premia were not significantly different between the two periods [fixed rate and floating] and in the case of Denmark, it was actually significantly lower in the

Table 21
Forward Exchange Contracts: Fixed Rate System vs.
Floating Exchange Rates

Covered Transactions	Number of Companies
	Significant Increase
Payments/Receipts from Import/Export Transactions	6[a]
Payments/Receipts for Commitments not Recorded in the Books	5
Net Exposed Balance Sheet Exposure	1[b]
Foreign Currency and/or Credit Swaps	1[c]
Sample Size: 8 companies	

[a] On this question, there are 9 companies in the sample.

[b] This company actually reduced the use of this strategy.

[c] Excluding one company which had not used this strategy in the fixed rate system.

flexible regime."[5] Similarly, the average difference between the forward rate and the spot rate prevailing at the maturity date (in Kohlhagen's studies, 90 days later) has not significantly increased (on a statistical basis) with floating exchange rates. This is true for any of the six currencies studied. On the other hand, whether the cost of forward cover is measured by the forward discount/ premium or the spread between the forward rate and the subsequent spot rate, under floating exchange rates, there is a higher probability that the variance about the mean is greater.

Kohlhagen's results and the findings of this study indicate that in the face of greater uncertainty in exchange rate movements, any increase in the cost of hedging foreign currency transaction (measured by forward discounts or premia) does not seem to be a sufficient deterrent to most of the companies in the sample. More strongly stated, most of the sampled companies apparently feel that the benefits from increased hedging of foreign currency transactions in the forward markets outweigh any cost increase.

On the other hand, greater uncertainty in exchange rate movements has rendered the cost of hedging the balance sheet exposure either prohibitively costly or unattractive to the sampled companies. The cost of this type of forward coverage is the difference between the forward rate and the subsequent spot rate. This is demonstrated in the previous chapters. As Kohlhagen's results pointed out, "the absolute values of the difference between the forward and subsequent spot rate have become larger (from 45% in the case of sterling to 225% for the Deutschemark)"[6] with floating exchange rates. From the standpoint of hedging, this conclusion is borne out by the fact that none of the sampled companies increased forward contract hedging of the balance sheet exposure whereas one company actually reduced to a significant extent the use of this strategy.

Pricing and inventory strategies

The number of companies which have significantly increased the use of these defensive strategies under floating exchange rates is markedly less than those increasing the use of forward exchange contracts. The fundamental reason appears to be in the competitive pressure in the market place. As the Treasurer in one company indicated, this is especially true for the markets of his company's products in European countries. However, in developing regions, this company has been able to effect price increases to local customers.

With regard to inventory adjustment, it is often explained that inventory is always kept at the lowest level possible. Consequently, it is not susceptible to changes for exposure management purposes. With respect to transfer prices, they are subject to negotiations between subsidiaries and are often scrutinized by local tax authorities. Accordingly, transfer pricing is often excluded as a defensive strategy.

These constraints notwithstanding, some companies have significantly increased the use of these pricing and inventory strategies to enhance the protection of their currency exposures in the face of greater uncertainty in exchange rate movements. Table 22 shows the exact number of companies which have significantly increased the use of these strategies.

Leads and lags

In view of the various constraints on the leads/lags strategies, it is remarkable that about half of the (effective) sample of companies have significantly increased the use of these strategies for hedging purposes. Obviously, greater foreign exchange risks under floating exchange rates have added motivation for these companies to use these strategies more than they had in the fixed rate system. In other words, in terms of risk versus return, whereas the risk has been greater under floating exchange rates, the cost of leading and lagging appears to remain stable, or at least not prohibitive to these companies. This is especially true for lagging of accounts payable where the direct cost is the opportunity cost of prompt payment discounts. Another way to look at this increase is that given greater foreign exchange risks, these companies began to search for new ways to hedge their currency exposures in areas where they had been less willing to exploit.

It is thus noteworthy that three of these 4 companies have less than 25 percent of their total purchases from non-local sources. One of these companies "usually" used leads/lags of third-party receivables/payables before floating exchange rates. Two companies "occasionally" used this strategy in the fixed exchange rate system. The fourth company increased the use of leads/lags from "occasionally" to "always". Two of these companies increased the use of the strategy of specifying billing currencies from "occasionally" to "usually," apparently feeling that the greater benefits of smaller currency exposures are worth the cost of customers/purchasers' resistance. Another company from this group had already "always" used this strategy before floating exchange rates. It also had "usually" used the strategy of changes in credit terms in the fixed exchange rate system. As to the strategy of changes in credit terms, one company which had never used it before began to use it since the emergence of floating exchange rates. Two other companies in the above group increased the use of this strategy from "occasionally" to "usually."

Table 23 shows the exact number of companies which have significantly increased the use of leads and lags strategies in response to greater foreign exchange risks.

Inter-company accounts' adjustment

Relative to leads and lags of third party receivables/payables, there appears to be a greater number of companies which have significantly increased

Table 22
Pricing and Inventory Strategies: Fixed Rate System
vs. Floating Exchange Rates

Strategies	Number of Companies Significant Increase
Increased Export Prices	3
Increase Selling Prices to Local Customers	3
Increase/Decrease Inter-Subsidiary Transfer Prices	2
Increase/Decrease Local/Foreign Currency Inventory Levels	1
Sample Size:	8

Table 23
Leads/Lags of Receivables and Payables with Third
Parties: Fixed Rate System vs. Floating Exchange Rates

Strategies	Number of Companies Significant Increase
Leads/Lags Receivables from/Payables to Third Parties	4
Specification of Billing Currencies	2
Extend/Receive More/Less Generous Credit Terms	2[a]
Sample Size:	8

[a] Excluding the company which had not used this strategy in the fixed exchange rate system.

the use of inter-company accounts' adjustment after floating exchange rates. The reason can be found in the little external constraint on these strategies and the relatively little direct cost associated with these strategies (which is the difference between the interest rate that the subsidiary from which cash is drained has to pay for borrowed funds and the return from short-term investments.) Table 24 shows the number of companies which have significantly increased the use of inter-company accounts' adjustment.

Like leads/lags of third-party receivables/payables, it thus seems that with the advent of floating exchange rates and associated greater risks, these five companies became more willing to undertake additional hedging activities in the area of inter-company flows where they had not fully been exploited in the fixed rate system. In this connection, it is remarkable that only two companies in this group have substantial amounts of inter-company transactions (constituting over 75 percent of their cross-border business.) One of these companies had already "usually" used this strategy in the fixed rate system. Two other companies increased the use of this strategy from "occasionally" to "usually."

In conjunction with inter-company import and export transactions, one company in this group also increased the use of adjusting the flows of remittances to the parent company, i.e., varying the amounts of remittances. Two others in the group have significantly increased the use of timing of remittances to the parent company to counter greater currency fluctuations.

Debt and working capital management

Consistent with the hypothesis—and the evidence supporting it—that companies would be less willing to accept additional risks in view of greater uncertainty in exchange rate movements, very few companies have increased the use of local/foreign currency borrowings for exposure management purposes. In fact, only one company in the sample indicated that it has increased the use of local currency borrowings from "occasionally" to "always" after floating exchange rates. The same company has also significantly increased the use of foreign currency borrowings. One other company in the sample increased the use of foreign currency borrowings for exposure management purposes from "occasionally" to "usually."

In contrast, four companies in the (effective) sample have significantly increased the use of maneuvering short-term assets and liabilities for exposure management purposes since the advent of floating exchange rates. As indicated earlier in Chapter III, the thrust of this strategy is in the management of cash balances and short-term investments. Due to the liquidity of these assets, the companies are able to move the exposures from one currency to another or simply invest the excess cash holdings in U.S. dollars, thereby avoiding exposure to foreign exchange risks to the same extent. Table 25 shows three

Table 24
Inter-Company Accounts' Adjustment:
Fixed Rate System vs. Floating Exchange Rates

Strategies	Number of Companies Significant Increase
Lead/Lag Inter-Subsidiary Receivables/Payables	5
Accelerate/Delay Remittances	3[a]
Adjust the Flows of Remittances to Parent Company	4
Sample size:	8

[a] Excluding the company which had not used this strategy in the fixed rate system.

Table 25
Debt and Working Capital Management:
Fixed Rate System vs. Floating Exchange Rates

Strategies	Number of Companies Significant Increase
Local Currency Borrowings	1
Foreign Currency Borrowings	2
Pre-payment of Bank Borrowings and Like Commitments to Third Parties	3
Adjust Local/Foreign Currency Long-term Debt	2
Reduce Short-term Assets and Increase Short-term Liabilities Denominated in Depreciating Currencies and Vice Versa	3[a]
Adjust Planned Parent Company's Dollar Investments	3
Sample Size:	8

[a] Excluding the company which had not used this strategy in the fixed rate system.

companies which have significantly increased the use of the strategy of adjusting the flows of dollar investments by the parent company. One of these companies has not increased the use of any strategies other than this one and forward exchange contract hedging on foreign currency transactions since the advent of floating exchange rates.

Table 25 shows the number of companies which have significantly increased the use of debt and working capital management strategies since floating exchange rates.

In summary, floating exchange rates have brought about a significant increase in the hedging activities of the sampled companies. This is manifested in the adoption of "new" defensive strategies and the significantly increased use of the "old" ones, most notably, forward exchange contracts on foreign currency transactions, inter-company accounts' adjustment, inter-currency netting, and, to a lesser extent, leads/lags of third-party receivables/payables. The analysis further suggests that, at least for these strategies, in terms of risk-return trade-off, greater uncertainty brought about by generalized floating has added a motivation for the companies to expand their hedging and search for new ways to protect their exposures.

A review of past research on multinational firms' hedging practices in the fixed exchange rate system and under floating exchange rates also reveals this trend. However, it should be noted that past data are not directly comparable and the basis of data measurement was the number of companies which used the defensive strategies. Thus, Jadwani's results indicated that most of the companies in his sample of 25 firms did not resort to any strategies other than forward exchange contracts and local borrowing to cope with the 1967 sterling devaluation.[7] On forward exchange contracts, about 80 percent of his sample of companies used this facility to hedge U.S. dollar loans, but just about one-half to hedge the balance sheet exposure and foreign currency transactions from import/export transactions. Similarly, 17 companies used local borrowing to build up their sterling liabilities. However, only nine companies varied the timing and/or the amounts of dividend remittances and one company built up its local inventory. No other defensive strategies were shown to have been used by any of these companies.[8] Similarly, Fieleke's investigation in February 1972 of 167 U.S. firms after the 1971 flotation of the Deutsche mark showed that of 73 firms which had some transactions with Germany, only 19 engaged in forward exchange contracts. On the strategies of leading/lagging, specification of the billing currency, and use of the currency clause, less than 15 percent of the 75 companies which responded to his question in this regard engaged in these practices.[9]

In contrast, judging from the number of companies which considered them useful, Jilling showed that 83 percent of his sample of 107 companies used forward exchange contracts and eight out of 10 companies engaged in local borrow-

ings at one time or another since the introduction of floating exchange rates.[10]
For the other defensive strategies which ranged from "practice intracompany
transfer pricing" to "adjust inventory," at least 5 out of 10 companies used
them.

The findings presented in this section are also confirmed by the five
foreign exchange consultants/bankers. To quote one banker:

> Clearly, after 1971 the volume of foreign exchange rose significantly. Last year or
> so, it has not risen. It peaked last year. Now, clearly if we come to another "crisis,"
> we are going to pick up again . . . Up to 1971, a lot of companies didn't hedge. A lot
> of them started hedging . . . some of them started hedging the balance sheet.

This same banker also said:

> People are becoming increasingly aware of achieving the same goal. If you structure
> your debt properly, you can get into a minimal exposure position where you don't
> have to hedge. We become very much aware of how long it takes between a devalu-
> ation and the time that you can change your prices in a given country. It is a very
> important factor to determine what your exposure is. Until you take that into
> account, any concept of exposure doesn't make any sense because you may be
> able to recuperate the next day by jacking up your prices. So, people are becoming
> more aware of "skinning a cat," than just killing it. The initial flurry to hit the
> foreign exchange markets has gone.

From the empirical findings, the results from past research and similar
comments of the consultants, it thus can be concluded that as a result of greater
uncertainty under floating exchange rates, companies have intensified their
hedging activities. This has occurred not only in the foreign exchange markets,
but companies have also become aware of and actually used other vehicles for
protection against foreign exchange risks.

However, like the interviewed executives, the consultants were quick to
point out that the advent of generalized floating has been less dramatically
impactive on their foreign exchange management than the adoption of FASB 8.
This is the subject for discussion in the next section.

FASB 8

In December, 1975, the Financial Accounting Standards Board finally
adopted FASB 8. This statement seeks to set forth the standards whereby the
results of foreign operations of U.S.-based multinational corporations are consolidated with the parent company's results. The purpose of this section is to
analyze the effects of these standards on the method of currency exposure
measurement and the defensive strategies of the sampled companies.

FASB 8's Standards

This statement consists of two principal divisions which are most relevant to the issues addressed in this study: (1) the exchange rate to translate the accounts of foreign financial statements and, (2) the timing for recognition of foreign exchange adjustments.

Translation rate

In elimination of the diverse translation practices by multinational firms prior to this statement, FASB 8 requires that the financial statements of U.S.-based multinational corporations' overseas subsidiaries be prepared with U.S. generally accepted accounting principles and that the resultant statements of financial conditions and profit and loss be translated in accordance with the temporal principle. This principle stipulates that cash, receivables and payables, and assets and liabilities carried at present or future prices are to be translated at the current exchange rate and assets and liabilities carried at past prices at applicable historical rates.

Specifically, with regard to foreign currency transactions of a U.S. operation (e.g., imports to and exports from the United States),

(a) At the transaction date, each asset, liability, revenue or expense arising from the transaction shall be translated (that is, measured in) dollars by use of the exchange rate *(rate)* in effect at that date, and shall be recorded at the dollar amount.

(b) At each balance sheet date, recorded dollar balances representing cash and amounts owed by or to the enterprise that are denominated in foreign currency shall be adjusted to reflect the current rate.

(c) At each balance sheet date, assets carried at market whose current market price is stated in a foreign currency shall be adjusted to the equivalent dollar market price at the balance sheet date (that is, the foreign currency market price at the balance sheet date multiplied by the current rate).[11]

For cash, receivables and payables denominated in a foreign currency but carried in the local books of the overseas subsidiaries, they must first be translated into the local currency at the current rate. These adjusted balances and like items denominated in the local currency then will be translated into U.S. dollars at the current rate.

For assets and liabilities of the overseas subsidiary other than those mentioned in the preceding paragraph, the particular measurement basis shall determine the exchange rate to be used for translation. Thus,

(a) Accounts carried at prices in past exchanges (past prices) shall be translated at historical rates.

(b) Accounts carried at prices in current purchase or sale exchanges (current prices) or future exchanges (future prices) shall be translated at the current rate.[12]

As to revenue and expense items, they shall be translated into U.S. dollars by using the average exchange rate prevailing in the particular period in question (e.g. quarterly average rate). On the other hand:

> Revenue and expense that relate to assets and liabilities translated at historical rates shall be translated at historical rates used to translate the related assets and liabilities.[13]

Table 26 shows the exchange rate to be used for translation of specific foreign financial statements' balance sheet accounts. For inventory, if it is carried at cost, the translation rate is the historical rate of exchange. If it is carried at current or future prices, the current rate will be the translation rate. However, due to the "lower of cost or market" rule, in either case, inventory is not exposed, i.e., inventory write-downs due to currency depreciations will be reported as inventory losses, not as part of foreign exchange adjustments. On the other hand, if the local currency appreciates, the lower value of inventory which is its historical cost will not be changed, i.e., no foreign exchange gain or inventory write-up will be recognized.

Thus, effectively under FASB 8's provisions, only cash, receivables and payables, and debts (excluding stockholders' equity) shall be translated at the current rate of exchange and therefore, are exposed to currency fluctuations. For the purpose of computing the translation exposure, all of the other assets and liabilities are not exposed as they are translated at historical rates.

Timing for recognition of foreign exchange gains/losses

This provision is probably the most controversial ruling of FASB 8. Whereas before the adoption of this statement, companies had the option of deferring exchange gains or losses, especially those arising from translation, effective January 1, 1976, these gains and losses shall be recognized as part of current income/expense. FASB 8 rules:

> Exchange gains and losses shall be included in determining net income for the period in which the rate changes.[14]

The above provision is also applicable to gains/losses on forward exchange contracts unless the contract is a hedge of an identifiable foreign currency commitment. For a forward contract to be considered a hedge of a foreign currency commitment, all of the following conditions must be met.

Table 26
Rates Used to Translate Assets and Liabilities

Assets	Current	Historical
	Translation Rates	
Cash on hand and demand and time deposits	x	
Marketable equity securities:		
Carried at cost		x
Carried at current market prices	x	
Accounts and notes receivable and related		
unearned discount	x	
Allowance for doubtful accounts and		
notes receivable	x	
Inventories:		
Carried at cost		x
Carried at current replacement price		
or current selling price	x	
Carried at net realizable value	x	
Carried at contract price (produced under		
fixed price contracts)	x	
Prepaid insurance, advertising, and rent		x
Refundable deposits	x	
Advances to unconsolidated subsidiaries	x	
Property, plant, and equipment		x
Accumulated depreciation of property,		
plant, and equipment		x
Cash surrender value of life insurance	x	
Patents, trademarks, licenses, and formulas		x
Goodwill		x
Other intangible assets		x
LIABILITIES		
Accounts and notes payable and overdrafts	x	
Accrued expenses payable	x	
Accrued losses on firm purchase commitments	x	
Refundable deposits	x	
Deferred income		x
Bonds payable or other long-term debt	x	
Unamortized premium or discount on bonds		
or notes payable	x	
Convertible bonds payable	x	
Accrued pension obligations	x	
Obligations under warranties	x	

Source: Financial Accounting Standards Board, *Statement of FASB 8,* p. 20.

(a) The life of the forward contract extends from the foreign currency commitment date to the anticipated transaction date or a later date.

(b) The forward contract date is denominated in the same currency as the foreign currency commitment and for an amount that is the same or less than the amount of the foreign currency commitment.

(c) The foreign currency commitment is firm and uncancellable.[15]

Thus, gains/losses on forward exchange contracts taken out as a speculation or for the purpose of covering the balance sheet exposure or a foreign currency transaction which do not meet all of the above conditions shall have to be recognized as part of current income/expenses.

These new currency accounting rules represent an important departure from prior translation practices by most of the sampled companies and have led to significant deterioraton of and fluctuations in reported earnings of some of them. Initially, the sample of companies was selected such that four companies had their reported earnings significantly impacted by FASB 8. In one company, the effect resulted in an increase of the 1975 fiscal year's earnings by 11.3 percent. In the other three companies, the effect was adverse, resulting in a decline in net income by 12.9 percent in one company (1974 fiscal year), 8.07 percent in another (1975 fiscal year), and in the last 5.3 percent (1976 fiscal year).

Of the 10 companies in the sample, 8 were selected because prior to FASB 8 they used translation methodologies that were different from the provisions of FASB 8. As it turns out, one company was dropped from the sample for the purposes of this analysis because it became a multinational corporation only shortly before FASB 8 was issued. Its exposure management activities before and after FASB 8 therefore are not sufficiently comparable. The other two companies were included in the sample because they used the monetary-non-monetary method for translation—which is effectively the same as FASB 8 rules—and therefore serve as a control group.

The hypothesis underlying this sampling procedure is that given significant earnings impact by FASB 8, those companies which used a translation methodology different from that of FASB 8 will undertake significant changes in their currency exposure measurement and, as the original discussion suggests, are motivated to abandon any defensive strategies that they used previously.

However, as the empirical findings indicate, none of the companies abandon any of the defensive strategies that they used previously as a result of FASB 8. And yet, partly confirming the original hypothesis, a couple of companies reduce the use of forward exchange contracts to hedge off-balance sheet items. For the most part, those companies whose earnings are significantly affected by FASB 8 actually step up their exposure management activities and increase the use of certain defensive strategies.

This is a result of the increased awareness of foreign exchange problems created by FASB 8. Furthermore, the effects of FASB 8 are more widespread—in terms of the companies which are affected—than originally anticipated. Part of the problem is that the base year is not sufficiently indicative of the earnings impact of FASB 8. In addition to the four companies that were identified, one other company which is included in the control group has experienced significant earnings impact by FASB 8. However, there seems to be no real solution to this problem because this company does not disclose this impact in its 10-K reports.

Another part of the problem of the extensiveness of FASB 8's effects is the existence of the reserve account. Thus, to the extent that a company deferred its translation gains/losses, from the standpoint of exposure management, effectively it excluded all of the balance sheet accounts from its currency exposure, regardless of the translation method that it used previously. With FASB 8, such a company has to recognize translation gains/losses as part of current income. Since exchange rate fluctuates, this provision leads to fluctuations in reported earnings which must be reflected in the statement of income. This is the reason for the increased awareness of foreign exchange problems.

Since not all companies which had a reserve account experience FASB 8's effects to the same extent, as the empirical findings suggest, another factor should be taken into consideration which is the amounts of local/foreign currency long-term debts. The disparate experiences of the two companies which had a reserve account and used the monetary-non-monetary method for translation prior to FASB 8 clearly point to this conclusion.

There seems to be another factor which influences the extent of FASB 8's effects. This is the geographical distribution of a company's international operations. Thus, a company of which the international operations are concentrated in depreciating currencies—in terms of the U.S. dollar—such as the Brazilian cruzeiro should experience a positive earnings impact, and therefore, would not undertake any increased defensive activities. On the other hand, a company which operates in a country such as Italy should experience violent earnings fluctuations, and therefore, would step up its defensive activities to counter FASB 8's effects. This factor, however, cannot be documented from the empirical findings.

The following sections will analyze the effects of FASB 8 on the nine sampled companies insofar as their currency exposure measurement and defensive strategies are concerned.

Currency Exposure Measurement

Before FASB 8, four companies in the sample used the current rate of exchange to translate their monetary assets and liabilities. They also used the current rate to translate their inventory. This is the modified monetary-non-monetary method. Two companies used the current-noncurrent method, two monetary-nonmonetary, and one current rate with the exception that stock-holders' equity and deferred charges were translated at historical rates. One company is excluded from this discussion because it became a multinational company—as defined in this study—only recently. It should be pointed out, however, that its exposure management activities are FASB 8 oriented and therefore, its currency exposure is defined in accordance with FASB 8 insofar as the balance sheet accounts are concerned. Thus, of the nine companies in the sample, seven had to change their translation practices to conform with FASB 8.

More importantly from the standpoint of exposure management is the effect of FASB 8 on the currency exposure measurement of these companies. In this respect, all of the nine companies have been affected by FASB 8.

Insofar as the balance sheet accounts are concerned, nominally, three of the modified monetary-nonmonetary companies have retained the original methodology to measure their currency exposures. That is, they include in their currency exposures inventory as well as the monetary assets and liabilities. One modified monetary-nonmonetary company, however, dropped inventory from its currency exposure and switched entirely to FASB 8. On the other hand, one current-noncurrent company now follows the modified monetary-non-monetary approach to define its currency exposure, regardless of the fact that it has to translate its foreign financial statements in accordance with FASB 8. The other current-noncurrent company accepts FASB 8 to define its currency ex-posure as well as to translate the balance sheet. As to the two monetary-non-monetary companies, both followed the modified monetary-nonmonetary method to measure the currency exposure. After FASB 8, one of these two companies dropped inventory from its currency exposure and has become entirely FASB 8-oriented for exposure management as well as translation purposes. The other company continues to follow its prior practice of including inventory for exposure management but excluding it for translation. Table 27 summarizes the nominal effects of FASB 8 on the currency exposure measure-ment of the nine companies in the sample. Hidden in this table is the fact that five of the nine companies had to change their currency exposure measurement after the adoption of FASB 8.

In actuality, FASB 8's effects on currency exposure measurement are more widespread and substantial. These effects can be examined from the stand-point of income recognition and exposure management orientation.

From the standpoint of income recognition, three of the nine companies used a reserve account to defer all of their unrealized (i.e., translation) foreign exchange gains and losses. In effect, this resulted in the exclusion of balance sheet accounts from their currency exposures. It is thus no surprise that these

Table 27
Nominal Effects of FASB 8 on Currency Exposure Measurement
(Balance Sheet Accounts Only)

Measurement Methodology	Number of Companies	
	Before FASB 8	After FASB 8
Monetary-nonmonetary	0	4
Modified monetary-nonmonetary	6	5
Current-noncurrent	2	0
Current rate (except stockholders' equity and deferred charges)	1	0
Number of companies affected:		5
Sample size:	9	9

companies had never used forward exchange contracts to hedge their balance sheet exposures, simply because there had been no exposure to hedge. From this basis, it would be appropriate to deduce that these companies have used this defensive strategy since FASB 8. Indeed, this has actually happened in all three companies. Of these companies, insofar as the balance sheet accounts are concerned, two presently follow the modified monetary-nonmonetary method to define the currency exposure. The other exclusively uses FASB 8 in its currency exposure measurement.

A fourth company also used the reserve account to defer its unrealized exchange gains/losses. Of the losses, if no reserve was available, they were deferred to the extent that they did not exceed the adjustment arising from the translation of long-term liabilities; the excess was then charged to current income. Thus, this company used the modified monetary-nonmonetary method for translation, but only to a very limited extent did it include the balance sheet accounts in its currency exposure. Presently it follows the modified monetary-nonmonetary method to define its currency exposure.

A fifth company charged unrealized foreign exchange gains/losses to current income, except those arising from long-term debts. From an exposure management point of view, it means that this company excluded long-term debts from its currency exposure, although for translation purposes it used the monetary-nonmonetary approach. For this company, this exclusion was very important because it has had sizeable amounts of long-term debts denominated in hard Euro-currencies such as the Swiss franc and the Dutch guilder. By excluding long-term debts, the Swiss franc and the Dutch guilder exposures came close to being neutral whereas the Belgian franc and the pound sterling exposures were cut by at least one third. Expectedly, it had never used forward exchange contracts to hedge the balance sheet exposure, but has engaged in this defensive strategy since the adoption of FASB 8. This is a very significant change for this company, given the fact that it is very reluctant to hedge in the forward exchange markets, even for foreign currency transactions. In fact, it is indicated by the foreign exchange manager that this company has never hedged these transactions by forward exchange contracts. Presently, it follows FASB 8 in its currency exposure measurement.

A sixth company recognized unrealized foreign exchange gains/losses as part of current income, except those arising from translation of long-term debts used for financing of capital assets. This portion of the balance sheet thus was effectively excluded from the balance sheet component of the currency exposure, although the company used the modified monetary-nonmonetary method to translate its foreign financial statements. After FASB 8, the modified monetary-nonmonetary method is again used to measure the currency exposure, regardless of the fact that this new accounting rule requires that inventory be translated at historical rates.

The three remaining companies have always recognized unrealized foreign exchange gains/losses as part of current income. One of these continues to measure its currency exposure in accordance with the modified monetary-nonmonetary method. The two other companies now are completely FASB 8-oriented. One of them used the modified monetary-nonmonetary method to define its currency exposure whereas the other followed the current-noncurrent method.

Table 28 summarizes the effects of FASB 8 on the currency exposure measurement of the sampled companies viewed from the standpoint of income recognition. This table also points out the fact that four of the five companies which presently follow the modified monetary-nonmonetary method in the definition of their currency exposures frequently falter between this approach and FASB 8. This fact was discussed in detail in Chapter III.

From the foregoing analysis, it is evident that from the standpoint of income recognition, FASB 8 has affected and actually altered the currency exposure measurement of the nine companies in the sample. Only two of these companies can be considered marginally affected.

Effects of FASB 8 on Defensive Strategies

As noted, FASB 8 has resulted in significant earnings impact on five of the nine companies in the sample. Additionally, partly due to the existence of the reserve account, the effects on currency exposure measurement are more wide-spread than originally anticipated. However, these changes have not led any company in the sample to abandon any of the defensive strategies that they used previously.

Whereas a couple of companies reduced the use of forward exchange contracts to hedge off-balance sheet items (which are not foreign currency commitments as defined by FASB 8), none of the companies ceased using this strategy. Additionally, two other companies indicated that they have become more conscious of the timing of the contract, i.e., they try to the extent possible to synchronize the anticipated receipt/payment date of such transactions with the maturity date of the contract. Beyond this fine-tuning, these companies reported that they do not find FASB 8 to be a constraining influence on the use of this strategy to hedge such transactions.

Furthermore, none of the companies abandoned or reduced hedging of the balance sheet exposure in the forward exchange markets. Of the six companies which included inventory in their currency exposures prior to FASB 8,[16] two companies continue to hedge this exposure component in the foreign exchange markets. (These companies translated inventory at the current rate of exchange and recognized translation gains/losses as part of current income, except that one company deferred that portion of translation adjustment

Table 28
Balance Sheet Components of Currency Exposures Affected by FASB 8

Company Code	Balance Sheet Accounts Included in Currency Exposures	
	Before FASB 8	After FASB 8
1st	None	Monetary-nonmonetary
2nd[a]	None	Modified monetary-nonmonetary
3rd[a]	None	Modified monetary-nonmonetary
4th	Modified monetary-nonmonetary less long-term debts	Monetary-nonmonetary
5th[a]	Modified monetary-nonmonetary	Modified monetary-nonmonetary
6th	Modified monetary-nonmonetary less long-term debts to finance capital assets	Modified monetary-nonmonetary
7th[a]	Very limited extent	Modified monetary-nonmonetary
8th	Modified monetary-nonmonetary	Monetary-nonmonetary
9th	Current-noncurrent	Monetary-nonmonetary

Sample size: 9 companies

[a] This company frequently falters between the modified monetary-nonmonetary approach and FASB 8.

arising from long-term debts used to finance plant and equipment.) Three companies in this group did not hedge any balance sheet components in the forward exchange markets. The remaining company actually reduced forward exchange contract hedging of the balance sheet components of its currency exposure well before FASB 8 was issued, due to large losses from such contracts. It recently ceased using this strategy altogether because of uncertainty in exchange rate movements, not FASB 8.

In lieu of reducing defensive activities, the nine companies in the sample actually step up their exposure management efforts to cope with FASB 8.

For the first company—refer to Table 27 for company code—the issuance of FASB 8 coincided with a change in the way the company sought to expand its international business. Before 1975-76, this company billed most of its exports in U.S. dollars. Also it has had sizeable amounts of equipment purchased from overseas which exposed the company to foreign exchange risks to the same extent if they were to be replaced. Under these circumstances, this company sought to protect its currency exposure by adopting the current rate method to translate its foreign financial statements as well as to manage the foreign exchange risks. Then came a decision to denominate its overseas billings in foreign currencies as a way to increase its export sales. About the same time, FASB 8 was promulgated. The changes in the translation method and timing of income recognition and the natural increase in transaction exposures cumulatively led to foreign exchange losses of almost 18 percent of net earnings in 1976. Although FASB 8's share of this impact was insignificant in this year, in 1975, FASB 8's impact amounted to 8.07 percent of net earnings. Under these circumstances, a decision was made to approach exposure management entirely on an FASB 8 basis. Presently, however, the company is considering adding back to its currency exposure that portion of inventory calculated on a quarterly average basis.

This change in exposure management strategy has led to a significant increase in the use of a great number of defensive strategies. Table 29 summarizes the strategies of which the use has been significantly increased. As it can be seen from this table, the effects of FASB 8 on its defensive strategies are widespread and significant. Missing from this list of affected strategies are leads/lags of inter-subsidiary receivables and payables simply because it has little of inter-company transactions, except with the parent company. To the extent that any transactions of the parent company exist, leads/lags of these fund flows have been increased. It has also pre-paid certain foreign currency and U.S. dollar debts and replaced them with local currency borrowings. In this respect, the company has become more conscious of the volatility of the financing currencies. Due to increases in foreign currency transactions, forward exchange contract hedging has also been increased. Furthermore, to protect its inventory, price increases have also been effected. In addition, it is now contemplating replacing its Swiss

Table 29
A Company's Changes in Defensive Strategies Due to FASB 8-I:
Significantly Affected Strategies

Accelerate/Delay Remittances to Parent Company

Pre-Payment of Bank Borrowings and Like Commitments to Third Parties

Increase Export Prices

Increase Billing Prices to Local Customers

Specify Currency of Billing in Import and Export Transactions

Increase/Decrease Local/Foreign Currency Inventories

Forward Exchange Contracts on Payments/Receipts for Commitments not Recorded in the Books

Adjust the Flows of Remittances to Parent Company

Adjust Planned Parent Company's Dollar Investments

Negotiate Foreign Currency and/or Credit Swaps

Reduce Short-term Assets and Increase Short-term Liabilities Denominated in Depreciating Currencies and vice versa

Adjust Local/Foreign Currency Long-term Debts

franc debt with borrowings denominated in some other currency.

Equally widespread but less visible are the effects on the defensive strategies of the second company. Officially, the company measures its currency exposure with inclusion of inventory. However, frequently this company has to move toward the FASB 8 approach in its exposure management orientation when potential translation effects on earnings are sufficiently large. This is due to the fundamental conflict between FASB 8 and the modified monetary-nonmonetary method. Table 30 shows the defensive strategies of which the use has been significantly increased as a result of FASB 8.

Table 30
A Company's Changes in Defensive Strategies Due to FASB 8-II:
Significantly Affected Strategies

Pre-payment of Bank Borrowings and Like Commitments from Third Parties

Foreign Currency Borrowings

Forward Exchange Contracts on Payments/Receipts Arising from Import and Export Transactions

Adjust Planned Parent Company's Investments

Missing from this table are those strategies related to pricing and inventory strategies, leads/lags of third-party receivables and payables, and inter-company accounts' adjustment. It appears that the little increase in the use of these strategies is a result of the fact that this company's exposure management approach is fairly decentralized with respect to transaction exposures—as compared to the other companies in the sample. In fact, it only occasionally used the strategies of price increases and "never" adjusted inventory levels or engaged in inter-company accounts' adjustment before FASB 8. In contrast, because the translation exposure is centrally controlled at the parent company's headquarters, debt management strategies have been increased to cope with FASB 8. Most notable are the strategies of debt pre-payment and foreign currency borrowings. In addition, an interviewee from this company indicated that in retrospect, it would have been beneficial if the company's Swiss franc debt was replaced by an obligation denominated in the U.S. dollar.

Similarly, the seventh company has concentrated on debt management aided by inter-company accounts' adjustment to manage its FASB 8 exposure. Presently, this company measures its currency exposure by including inventory but also is concerned about the translation effects of exchange rate changes, and therefore, has increased the use of inter-company accounts to move exposures among currencies. Table 31 summarizes the defensive strategies of which the use has been significantly increased due to FASB 8.

Table 31
A Company's Changes in Defensive Strategies Due to FASB 8-III:
Significantly Affected Strategies

Lead/Lag Inter-Subsidiary Receivables/Payables

Accelerate/Delay Remittances to Parent Company

Local Currency Borrowings

Foreign Currency Borrowings

Adjust the Flows of Remittances to Parent Company

Forward Exchange Contracts on Net Balance Sheet Exposure

Noteworthy is the company's increased use of forward exchange contracts to hedge its balance sheet exposure. It also has decreased local currency borrowings. In addition, borrowings denominated in foreign currencies other than the Swiss franc have been increased. On the other hand, its Swiss franc debt has been replaced by borrowings denominated in the U.S. dollar.

As to the ninth company, the actions taken so far to manage its FASB 8 exposure have not been very significant, although since FASB 8 it has begun to use changes in credit terms occasionally. On the other hand, it has reduced buying/selling foreign currencies forward on off-balance sheet items. It has also taken out forward exchange contracts to hedge its FASB 8 exposure, a strategy it did not use before FASB 8.

However limited these actions may be, substantial changes are expected in the near future as it has begun to review its exposure management orientation, strategies, objectives, and organization. One of the areas that will be affected in this review is the parent company's relationship with the overseas subsidiaries in terms of defensive strategies. At the time of the interviews, no guidelines and policies existed concerning the extent that the overseas subsidiaries can act to cover the parent company's balance sheet exposure. For example, presently the overseas subsidiaries are not authorized to change inter-company payment terms without consent from the parent. What is being reviewed is the extent to which the subsidiaries can take independent actions in this area without prior approval from the parent company.

Also under review is the objective(s) of its foreign exchange management, e.g., whether foreign exchange risks should be managed on the basis of FASB 8 or from an economic standpoint. Once the organization and objective(s) are established, a number of actions could be taken. The company's Assistant Treasurer gave some examples:

> Let us say we have a German subsidiary and that German subsidiary has a net exposed liability position in Deutsche marks and we believe the Deutsche mark is going to strengthen against the dollar and therefore we do not want it to have that net liability position. There are a number of things that can be done. One of them would [be to] have the German company borrow U.S. dollars and pay off the Deutsche mark debt. If on the other hand the company had a flat position, and we believe the Deutsche mark was going to depreciate against the dollar and we would like that company to have debt in Deutsche marks, arrangements could be made to reduce its inter-company payment terms from the U.S. or some sister subsidiary from . . . six months to three months. This would necessitate it borrowing locally in Deutsche marks enough to pay down its inter-company debt. This then would produce the favorable position that we were aiming at. Or you could have it borrow Deutsche marks and invest the proceeds in dollars or Swiss francs or some other currency.

While FASB 8's effects on the defensive strategies of these four companies are extensive, they are not unexpected in view of the significant impact on their earnings. Unanticipated are the effects on debt management strategies of the fourth company. They are unanticipated because this company does not disclose earnings impact by FASB 8 in its 10-K reports, therefore, was not identified as such. As it turns out, this company has suffered significant earnings fluctuations from the removal of the reserve account which was used to defer translation gains/losses on its sizeable amounts of long-term debts denominated in such strong Euro-currencies as the Swiss franc, Dutch guilder, etc.

Specifically, since FASB 8 this company has stepped up the use of local and foreign currency borrowings to change its debt structure, although these strategies have already been used rather extensively before. The reason for this limitation to debt management strategies to manage the FASB 8 exposure is that such strategies as leads/lags of third-party receivables/payables and inter-company accounts' adjustment have already been used to the extent possible. In addition to borrowings, it has also begun to engage in forward exchange contract hedging of the balance sheet exposure and off-balance sheet items, practices it did not use before FASB 8.

With respect to debt management, the company has increased local currency borrowings in the subsidiaries which have offsetting exposed asset positions. In the Canadian case, it has issued commercial paper in Canadian dollars and used the proceeds to pay off U.S. dollar debts. Furthermore, when currency relationships permit, it has built up Deutsche mark deposits to offset its short position in Swiss francs. At times, these movements of funds amounted to tens of millions of dollars.

The experience of this company is even more remarkable when compared to the little impact of FASB 8, if any, on the defensive strategies of the third company, even though both used the monetary-nonmonetary method for translation and measured their currency exposures according to the modified monetary-nonmonetary method. What seems to have made the difference is the existence of the much larger amounts of hard Euro-currency long-term debts in the fourth company.[17]

In fact, a review of the debt structures of the companies—as disclosed in their 10-K reports and the information obtained in the interviews—which reported significant changes in their defensive strategies as a result of FASB 8, reveals that they all have sizeable amounts of long-term Euro-currency debts and used a reserve account to defer translation losses.[18] It appears that neither of these two factors is sufficient for a company to change its defensive strategies, especially on their borrowing and debt structure strategies. However, when combined, they produce a powerful impact on the earnings which fluctuate with changes in exchange rates. In this connection, it is worthy to note an executive's view on the relationship of a subsidiary's financial structure and the exposure problem:

> My basis view is that a foreign subsidiary which is appropriately capitalized and has an ordinary appropriate financial structure does not create enormous balance sheet exposures. They may be large, but you do not have this substantial exposure number which is created so often when for instance a manufacturing operation is primarily funded through local long-term debts and has a minimum of capital. That is the type of situation where you have substantial exposure problems. If you have a more or less normally financed entity, the problems are what I would call manageable.

To a much lesser extent are the effects on defensive strategies of the fifth and eighth companies. Where they exist, the effects seem to be isolated. At the fifth company, it has ceased to sell/buy foreign currencies forward to hedge the balance sheet exposure. This change, however, seems to be more attributable to uncertainty in exchange rate movements than FASB 8 in view of the fact that forward exchange contract hedging of the balance sheet exposure was already significantly reduced prior to FASB 8.

At the eighth company, the exposure management approach is basically FASB 8-oriented as it seeks to protect its overall earnings against quarterly fluctuations. This philosophy of profitability management is quite strong regardless of the fact that FASB 8 did not result in any material impact on its 1975 earnings. Actually, the only currency exposure measurement effect was the exclusion of inventory. In terms of defensive strategies, FASB 8's effects are real but not apparent. One actual case will illustrate the point. Consider the situation where a currency is forecast to be depreciating and the company is short on an FASB 8 basis but long when inventory is added. The problem arises when there is a large unbooked receivable exposure created by a sale contract. Normal company practice would dictate forward selling of the currency to protect the gross margin. But from the viewpoint of FASB 8, this action is not called for. After much debating which involved the very top level of the company's management, the decision was to sell the foreign currency forward. At the last minute, this decision was reversed at the same management level.

To examine the effects of FASB 8 on the sixth company's defensive strategies, its internal exposure reports were reviewed, in addition to the taped interviews and conversations over the telephone and lunches. These reports include data on the amounts and directions of exposures in 17 currencies, forecasts of their exchange rates against the U.S. dollar, and contemplated hedging actions and their costs. These reports covered the last half of 1977. From the cumulative evidence, it is believed that this company is firmly entrenched in its policy of disregarding FASB 8 in its exposure management strategy. This policy, however, seems to be aided by two related factors:

1. It has no long-term debt denominated in hard Euro-currencies
2. In several important currencies, its FASB 8 exposures were in the same direction as its economic exposures.

The Environment of Foreign Exchange Management Under FASB 8

As it has been pointed out on several occasions, before FASB 8 was issued, companies had several options to recognize the earnings effects of foreign exchange risks. When the reserve account was used and long-term debts were translated at historical rates, effects of currency fluctuations were not striking, at least from the viewpoint of behavior modification. Furthermore, if the translation was appropriately selected—for example, monetary-nonmonetary method with translation adjustments deferred—even if the company had large amounts of foreign currency debts, translation gains/losses were hardly recognized until they became realized. For long-term debts, currency effects could be deferred for years.

After FASB 8, the environment of foreign exchange management has been changed. Probably the most powerful impact of FASB 8 has been that the companies' top management personnel become increasingly aware of foreign exchange problems since they are translated directly into earnings-per-share data. Analyzing this aspect of FASB 8's effects, an executive said:

> It has been the foundation for virtually everything you do today within exposure management. It has become a primary issue in our decision-making as much as what price can you get for your products and what is gross margin . . . It is also what is the translation impact and have you considered it in what you are doing? I think it is the most important element in terms of the additional awareness and additional work we do in exposure management. I think that what it has done . . . first, it triggered a reaction which said I've got to be sensitive to my translation adjustment, my shareholders are now going to be probably sensitive to the market . . . It has opened up a whole other area of business decisions that hasn't been fully thought out before.

Along the same lines, another executive said:

> I think that FASB 8 forces you to look at the raw numbers that are cranked out. You may say I don't believe that that is an economic loss. But you have to look at it nevertheless. It put a lot more emphasis on our monitoring of exposures.

Added to this awareness is a perception that fluctuations of earnings, although they are only accounting entries and may be reversed in the future, would have negative effects on share prices. However, none of the executives of the companies whose earnings have been significantly affected by FASB 8 would comment specifically as to whether or not quarterly fluctuations have depressed their companies' share prices, citing that this cannot be substantiated either way. Nevertheless, three of these executives were convinced that securities analysts do not fully understand the effects of FASB 8 on their companies' earnings. Actually, securities analysts have not responded sympathetically to their explanations that under floating exchange rates their companies' misfortunes would be reversed in the future. As a result, these companies have abandoned efforts to explain FASB 8's effects to the investment community.

Under these circumstances, the sampled companies have stepped up their exposure management activities. The first step is to improve the reporting system. At one company, prior to FASB 8 the information system was so inadequate that often decisions were made that were "180 degrees wrong." At another company, the ongoing reorganization would not have been contemplated—or at least would have been further delayed—had FASB 8 not been issued. At the other companies, changes have been made in the information systems to improve the information flows and increase central control over exposure management activities of the overseas subsidiaries, primarily in the area of inter-company settlement terms.

The second step is to strengthen the monitoring of FASB 8 exposures. This is true in all of the sampled companies whether or not they are FASB 8-oriented or however insignificant their earnings have been impacted by FASB 8. In the more affected companies, the use of certain defensive strategies has been increased, e.g., forward exchange contracts on foreign currency transactions, although there is no inherent reason in FASB 8 that these changes should occur.

Confirming the finding that there has been a change in the environment of foreign exchange management brought about by the introduction of FASB 8 under conditions of floating exchange rates, a banker said:

> I think that is true. Floating exchange rates is one factor . . . which gave you greater volatility . . . then you came up with the reporting requirements, a change in accounting standards which were significant because you could not anymore reserve for foreign exchange losses.

Another banker said:

> These are the two things that happened and both of them together have the impact of creating the sensitivity and reaction in the companies that you have seen . . . I would think that even today, there would be less of an effort, less sensitivity on the part of senior management if it were not necessary for companies to report foreign exchange gains and losses in the annual report . . . We spoke to presidents of good-sized companies that are very much interested in this, and I am not sure that it would have happened without the accounting change.

This environmental change has created necessary conditions for companies to re-orient their foreign exchange management program and approach:

> FASB 8 came along and it was discovered that the reporting system was not adequate. People staffing the treasury function generally did not have experience in third-currency financing. They were familiar with domestic affairs, off-shore financing, but little with third-currency financing. As a result, they went in to borrow Swiss francs, attracted by the low interest rate in the Swiss market, with little thought given to the long-term effects of exchange rate fluctuations. Five years later, they took a beating on Euro-currency issues.

As part of this re-examination of their foreign exchange management program,

> The companies are re-examining how they evaluate their subsidiaries. This is something that was started a couple of years ago which they are still not on top of yet. Two, departments have been created now to follow foreign exchange movements when those departments did not exist before and they try to centralize exposure management, not just hedging, but exposure management strategies. Three, there has been a greater awareness of vulnerability to exchange rates in terms of intracorporate trade as well as external trade, all of which requires a centralized approach which companies are beginning to take. And fourthly, there has been a general shift in philosophy . . . because they were after markets and now they are after a centralized approach because they want more financial control. They are trying to achieve both, so you have a philosophical change in the approach to management in general.

And these changes do not appear to be limited to the sampled companies for as the consultants indicated, in terms of the frequency distribution, their corporate clients have had the same experiences as those found in the sampled companies.

Thus, in view of these improvements in the foreign exchange management program, it is not possible on the basis of the collected data to suggest whether or not FASB 8 has resulted in companies taking actions which are inconsistent with their economic objectives. In fact, at the outset of this research, an implicit assumption was that prior to FASB 8, companies have best approximated their economic exposures by using one of the then accepted methods of translation. When this assumption was discussed with the consultants, some of them said that while the assumption was reasonable, it was not realistic. They then pointed to the inadequacy of companies' reporting systems and little thought given to the economic implications of the adopted translation methods. In other words, unless it can be established that the original assumption is tenable and realistically descriptive of the situation before FASB 8, it seems not possible to conclude that FASB 8 has resulted in uneconomic behavior on the part of the companies.

On the other hand, as pointed out above, FASB 8 has resulted in certain improvements made by the sampled companies and by others, as it was indicated by the consultants, to bring about a better reporting system, more frequent monitoring of exposures, and involvement of top management in foreign exchange problems and financial policies. In fact, the consultants pointed out that as a result of FASB 8, companies began to take a closer look at the use of debts to finance overseas operations. Furthermore, they became more aware of the opportunities to manage foreign exchange exposures by financial planning, rather than simply relying on traditional strategies such as forward exchange contracts. In contrast, as one consultant suggested, before FASB 8, companies often did not give enough thought to the effects of foreign exchange on their debt and financing policies. They were simply more concerned and occupied with the levels of interest rates. Whether or not this was true in most companies, this empirical research cannot substantiate. However, based on some scattered evidence collected in the interviews, it appears that this situation prevailed in many companies.

The preceding evidence suggests that FASB 8 has brought some positive changes in the financial policies and foreign exchange management activities of multinational firms. This is not to say, on the other hand, that FASB 8 is "the ultimate wisdom," to use the terminology of one executive, or that companies are happy with it. Since a further discussion of this subject matter goes beyond the scope of this study, it suffices to say that even in this respect—the merits of FASB 8—the reaction of the interviewed executives was also mixed and differed for various reasons.

Summary and Conclusion

This chapter has been devoted to the analysis of the effects on foreign exchange management of two major developments in the environment of FASB 8. The first half of the chapter concentrates on the effects of floating exchange rates. The empirical findings presented herein and scattered throughout this study indicate that as a result of large swings of exchange rates, the sampled companies found it much more difficult to forecast future exchange rate movements. Another way to look at the same problem statistically is to say that exchange rate movements have exhibited a larger degree of uncertainty than that which prevailed in the fixed exchange rate system. As risk becomes greater with associated larger potential foreign exchange losses, the sampled companies have intensified their hedging efforts. This is accomplished in two ways: by creating new defensive strategies and increasing the use of existing ones.

Two companies in the sample were found to resort to some strategies that they had not used in the fixed exchange rate system, although these strategies are traditionally available and used by the other companies. In addition, most of the companies have resorted to the strategy of inter-currency netting. Basically, this is a willingness to leave open an exposed position in one currency in the hope that losses from this exposure are offset or reduced by gains from exposures in other currencies, so that the net result is that the global foreign exchange adjustment is tolerable. Such a strategy was simply not possible in the fixed exchange rate system. Furthermore, a couple of companies have created the facility of "internal hedge" to make it possible to net out transactions with third parties.

More remarkable is the fact that most of the sampled companies have intensified the use of traditional defensive strategies to cope with greater uncertainty. Most notable is the increased use of forward exchange contract hedging and inter-company accounts adjustment. The former has been increasingly used as the cost of hedging on foreign currency transactions under floating exchange was not significantly greater than that in the fixed exchange rate system, although the risk is greater. For the same reason, hedging the balance sheet exposure was not increased because the cost had been significantly higher; this did not justify the outflow of cash funds to protect accounting adjustments. In fact, one company actually reduced the use of this strategy and recently abandoned it completely. Likewise, the use of inter-company accounts' adjustment has been significantly increased because it does not entail much direct costs and yet the benefits are to reduce the exposures. This risk-return trade-off also explains why borrowings have not been increased for use as defensive strategy as it entails additional exposure. The operating strategies of lead/lags and pricing and inventory adjustments were found to be not as significantly

affected—in terms of the number of companies which increased their usage—
due to internal and external constraints.

The problems of foreign exchange, however, did not manifest themselves
strikingly or powerfully, and receive the full attention of top management
until the adoption of FASB 8. Because this accounting rule requires companies
to recognize translation adjustments as part of currency income, and estab-
lishes a uniform standard for companies to translate their foreign financial
statements, it brings about an awareness that rightly or wrongly, the fluctuations of exchange rates do affect their reported earnings; in fact, their earnings
fluctuate with every change in the exchange rates. Most affected were those
companies which used a translation method different from that of FASB 8,
which extensively used a reserve account to defer their translation adjustments,
and which have large amounts of local/foreign currency debts. All of these
companies, as a result, began to direct greater attention to the effects of foreign
exchange on their reported earnings and started to have the involvement of top
management in foreign exchange problems. This environment of concern and
awareness has resulted in even greater hedging activities in some companies.
Most remarkable is the attention that has been paid to the currency denomination of their debts and the financial structure of their overseas subsidiaries.
This is a major development that is unprecedented since companies seemingly
were not very concerned about the short-term fluctuations of exchange rates
when they took out foreign currency long-term debts.

Coupled with this intensified hedging effort and concern over the debt
structure is a program to continue updating the reporting systems and monitoring of exposures. This is true whether or not a company has changed in any significant way their defensive strategies or is affected by FASB 8's earning effects.
Thus, whereas it is not possible to determine whether FASB 8 has resulted in
misdirection of exposure management efforts with adverse consequences on the
resource allocation in the economy, it is evident at least that it has caused a
presumably better and more organized foreign exchange management program.

Chapter VI

Applications and Implications

The three preceding chapters provide an analysis of the empirical findings on the behavior of a sample of large multinational manufacturing companies under conditions of foreign exchange risks. Their behavior has been examined with respect to the ways they measure their currency exposures, their foreign exchange management objectives, the defensive strategies that have been used to achieve these objectives, and the factors constraining these strategies. The analysis then attempts to establish the relationships among these elements by studying the information systems which collect the data on currency exposures and risk/cost consequences of the defensive strategies, and the processes whereby the risk-return trade-off is evaluated and decisions are made. Finally, the investigation is focused on the effects of greater uncertainty in exchange rate movements under floating exchange rates and the new currency accounting rules espoused by FASB 8 on the foreign exchange management efforts of the sampled firms.

As it has been demonstrated, the foreign exchange management behavior of the sampled companies largely follows the reactive model suggested at the outset of this study. However, the results of the empirical research indicate some areas of discrepancies as well as offer new insights into the process of foreign exchange management. For this reason, a reformulated descriptive model of the foreign exchange management process will be attempted in this chapter. This reformulation will also serve as a generalization of the empirical findings. In the second half of this chapter, an attempt is then made to derive the implications of the findings on the international monetary system, foreign exchange and capital markets, and the multinational firm.

A Descriptive Model of the Foreign Exchange Management Process

As a foreword to this discussion, it is necessary to examine the extent to which the findings can be generalized. The sampling procedure used in this study is quota sampling. The justification for this procedure is discussed in Chapter II. As then noted, this sampling procedure does not produce a representative sample in the statistical sense. However, recognizing this problem, care has been taken to include in the sample a sufficient number of companies such that they constitute a cross-section of the population of large multinational manufacturing firms subject to this study. Furthermore, the major empirical findings were then discussed with five foreign exchange consultants/international bankers who have been active in this area of international corporate finance. Among other things, the frequency distribution of the sampled firms in the various foreign exchange management factors and the effects of floating exchange rates and FASB 8 were confirmed by these consultants. Past studies were then reviewed when it was possible or relevant to verify the validity of the empirical findings. Writings or seminar presentations of corporate financial officers, when they existed, were also incorporated into the analysis. The empirical and verification results were then compared with the tentative hypothesis generated by the conceptual model which embodies the literature directly and indirectly related to the subject area of foreign exchange management.

In view of the above, it is not warranted to generalize the findings in statistical terms. It seems reasonable, however, to suggest that the results of the empirical research and the reformulated descriptive model realistically portray the behavior of large multinational manufacturing firms under conditions of foreign exchange risks in the environment of floating exchange rates and FASB 8. On the other hand, the verification procedures confirm the reliability and validity of the empirical findings insofar as the sampled companies are concerned.

In any event, this reformulation constitutes a series of revised and empirically supportable hypotheses about the behavior of multinational firms under conditions of foreign exchange risks. However, before being accepted as scientific evidence, they should be subjected to further and more rigorous testing, preferably under controlled and statistically derived sampling procedures.

Figure 13 depicts the reformulated descriptive model of the foreign exchange management process. Like the original conceptualization, the model has three major interactive components: the internal and external environments, diagnosis of the effects of the external environment, and response. However, the interaction between these components appears to be more complex and dynamic than that implied in the original conceptualization. In actual practice, the foreign exchange management process consists of a series of decisions; many are subject to constraints by the internal and external environments and are affected by those preceding and in turn will affect those succeeding them as well.

In other words, foreign exchange management is an ongoing process over time. Being necessitated by continual changes in the exchange rates, it is both a dynamic and adaptive process for the adjustment of the aggregate of currency exposures in response to foreign exchange risks. In this process, the natural changes in the currency exposures—that is, those caused by sale and financing operations—are captured in the information systems which also process the data on future exchange rates. In this regard, FASB 8 plays an important role in the definition of currency exposures and what the objectives should be. Should there be an unacceptable inconsistency between potential foreign losses and the profit/earnings objectives, defensive strategies will be considered to alter the currency exposures. Likewise, if FASB 8 has a significant impact on earnings, the FASB 8 approach will be followed to define the currency exposure. This is true even if the currency exposure measurement normally disregards this accounting rule.

In the identification phase of the defensive strategies, those related to pricing/inventory and inter-company accounts' adjustment are defined to a large extent in terms of their feasibility and the amounts of possible adjustment in the sale and supply/distribution plans. The identified stategies are then evaluated following an upward path in the company's organizational hierarchy in terms of their risk/cost consequences in light of the objectives. From this evaluation will emerge a set of selected defensive strategies which will alter the currency exposures in the direction and possibly the magnitudes that are required by the forecast changes in the exchange rates. These strategies in turn will necessitate a revision of the currency exposures if the exchange rate forecasts for the next decision period render these exposures unacceptable in terms of their implications on potential foreign exchange losses.

The following provides a detailed discussion of the major components of this model of the foreign exchange management process by looking at the constituent elements and the relationships among them.

Currency Exposure

While the economic and accounting schools of thought debate the correct method of measuring a foreign operation's exposure to currency risks, there seems to be little disagreement among corporate executives. The empirical research indicates that, according to these executives and the consultants, the following should be included in the computation of a currency exposure:

1. All monetary assets and liabilities denominated in the local and foreign currencies.
2. Exposed earnings being net income plus those expenses related to the assets/liabilities that are translated at historical rates of exchange, e.g., depreciation.
3. Inventory, both from local and foreign sources. In this regard, some companies use the inventory turn-over rate to exclude that portion left over from the prior accounting period.
4. Off-balance sheet items being such transactions as confirmed orders and purchase agreements not yet recorded in the books; future sales and purchases which are not firm commitments are excluded.
5. Remittances of dividends and the like.
6. Income tax effects.

Figure 13
A Descriptive Model of the Foreign Exchange Management Program

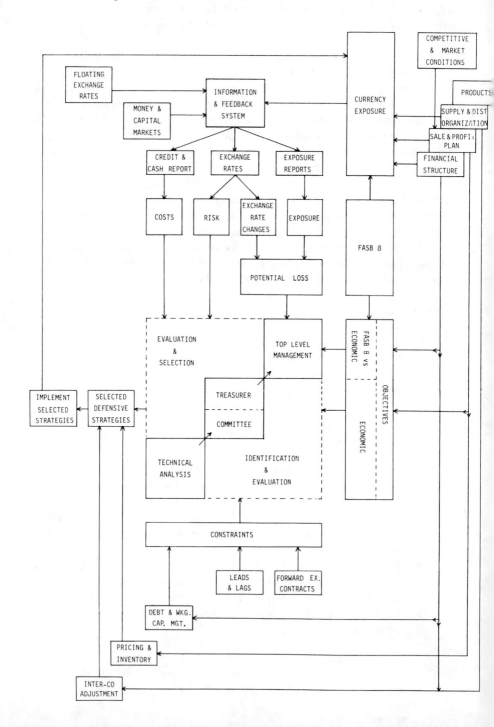

The fact that some of the sampled companies exclude one or more of the above components from the measurement of their currency exposures does not negate the above conclusion. As noted in Chapter III, the exclusion of inventory, for instance, reflects the differences in the foreign exchange management objectives of the companies rather than their operating characteristics or theoretical justification. In this regard, FASB 8 plays a critical role; four companies in the sample completely exclude inventory from their currency exposures although they do recognize that inventory is an exposed item. On the other hand, exposed earnings is excluded because most companies do not consider this item to be of material consequence. It should be reiterated that a substantial portion of this exposure component has been taken into consideration by including off-balance sheet items and forward exchange contract hedging of foreign currency transactions. With respect to income tax effects, as explained by an interviewed Treasurer, the reason is that his company does not use such defensive strategies as forward exchange contract hedging of the balance sheet exposure which render this consideration less important.

The amount and direction of a currency exposure is largely determined by the internal environment of the firm. Of major importance are the financial structure of the overseas subsidiary, the sources of its supplies, the markets where it sells its products, and the amounts of its transactions with its sister subsidiaries in other countries. The last three factors determine the amounts of cross-border business and, therefore, the amounts of exposures arising from foreign currency transactions. While the subsidiary's financial structure also determines the amounts of the translation and transaction exposure, under FASB 8 the long-term debt component has a significant influence over the method that a multinational firm uses to measure its currency exposure.

Thus, although the economic approach to currency exposure measurement, i.e., discounted net present value of cash flows, is not found in practice, FASB 8 is rejected as not sufficiently reflecting the economic exposure to foreign exchange risks.

Objectives

The objective of foreign exchange management is minimization of foreign exchange losses and avoidance of earnings fluctuations due to exchange rate changes. This is especially true with respect to translation adjustments. With respect to transaction gains and losses, this defensive posture is abated for the companies are prepared to take advantage of profit-making opportunities when they arise, but not to the extent of engaging in speculative practices. An indicator of this aversion to speculation is the relatively little use of forward exchange contracts to hedge the translation exposure. Furthermore, the companies are as much concerned with the economic effects of exchange rate fluctuations

as with the impact on reported earnings. However, due to the differences between the accounting and economic approaches in currency exposure measurement, often there is a conflict between the reported earning (accounting) objective and economic performance.

In resolving this conflict, it appears that the financial and profitability
plan play a significant role. In this connection, it is worth repeating that a company tends to be more inclined toward minimizing translation adjustments if it
(1) is sensitive to earnings per share; (2) has Euro-currency debt issues; or
(3) has strong earnings but large exposures. Additionally, the resolution for this
conflict often attracts the involvement of top level management.

Defensive Strategies and Constraints

A host of defensive strategies are available to multinational firms for protection against exchange rate risks. These strategies range from foreign exchange
market operations to price increases. The empirical evidence suggests that large
multinational firms are actively engaged in these defensive actions for the
purposes of changing the balance sheet structure, matching inflows of funds with
outflows and exposed assets with exposed liabilities, and buying "insurance"
by forward exchange contract hedging. The use of these strategies is thus consistent with the expressed concern for the translation as well as transaction and
economic losses due to exchange rate fluctuations.

The use of these strategies is expectedly subject to a variety of constraints,
internal and external to the firm. It appears that these constraints influence to
a significant extent the frequency that a strategy is used. Thus, in declining
order, the most frequently used (groups of) strategies are:

1.   Debt and working capital management techniques
2.   Inter-company accounts' adjustment, and inter-currency netting
3.   Forward exchange contracts

Within these groups, the most frequently used strategies appear to be local/
foreign currency borrowings and short-term assets/liabilities management, followed by inter-subsidiary leads/lags of receivables/payables and forward exchange contract hedging of foreign currency transactions. Also used but to a
lesser extent are those related to pricing and inventory and leads/lags of third-
party receivables/payables strategies. On the other hand, although internal hedge
is used by only two companies in the sample, as its usefulness is increasingly
recognized, it is expected that more companies will institute this arrangement
to reduce hedging costs.

Two recent developments in the environment of international corporate
finance are found to have contributed to a significant increase in the use of:

(1) debt and working capital management techniques; (2) inter-currency netting; (3) intercompany accounts' adjustment; and (4) forward exchange contracts to hedge foreign currency transactions. They are the regime of floating exchange rates and FASB 8.

Most impacted by greater uncertainty of exchange rates are the last two groups of strategies. As they serve different purposes and involve different exposure components, their uses have been equally increased to cope with the effects of greater exchange rate variability on foreign currency transactions with third parties and among sister subsidiaries. As to inter-currency netting, it emerges only recently after the introduction of the regime of floating exchange rates.

However, the issuance of FASB 8 has driven debt and working capital management techniques to the forefront of exposure management defensive strategies as companies are required to recognize the effects of foreign exchange on local/foreign currency long-term debts as part of their current income. Gaining importance with these strategies are those related to inter-company accounts' adjustments as they all serve to restructure the balance sheet exposure such that the resultant translation effects are minimized. In this respect, the companies which are most affected, in terms of their defensive strategies, are those which used a translation methodology different from that prescribed by FASB 8, had a reserve account to defer translation adjustments, heavily engaged in long-term borrowings outside of the U.S. capital markets, and consequently experience earnings volatility with exchange rate fluctuations.

The cumulative effects of floating exchange rates and FASB 8 thus have led companies to use these foreign exchange and money/capital markets facilities and inter-company accounts to the extent possible, subject only to the availability of cross-border transactions and risk-return trade-off considerations. A major exception to this statement is that all defensive strategies are subject to constraint by some rules or regulations imposed either by the local or host government. Prime examples are foreign exchange controls and local tax regulations. However, since these constraints are so paramount and fact-of-life, for the purpose of this modeling, they are hardly revealing.

Of greater interest is the division of responsibility over exposure management activities between subsidiaries and the parent company's headquarters, between operating management and treasury/exposure management staff personnel, and the constraints of market conditions.

Cumulatively, these factors appear to place a significant limitation on the use of those strategies which affect customer/vendor relationships, or the profit-making activities of the subsidiaries. Thus, leads/lags of third-party receivables/payables, price changes, and adjustments of inventory levels have not been used for exposure management purposes as frequently as those which involve inter-subsidiary transactions and foreign exchange and money/capital markets. The former groups of strategies are used for defensive purposes only as part of profitability management planning in the annual budgeting process. Although the treasury/exposure management staff are frequently consulted before the plan is finalized, changes are not subject to their approval. In fact, they do not have access to these strategies without the consent and cooperation of operating managements. Such may be the case; the use of these operating strategies— i.e., price changes, etc., so called for a lack of a better name—is relatively infrequent. This is understandable because competitive strength is difficult to assess and it is commonly believed that the treasury staff does not have sufficient expertise to perform this task.

On the other hand, the treasury staff at the headquarters have complete control—as compared to that of operating and subsidiary managements—over the strategies of inter-company accounts' adjustment, forward exchange contracts and borrowings. In fact, even when these strategies are undertaken by the overseas subsidiaries, they must first obtain consent from the parent headquarters. In this regard, several constraints limit the use of these strategies. Of significance are the availability of inter-company transactions, existence of forward exchange market facilities, loan covenants, and consideration for the credit worthiness of the subsidiairies.

Unexpectedly, the empirical research does not uncover a grave concern on the part of the sampled companies for such considerations as "good citizenship" or relationships with the local banking community in their exposure management defensive activities. When such considerations enter the decision-making process, they do not result in any restraint to borrow solely for defensive purposes or engage in foreign currency transactions which conceivably may contribute to further strengthening or weakening of a currency under pressure. Whereas these factors were documented to have had a restraining influence in the past, the potentially large foreign exchange losses under floating exchange rates and FASB 8 may have contributed to their little effect on multinational firms' foreign exchange management activities.

Information System, Risk Analysis and Selection of Defensive Strategies

The information systems for currency exposure data gathering and exchange rate forecasting play a central role in the foreign exchange management process. As a result of FASB 8, the need for close monitoring of currency exposure has increased and hence the emergence or refining of reporting systems of currency exposures on a world-wide basis.

The process of exposure data gathering starts with an exposure report sent monthly to the parent headquarters by the overseas subsidiaries. These reports are derived from the subsidiaries' financial statements and include all of the exposure components, broken down currency by currency. At the headquarters, the subsidiaries' reports are consolidated to produce a company-wide exposure profile. Since exchange rate fluctuations affect future exposed positions, either the subsidiary or the headquarters' staff provide for forecasts of future exposures. With the exposure reports, usually the overseas subsidiaries also submit a report of the cash balances and credit lines outstanding and associated interest costs. Sometimes, reports of cash flows are also incorporated in this reporting system.

With the floating rate regime, forecasting exchange rate and the associated analysis of risk-return trade-offs have gained added importance. This process of exchange rate forecasting consists of two distinct phases: technical analysis and decision-making.

In the phase of technical analysis, the treasury/exposure management staff collect input on future exchange rate movements from all available sources, e.g., in-house economists, foreign exchange consultants, banks, etc. These forecasts are then put through the second phase of the process in which they are subject to consolidation and evaluation by the staff with consideration for such factors as fundamental economic forces or simply intuition. However, before these forecasts are accepted as final, they are brought to discussion in a group. The purpose of this group effort is to bring into play the host of available technical expertise, experience and insight of the participants in this process in the hope of producing "best effort" forecasts under conditions of exchange rate uncertainty.

In this environment, the selection of defensive strategies is a process of decision-making under risk. In this process, the risk/cost consequences of defensive strategies are analyzed following an upward path in the organizational hierarchy, and risk is explicitly recognized, although in a qualitative form. The criteria of this risk-return trade-off analysis are found to be: feasibility; cost versus benefits; probabilistic estimates; and flexibility.

These decision criteria are present in all stages of the process, although the role of quantitative estimates of risk declines in importance as the decision problem travels further up in the organizational hierarchy. Nevertheless, the mode of decision-making has all the characteristics of a risk-return model. In this framework, the decision-maker attempts to rank the choice alternatives in terms of their risk and return, such that he retains for consideration only those feasible alternatives compared to any one of which there is no other alternative which gives either (a) a higher expected return and the same degree of risk, or (b) a lower degree of risk and the same expected return. Among these alternatives, the decision-maker chooses the alternative which is consistent with his attitude toward risk.

However, this modeling suggests that the risk-return ranking of alternatives is more involved and broad-based as it requires the participation of staff personnel and higher levels of management. Thus, the choice alternatives are identified at the staff level where the risk/cost consequences are identified and evaluated. This evaluation may be rudimentary or sophisticated, and may or may not involve quantitative techniques of analysis. In any event, the alternatives are then subject to further consideration and evaluation by a group of which the membership consists of staff personnel as well as decision-making authorities in the treasury department, e.g., the Treasurer. Depending on the magnitude (i.e., amounts of exposures and potential losses) and nature (i.e., translation versus economic) of the problem, the final decision rests with a senior financial officer, e.g., the Treasurer, or requires the approval of the very top level management, e.g., the Chairman of the Board. At any rate, in the identification-evaluation-acceptance cycle, the decision-making process involves far more than one individual and is more broad-based than any quantitative decision model can provide.

A Reactive Model

The above discussion delineates the major elements of a descriptive model of the foreign exchange management process in large multinational firms. It seeks to portray foreign exchange management as a process of decision-making reactive to the uncertainty in exchange rate movements for the overall purpose of minimizing the effects of foreign exchange risks on the firm. Toward this objective, the firm undertakes a variety of actions, all subject to some kind of constraints which limit its ability to act. In this connection, floating exchange rates and FASB 8 have emerged as major changes in the environment external to the firm. They have played a major role in bringing about significant changes in the thrust of the defensive strategies and the extent of their usage.

A question then arises: what are the implications of these changes on the foreign exchange and international capital markets and resource allocation in the economy? This is the subject of discussion in the remainder of this chapter.

Implications

From the preceding analysis of the various elements of the foreign exchange management process, several implications on the behavior of the multinational firm under conditions of foreign exchange risks, and the foreign exchange and capital markets can be derived.

On the one hand, if the experiences of the sampled companies are fairly representative of large multinational firms, it is reasonable to conclude that such firms have mounted a sophisticated and organized effort to cope with uncertainty of exchange rates and the earnings impact of FASB 8. This effort is characterized by the following: (1) a conscious choice of the method to define the currency exposure; (2) extensive use of defensive strategies except when severely limited by internal and external constraints; (3) a complete information system to gather the data on the currency exposures and exchange rate developments; (4) centralized control and coordination of exposure management activities of the overseas subsidiaries; and (5) top-level management involvement.

On the other hand, there are still areas that are worthy of improvement. For example, the facility of internal hedge has been recognized as useful, but not used very extensively. However, it is expected that more companies will institute this arrangement as their exposure management efforts continue to be expanded.

Other areas that seem worthy of improvement are as follows:

(1) Income tax effects on currency exposures are omitted in some companies. As it has been noted, whereas translation gains/losses are generally not taxable/deductible, tax effects are very real on inter-company transactions. Insofar as a company should be concerned with its after-tax earnings, exclusion of tax considerations might result in sub-optimal, and possibly erroneous, decisions.

(2) In the course of the interviews, several executives and consultants indicated that there is an over-emphasis on exposure management as an activity separate from the marketing and production strategies. While they do not suggest that exposure management is not useful and productive, in their opinion, companies often do not sufficiently take into consideration the effects of foreign exchange on their production and marketing strategies. From the empirical research, it is evident that the thrust of exposure management in the sampled companies is financial and the involvement of the treasury/exposure management staff in operating decisions, in most cases, is at best *ad hoc*. In this connection, it is interesting to note a case example as to how a financing decision can have a bearing on local pricing strategies: on the verge of the recent massive Mexican devaluation, a company in the sample decided to have its Mexican subsidiary increase borrowings in Mexican pesos. Of course, an objective was to hedge the Mexican exposure. There was, however, an additional consideration

> that was that the cost of funds is an integrated part of doing business, or the cost of sales. In order to emphasize to the Mexican management that possibly they were pricing their products too low. This "increased Mexican borrowing" was a very good way to make a point.

Also, there might have been an over-reaction to the effects of FASB 8. As companies become suddenly aware of the impact of foreign exchange on their earnings, an awareness brought about to top management by FASB 8,

> . . . there is a tremendous amount which is focused in this area. I think what has happened is that people have reacted so strongly to this issue, both people in the corporate position as well as people in the foreign exchange markets, that there is more speculation today than there has been in the past.

Whereas this reaction might be justifiable in view of the volatility of exchange rate movements,

> I don't think as a corporate treasury person, my responsibility is to play the end of that volatility. I think my responsibility lies in the longer-run decision. For example, in light of what I see in way of the currency movements over time, how do I structure my balance sheet? Whether or not I want to invest in that country?

(3) This brings us to the fundamental question of "What should be the objective of foreign exchange management?" There has been a significant amount of discussion in the literature on this very subject area which is related to the problem of appropriately measuring the exposure to currency risks. Since this aspect is beyond the scope of this research, it suffices to suggest that an appropriate measure of the currency exposure appears to lie somewhere between the future cash flow approach and the accounting methodology.

(4) The organization of a formal foreign exchange committee seems to be gaining popularity among companies as it allows a forum for the integration of the controllership function, treasury, and legal expertise in the problem-solving process and broadens the perspective of the foreign exchange management function. However, in most companies, this organization is not yet in place. Where it exists, in most cases, the membership is limited to the treasury department thereby not fully considering the effects of exposure management activities on marketing and production operations of the company.

(5) There is reason to suggest that benefits can be derived from more in-depth and structured use of analytical and quantitative methods for the evaluation of defensive strategies, at least at the staff or "technical analysis" phase— as defined in Chapter IV—of the decision-making process. Often this task is not carried to sufficient lengths to provide the technical support and the evaluated and integrated information that the final decision-makers need or deserve. In this regard, management science models appear to hold great promises, notwithstanding the finding that few companies use mathematical models to aid their decision-making.[1]

However, some companies in the sample appear to have instituted a well-organized and sophisticated system of foreign exchange management that can potentially serve as a model for other multinational firms. This is one of the reasons for having selected the Fortune 100 multinational manufacturing firms for the purposes of this study. The assumption is that being sufficiently motivated by large amounts of foriegn exchange exposures, these large companies have the capability and resources to institute whatever is needed to bring about a successful foreign exchange management program. Whether or not they have succeeded in this objective, it can not be reasonably suggested from this empirical research. It appears nevertheless that the organization that they have installed has been conducive to whatever benefits that they have enjoyed.

For theory construction, two major applications emerge from the empirical research.

(1) The findings in this study indicate that in the decision-making process whereas the final approval usually rests with a senior financial officer such as the Treasurer or the Financial Vice President, the process leading to this outcome involves a group of executives or analysts. Inasmuch as a decision has been reached before it is presented for approval by the relevant authority—except when it involves a change in the policy—the attitude towards risk of a company as an organization should not be equated to that of any particular individual.

(2) A more fruitful approach for the formulation of normative decision models appears to require the incorporation of the heuristic nature of the decision-making process. This would involve a procedure to rank the choice alternatives in terms of their risk-return trade-off without specifying a deterministic solution. From this ranking, the analyst/decision-maker would derive an efficient alternative which is consistent with his perception of the organization's attitude toward risk—which might be indistinguishable from his own. Such efficient alternatives will constitute the range of decision choices for the organization as a whole. If the identification of the alternatives is exhaustive and only efficient alternatives are retained for consideration, this procedure will generate a decision which is efficient and consistent with the risk acceptance level of the organization, which might be simply some average of the analysts.

On a macro-economic level, the exposure management activities of multinational firms as documented in this research have several important implications.

(1) The findings in this study indicate that the emergence of floating exchange rates with associated increase in uncertainty has resulted in more hedging by multinational firms, both in the foreign exchange markets and restructuring of exposures. From this, it can be inferred that multinational firms are capable of coping with the greater uncertainty without resorting to reduction of their international operations, hence adversely affecting international trade. On the other hand, it can also be said that this result is achieved only by an increase of the cost of doing business overseas. Since this incremental cost is eventually manifested in reduced cash flows, unless the firm can raise prices to compensate for the cost of protection against uncertainty, not exchange rate devaluations or revaluations, its value will be affected. If the stock market reacts by discounting the share prices of such multinational firms, because of the same or higher level of risk but lower return than it would be in the absence of exchange rate uncertainty, capital funds will be diverted from the international trade sector and channeled to domestic firms. Thus, via the stock market, greater exchange rate uncertainty brought about by floating exchange rates might be detrimental to international trade.

(2) Hedging activities by a multinational firm affect the external value of

a foreign currency in two ways. First, by using the forward exchange market, it increases the future supply of the foreign currency if it contracts selling forward, or increases its future demand in the case of forward buying. The spot rate of the currency is affected if the firm sells and buys spot to shift one currency denomination to another. Likewise, demand for and supply of the foreign currency in the spot market are affected if the firm accelerates/delays payments in anticipation of the foreign currency's further appreciation/depreciation. In any case, the supply of and demand for the foreign currency are affected. Second, if the firm engages in borrowings denominated in the foreign currency for hedging purposes, the demand for funds would rise above the level that would prevail should demand for credit be determined solely by investment and consumption requirements. Likewise, leads and lags would increase/decrease the demand for credit by importers/exporters to cope with shortage or surplus of receipts. When the demand and supply forces in the financial market are sufficiently altered, interest rates will inevitably rise or fall accordingly, ultimately leading to changes in the external value of the foreign currency in question.

The evidence uncovered by this research indicates that large multinational firms—if the experience of the sampled companies is representative—are actively engaged in these practices to cope with foreign exchange risks, which have been increased significantly as a result of floating exchange rates and FASB 8. It thus can be suggested that multinational firms' exposure management activities contribute to the further weakening or strengthening of a foreign currency, especially in view of the large amounts of funds they can move across currencies. Additionally, since multinational firms' hedging horizon is usually quarterly, there is reason to suggest that their defensive actions contribute to sustained fluctuations of a currency for some length of time.

(3) With respect to the implications of multinational firms' reaction to FASB 8, the findings indicate that half of the sample of companies resort to increased use of borrowings to counter FASB 8's effects on their earnings, and all of these companies have sizeable amounts of local/foreign currency long-term debts. Accordingly, they have switched from local currency to U.S. dollar debts or from foreign currency to local currency or U.S. dollar obligations when it is determined that the debts denominated in the relevant currency are not sufficiently supported by the underlying assets. The implications of these practices on the international capital markets are profound since they may lead to a greater outflow of U.S. dollars for overseas investments than it would be in the absence of FASB 8. In other words, the demand for Eurodollar debts may be increased as multinational firms seek to replace their local/foreign currency debts by those denominated in U.S. dollars. Likewise, the demand for hard Euro-currencies such as the Swiss franc and the Deutsche mark may be reduced as companies try to avoid financing operations in weak currencies by debts denominated in hard Euro-currencies. To the extent that weak currency areas

such as developing countries do not have sufficient funds for multinational firms to borrow, a greater outflow of U.S. dollars will result. Alternatively, local firms which cannot compete with multinational companies for local funds will be deprived of needed capital. In this case, the keen competition for local funds would lead to higher interest and inflation rates in the local economy.

(4) With respect to the effects of FASB 8 on resource allocation in the economy, this research started out with the implicit assumption that prior to FASB 8, companies effectively approximated their economic exposures to foreign exchange risks by adopting one of the then accepted methods of translation, and managed their exposures accordingly. If FASB 8 leads companies to change their currency exposure measurement such that, under this assumption, their economic exposures are misstated, thus leading to defensive actions which are not consistent with their economic objectives, the allocation of resources in the economy will be affected. The interviewed consultants are divided on this issue, i.e., whether companies correctly measured their economic exposures prior to FASB 8. Two consultants pointed out that before FASB 8, many multinational companies had reporting systems which were far from adequate to provide an accurate measure of their economic exposures. Furthermore, they adopted translation methodologies which did not necessarily reflect the true extent of their economic exposures. Two other consultants to whom this question was addressed held the opposite view. Although the empirical findings from this research appear to support either view, the probing was not sufficiently in-depth to establish conclusively—for the sampled companies—as to which view/assumption is better descriptive of the reality before FASB 8. This lack of evidence thus precludes the suggestion that the switch of currency exposure measurement as a result of FASB 8 leads companies to behave inconsistently with their economic objectives. One change, however, is certain: many companies in the sample have refined and improved their reporting systems to obtain a better diagnosis of their exposures, and top management has become more aware of the effects of foreign exchange on earnings. If—and this is a big if—this means that as a result companies better manage their exposures, FASB 8 has resulted in more, not less, efficient allocation of resources in the economy.

Summary

This chapter is devoted to the discussion of a model of the foreign exchange management process in multinational firms. This model has the following major elements:

A. Currency exposure
B. Objectives

    C.   Defensive strategies and constraints
    D.   Information system, risk analysis, and selection of defensive strategies

It is then concluded that foreign exchange management is a decision-making process reactive to exchange rate uncertainty for the purpose of minimizing the effects of foreign exchange risks on the firm.

Subsequently, the discussion is focused on the implications of the findings on the behavior of the multinational firm, for the purposes of theory construction as well as practical foreign exchange management, and on the foreign exchange and capital markets.

Chapter VII

Conclusion

The subject of this study was focused on foreign exchange management decision-making in multinational firms and the effects of accounting rules on economic behavior. The purpose of this research effort was: (1) to examine the process of and the factors involved in the management of foreign exchange in large multinational companies in a multicurrency context under floating exchange rates; (2) to analyze the effects of floating exchange rates on their defensive strategies; (3) to study how these companies are affected by FASB 8 in regard to the measurement of their currency exposures and the ways they hedge; and (4) based on the empirical findings, to develop a model descriptive of the foreign exchange management process.

The data were obtained in in-depth interviews with financial executives of a sample of 10 multinational manufacturing companies on the 1977 Fortune 100 List, thus constituting a little over 16 per cent of the population of such companies. The interviews were conducted in spring and summer 1978, mostly with two executives in each company, one of whom had the title equivalent to "Foreign Exchange Manager" or "Manager of International Finance," and the other was an Assistant Treasurer or Vice President. Except in one case, in single interviews, the interviewees had the rank of Assistant Treasurer or above. In addition, five foreign exchange consultants and international bankers with a better-known foreign exchange consulting firm and four major multinational banks were interviewed for validation of the data and to obtain an overall perspective of the foreign exchange management process. Past research literature, conceptual and normative, was also reviewed to provide a theoretical framework for the research and verification of the data. Where it was relevant and available, the findings of past empirical studies were compared with the evidence from this investigation for further validation.

The study was begun with the formulation of a conceptual model descriptive of the process of foreign exchange management in multinational firms. This model suggested that the behavior of multinational firms under conditions of foreign exchange risks is of a reactive nature. In the measurement of its exposure to foreign exchange risks, a multinational company faces certain discrepancies between the accounting and economic approaches which it must resolve. However it measures its currency exposures, a company would attempt to reduce or eliminate its exposure by undertaking a variety of defensive strategies. The selection of these strategies is subject to certain internal and external constraints and goes through an evaluation process whereby they are ranked in terms of their expected return and risk. As a result of this ranking, an efficient decision alternative is selected. This decision choice, according to this model of risk analysis, not only is consistent with the decision-maker's attitude toward risk, its risk-return trade-off is such that there is no other alternative which either has a higher return with the same level of risk or the same return with a lower level of risk. Furthermore, due to greater uncertainty under floating exchange rates, companies would either increase the use of existing defensive strategies and/or devise new ways to counter this greater risk. Additionally, FASB 8 has created conditions for companies to change the way they measure their currency exposures as well as abandon the use of certain defensive strategies if they result in untimely recognition of currency effects on earnings.

The empirical findings suggest that this is a realistic portrayal of the behavior of large multinational firms under conditions of foreign exchange risks. However, they also necessitate some revision in the conceptual model of risk analysis and indicate more widespread effects on the sampled companies' currency exposure measurement and their defensive strategies than originally anticipated.

With respect to currency exposure measurement, none of the sampled companies measure the currency exposure based on future cash flows. However, they do go beyond the balance sheet to get at the overall effects of exchange rate fluctuations. This can be accomplished, all of the companies agree, by including inventory, monetary assets and liabilities, exposed earnings, off-balance sheet items such as confirmed orders, and remittances of dividends. In actual practice, differences exist in the treatment of inventory and exposed earnings. In the case of the former, because the companies which exclude it— of which there are four—are quite concerned with the translation effects on their earnings, they consequently attempt to manage their exposures without regard to the economic effects of exchange rates changes on inventory. Those companies which include inventory, however, do not follow the economic distinction of those inventories which are subject to price controls, or other types of pricing inflexibility, and those which are not. They either include all inventories or calculate the exposed portion based on the inventory turnover rate. In the case of the latter—exposed earnings—nine companies exclude it from their currency exposures because, some of the executives explained, this component does not constitute a significant part of their exposures. With respect to off-balance sheet items, all of the companies consider this component exposed and actively manage it, although only one company in the sample formally includes it in its currency exposure.

Given this definition of the currency exposure, the companies seek to minimize their foreign exchange losses. From the viewpoint of translation losses—defined in accordance with FASB 8—this objective is paramount. An exception is one company of which the earnings have not been significantly affected by FASB 8. This company has chosen to disregard FASB 8 in its exposure management orientation. However, there are three other companies which have had the same experience, yet are also concerned with the translation effects. This points to the fact that there is often a conflict between the reported earnings (accounting) objective and economic performance, a conflict which is difficult to solve and frequently leads to the involvement of top management in the exposure management activities. As a result of this conflict, four of the companies which have chosen to define their currency exposures differently from FASB 8—as far as the balance sheet accounts are concerned—have found themselves moving back and forth between the "FASB 8" and "FASB 8 plus inventory" approaches in the management of their foreign exchange losses. This is not to say that this conflict does not exist in the other companies. It only means that the conflict is not manifested in any shift in the definition of the currency exposure.

With respect to transaction gains/losses, the companies attempt to profit from their foreign currency transactions to take advantage of currency movements; however, they do not do so in such aggressive a manner as to create exposures. Notwithstanding this more aggressive posture, the overall exposure management activities of the companies are of a preservative nature, and are not directed toward profit-making.

To achieve these objectives, the companies have used extensively, unless constrained by internal operating conditions and/or external factors, the following groups of defensive strategies which are shown in declining order of the frequency of their usage:

1.   Debt and working capital management techniques
2.   Inter-company accounts' adjustment and inter-currency netting
3.   Forward exchange contracts
4.   Pricing and inventory strategies
5.   Leads and lags of third-party receivables and payables
6.   Internal hedge

Within these groups, the most frequently used strategies appear to be local/foreign currency borrowings and short-term assets/liabilities management, followed by leads/lags of inter-subsidiary receivables/payables and forward exchange contracts on foreign currency transactions.

Pricing and inventory strategies are defined at the annual budgeting/planning stage. Thus, by and large, when such strategies are used, they follow the plan guidelines which have presumably taken into consideration local pricing regulations and competitive conditions in the local/export markets. Furthermore, these strategies are subject to the constraints by competitive pressure which appears to be greater in developed than in developing countries. Leads and lags of third-party receivables and payables are subject to sensitivity to resistance from customers and vendors and to a limited extent to local regulations governing leading and lagging. In most developed countries, however, these local rules do not appear prohibitively restrictive. Another constraint on leads/lags is the availability of cross-border transactions with third parties. An additional consideration is the fact that, like in the case of pricing and inventory strategies, leads/lags are within the purview of local/operating managements, and therefore, the treasury department does not actively and routinely consider for these defensive alternatives in its day-to-day exposure management decisions.

External constraints, however, appear to be less limiting on the use of the defensive strategies which involve inter-company transactions and foreign exchange and money/capital markets. A basic constraint on the use of inter-company accounts' adjustment is the availability of inter-subsidiary cross-border transactions. Once this condition is satisfied, it remains to properly control the settlement of inter-company payment terms so as to avoid unintended exposures. Likewise, the use of debt and working capital management for defensive purposes is more limited by internal policy than external factors as it is subject to plan/policy guidelines such as "proper balance sheet structure." Furthermore, working capital management seems to be used more frequently for defensive purposes in those companies which centrally control this strategy at the parent headquarters than in those which delegate this responsbility to the overseas subsidiaries. On the other hand, hedging in the forward exchange markets is not possible in countries where this facility does not exist. Finally, inter-currency netting has been used primarily among selected currencies in the "snake" group for their movements have exhibited sufficient correlation to warrant the use of this strategy.

Overall, multinational firms operating in different parts of the world have a number of constraints and the above are only a few of those for which the direct effect can be established from the empirical research. However, there are others which might be more important in terms of their limitation on the use of defensive strategies such as local and home country's laws and regulations. Yet, their effects can only be discussed in a general manner. In this connection, it is interesting to note the ineffective constraining influence of the so-called "good citizenship" consideration and concern for relationships with the local banking community on the exposure management activities of the sampled firms.

Notwithstanding these internal and external constraints, the sampled multinational firms have used extensively the mentioned defensive strategies to protect their currency exposures. These defensive actions are backed up by information systems designed to capture their translation, transaction, and

inventory exposures on a currency-by-currency basis. When any of these exposures components are negligible—such as inter-company transactions—they are
omitted. But, by and large, the information systems seem adequately designed
to capture the necessary exposure data. Simply enough, these data are taken
off the balance sheet which are broken down by currency and sent periodically
from the overseas subsidiaries. They are then consolidated on a currency-by-
currency basis at the headquarters which also project these data into the future
if these forecasts are not already provided by the subsidiaries. The subsidiaries
also provide information on interest costs of their credit facilities.

   To obtain information for the development of exchange rate forecasts,
most companies employ the services of foreign exchange consulting firms. All
rely extensively on banking sources for exchange rate input. A few also employ
internal economists, and a couple of companies use mathematical models to
forecast exchange rates.

   Wherever the companies obtain the forecasting input, the treasury/exposure
management staff play a major role in the development of the final forecasts for
planning as well as hedging purposes. This is called the decision-making phase as
opposed to the step preceding it which is basically data gathering an.' evaluation.
In the decision-making phase, the staff first attempt to evaluate the initial forecast by filtering them through what may be called the staff's perception of the
factors, and their relative importance, which determine the exchange rate movements. Once the forecasts are evaluated, they are consolidated and subjected to
further evaluation in so-called "group discussions." In this final phase of the
forecasting process, the consolidated forecasts are subject to scrutiny by a group
of which the members include the highest level of management in the treasury's
organizational hierarchy, and sometimes higher levels of management or representatives from the controller function. The results of the group discussion are a
set of official forecasts accepted for distribution and used for decision-making
purposes. Whereas this forecasting procedure is more involved than mere mathematical modeling or "calling up the banker," no attempt is made to present the
forecasts in a form which can be translated into probabilistic statements or other
forms of risk measurement. Instead, the companies seek to determine the direction and trend of a currency's movements. When hedging is contemplated,
several rates are obtained, and thus conceivably probabilities can be derived;
however, they are not presented in these terms.

   Nevertheless, the risk factor is well recognized and dealt with in the form of
probabilistic analysis, subjective judgment of the evaluator, and group discussion. Probabilistic analysis is performed mostly on forward exchange contract
hedging and borrowings. For the other types of defensive strategies, feasibility
is a more important consideration. When hedging in the forward exchange
markets or borrowing is contemplated, the quantitative analysis can be quite
elaborate and formal. However, as the decision problem goes up the organiza-

tional ladder, subjective judgment of the more senior evaluator begins to overtake technicalities. In this respect, "flexibility" or the ability to undo a particular decision was found to be an important analytic criterion. Thus, the sampled companies do not use mathematical modeling to assist their decision-making. However, the process was found to be more involved and broad-based as the next step is that the decision alternatives are subject to "group discussion" in a formal or *ad hoc* foreign exchange committee. It is this "consensus of opinion" approach that seems to substitute for any explicit recognition of risk because of the difficulty in making such an explicit estimate of risk under floating exchange rates and the absence of any quantitative measure of a company's risk attitude.

However, in terms of the trade-off between risk and return, it is not possible to determine the amount of additional return that is required to compensate for the incremental risk, although some numbers were mentioned. On the other hand, it appears that the plan/budget guidelines provide a powerful guide to determine whether a translation loss is acceptable.

As a result of this "group discussion," a decision is reached in the committee, though subject to approval by a higher level of management, e.g., the Treasurer if he is not a member of the committee. Invariably, if the exposure is large, the final decision is made by this officer although he may also seek the guidance of his superiors, e.g., the Financial Vice President or the Chairman of the Board. The involvement of the very top level of the management structure, however, is not frequent, and usually occurs only when the decision problem involves translations versus economic losses.

Inasmuch as the management of foreign exchange receives attention from the very top level of a company's management hierarchy, the exposure management activities of the subsidiaries are also centrally controlled at the parent headquarters. Invariably, the translation exposure is the responsibility of the parent company whereas the transaction exposure is controlled via reporting requirements, plan/budget guidelines, and frequent consultation between the headquarters' staff and subsidiaries' managements. As to defensive strategies, although the subsidiaries have greater latitude in the use of operating strategies such as pricing and inventory strategies, they are limited by plan guidelines. In all cases, they must obtain prior consent from the headquarters staff before they can engage in borrowings or forward exchange contract hedging.

From the evidence, it is concluded that indeed the companies approach risk-return trade-off analysis and selection of defensive strategies by ranking them in terms of risk and return. The process as found in actual practice, however, is more involved and broad-based than mathematical modeling such as the expected return-variance framework. Furthermore, the decision-making is closely controlled by top management and centrally located at the parent company.

In most companies, the increased uncertainty under floating exchange rates has led to increased hedging in all defensive strategies. In two companies, certain defensive strategies which had not been used in the fixed exchange rate system have been used since floating exchange rates. In addition, inter-currency netting and internal hedge are the products of the floating rate regime. Significantly, as compared to the other defensive strategies, the use of forward exchange contracts, inter-company accounts' adjustment and management of short-term assets/liabilities has been most increased to cope with greater currency risks. Least affected by floating exchange rates is the use of local/foreign currency borrowings. Leads/lags and pricing and inventory strategies have also been increased but not to as great an extent as that in the use of forward exchange contracts and intercompany accounts' adjustment.

For the majority of the sampled companies, floating exchange rates have had less dramatic impact on their management of foreign exchange than FASB 8. Not only those companies of which the earnings have been adversely affected by FASB 8 have changed their currency exposure measurement and defensive strategies as a result, but also those that have been insignificantly affected have reacted to this accounting ruling. First, except in one company, across the board, FASB 8 has led to changes in the way these companies define their currency exposures. This greater-than-expected effect was found to result from the widespread use of the reserve account to defer translation adjustments before FASB 8. Second, the five companies which have experienced earnings fluctuations due to FASB 8 have increased the use of a number of defensive strategies to smooth out their earnings fluctuations. Most notable is the increased use of borrowings and inter-company accounts' adjustment. These strategies are directed toward moving exposures across currencies and replacing debts denominated in hard Euro-currencies such as the Swiss franc by debts denominated in the local currency or the U.S. dollar. There are also instances of debt substitution between the local currency and the U.S. dollar and vice versa. Two other companies have also increased the use of certain defensive strategies in significant ways to counter FASB 8's effects. These changes, however, are to a lesser extent than found in the other five companies. Only in two companies that FASB 8's effects on their defensive strategies can be considered marginal. The disparate experiences of these companies, especially among those which used similar methods for translation and recognition of translation adjustments, point to the role of local/foreign currency long-term debts in determining the extent of FASB 8's effects. Those companies which have larger amounts of such debts experienced more significant impact on their earnings and have resorted to greater use of debt and inter-company accounts' adjustment.

However, the fact that the use of certain defensive strategies such as forward exchange contract hedging of foreign currency transactions has been increased points to a significant change in the environment of foreign exchange management under FASB 8. This accounting convention has created an increased awareness of foreign exchange problems and their effects on earnings.

This awareness has attracted greater attention by top management to the problems of foreign exchange and as a result led companies to update and refine
their reporting systems and spend greater amounts of resources on foreign
exchange management. In some companies, certain defensive strategies become
more extensively used although this increase cannot be explained by the earnings
impact of FASB 8.

On the basis of these findings, it is concluded that the behavior of the
multinational firm under conditions of foreign exchange risks largely follows the
conceptual model formulated at the outset of the study. With additional insight,
a model descriptive of the foreign exchange management process is formulated
to incorporate the heuristic process of risk analysis and selection of defensive
strategies as found in practice. This reformulated model, like the original conceptualization, depicts foreign exchange management as a decision-making
process reactive to the uncertainty in exchange rate movements for the overall
purpose of minimizing the effects of exchange rate fluctuations on earnings.
Toward this objective, the firm undertakes a variety of defensive strategies,
all subject to some kind of internal and external constraints which limits its
ability to act.

The results of this empirical research thus indicate that multinational
firms are well conscious of the economic impact of exchange rate fluctuations
as well as the resultant translation losses. The fact that some companies are more
concerned with translation losses does not negate this conclusion. On the other
hand, the general agreement on how best to measure the economic exposure
is obviously divergent from the economist's definition based on future cash
flows. It thus remains an area for additional research to reconcile the gap between the practitioner's definition and that of theorists.

In any event, the companies have implemented a well-organized effort to
manage their exposures which includes active use of various defensive strategies,
a sophisticated information system to collect the data on the exposures, central
control and coordination of subsidiaries' exposure management activities, and
active involvement by the top level of management. The evidence further indicates that this sophistication is a product of greater uncertainty under floating
exchange rates and the awareness of foreign exchange problems brought about
by FASB 8.

This reaction on the part of multinational companies will have profound
implications on international trade as inevitably it leads to reduced cash flows.
If the stock market discounts the share prices of such firms as a result, capital
funds will be diverted from the international trade sector. There is also reason
to suggest that active defensive actions by multinational firms contribute to
sustained fluctuations in the foreign exchange markets, rather than stabilizing
exchange rate movements. Their actions may also lead to future profound
changes in the movements of international capital; the most significant

possibilities are increased use of U.S. dollars to finance investments in countries with strong currencies, and use of local and dollar financing, in lieu of Euro-currency debts, for their operations in developing countries of the world.

In conclusion, this empirical study has presented evidence on several important issues that are heretofore undocumented or inadequately analyzed:

1. How multinational firms measure their economic exposures to foreign exchange risks.
2. What are their foreign exchange management objectives?
3. How frequently or extensively they use a certain defensive strategy.
4. How they approach the problem of risk analysis and the procedures/ organization that they set up to make decisions under conditions of exchange rate uncertainty.
5. The information systems they establish to collect the data on currency exposures and the procedures for development of exchange rate forecasts.
6. The effects of greater exchange rate uncertainty and the accounting rule changes embodied in FASB 8 on their foreign exchange management policies and strategies.

The study also attempts to synthesize the empirical findings into a model descriptive of the foreign exchange management process in the multinational firm.

On the other hand, the analysis brings up more questions than answers. Accordingly, in the remaining pages, areas for additional and future research are suggested:

(1) For the purpose of theory construction, it seems fruitful to replicate this study to derive a general model descriptive of the foreign exchange management process in the multinational firm. It is believed that only with such a detailed understanding of this process can normative models be constructed which are capable of being put into practical application. There are two basic steps to achieve this objective. The first is to replicate this study, but on the entire population of multinational firms. The second is to concentrate on select areas such as the decision-making process. Obviously, the second cannot be done without the first, if one accepts the proposition that all parts are related and interdependent.

This study indicates that the decision-making process involves more than one individual. Furthermore, whereas a senior financial officer must approve a decision and may actively take part in it, he may not make the decision himself. As such, how can recent advances in mathematical decision modeling be reformulated to be operational without being overly complex, or without having to make simplifying assumptions such as a company's attitude toward risk is equal to that of, say, the Treasurer?

(2) The issue of "How to measure an exposure to foreign exchange risks" has occupied much discussion in recent years. This study shows how the sampled companies approach this problem. Their experience suggests that the original question should be dissected into several subsidiary research questions to be manageable:

1. Within the decision-making horizon of a multinational firm, what is convertible into cash (or, for a U.S. dollar-based corporation, into U.S. dollars)?
2. What should be its decision-making horizon? and what length?
3. What does it mean by its short- and long-term objectives?
4. Given these objectives, how many decision periods should it consider?

It may very well turn out that in a multi-period decision model and with a sufficiently long horizon, the method adopted by the sampled companies approximates the future cash flow approach. This result is expected for consideration of the fact that a trade receivable is convertible into cash within about one quarter, or perhaps in less time, and a long-term debt represents a cash outflow outside of the one-year period. If a firm's decision-making horizon is greater than one year, these balance sheet items represent cash flows, and thus are economically subject to foreign exchange risks. To the extent that, as a result of a revaluation, the firm decides to build up its receivables and replaces its foreign currency debts by U.S. dollar loans, its dollar cash flows are affected. Similar analyses will help establish the cash flow nature of the balance sheet and statement of income accounts. Since some can be converted into cash within a fairly short period while others take more time, it is necessary for a firm to decide on the proper or desirable decision-making horizon, hence the above questions. On the other hand, the issue of foreign exchange exposure is much complicated by considerations for the Fisher Effect and the Purchasing Power Parity theory.

(3) Given the effects of floating exchange rates and FASB 8, how do multinational firms measure and control the performance of the overseas subsidiaries? And how should this be done?

(4) What are the pricing strategies of multinational firms under floating exchange rates? In developed countries? In developing countries?

(5) What is the impact of multinational firms' defensive strategies on foreign exchange markets? Fluctuations of exchange rates?

(6) What effects do multinational firms' borrowing policies and practices have on the Euro-currency markets? The U.S. balance of payments? The supply of credit to local firms in developing countries? Before and after FASB 8?

(7) Does indeed FASB 8 lead companies to define their currency exposures such that they are inconsistent with the economic objectives?

(8) What effects does FASB 8 have on the investment policies of multi-

national firms? On their capital and debt structure?

(9) What are the effects of FASB 8 on share prices of multinational firms? What are the implications on the efficient market hypothesis?

Hopefully, these questions will stimulate further research on the effects of multinational firms' behavior on the world economy.

Notes

CHAPTER I

1. Trevor G. Underwood, "Unfinished Business: Making Floating Exchange Rates Work," *Euromoney* (October 1974), p. 68.

2. Michael Jilling and William R. Folks, Jr., "The Emergence of the Foreign Exchange Risk Management Function" (Working Paper II: Foreign Exchange Risk Management Project, University of South Carolina, n.d.), p. 1.

3. A.R. Prindl, *Foreign Exchange Risk* (New York: John Wiley and Sons, 1976), pp. 152-58.

4. Margaret G. deVries, "The Magnitudes of Exchange Devaluation," *Finance and Development* 5 (June 1968):8-12.

5. Steven W. Kohlhagen, "The Performance of the Foreign Exchange Markets: 1971-1974," *Journal of International Business Studies* 6 (Fall 1975): 33-39.

6. The same results for the Danish krone, the French franc, the Deutsche mark, the Swiss franc, and the British pound sterling during the period 1973-1974 are indicated in Kohlhagen, "The Performance of the Foreign Exchange Markets: 1971-1974," pp. 35-36.

7. International Monetary Fund, *Annual Report of the Executive Directors for the Fiscal Year Ended April 30, 1977* (Washington, D.C.: International Monetary Fund, 1977), p. 28.

8. According to Kohlhagen, "The Performance of the Foreign Exchange Markets: 1971-1974," p. 35, the mean absolute difference between the three-month forward rate and the subsequent spot rate for the French franc, the Deutsche mark, and the Swiss franc was computed to be less than one percent for 1971-1972 period. In the same period, the British pound sterling averaged 6.305 percent.

9. These data are extracted from the companies' annual 10-K reports. The foreign exchange gains/losses are reported uniformly in accordance with FASB 8. Some more examples of these gains (losses) in millions of U.S. dollars are shown below:

	ITT	Continental Group	Union Carbide	Warner-Lambert
Rank[a]	11	17	21	93
1975	(52.5)	12.2	10.4	(7.9)

| 1976 | (13.2) | (11.4) | 9.6 | (20.8) |
| 1977 | (66.9) | (13.4) | (26.5) | (9.8) |

[a] Rank means the company's rank on the 1977 Fortune 500 List

10. By comparing the findings of H.J. Jadwani, "Some Aspects of the Multinational Corporations' Exposure to Exchange Rate Risk," (DBA dissertation, Harvard Business School, 1971), pp. IV-1 through IV-57 with those in Michael Jilling and William R. Folks, Jr., "Practices of American Corporations in Foreign Exchange Risk Management," (Working Paper II: Foreign Exchange Risk Management Project, University of South Carolina, n.d.). See also Michael Jilling, "Foreign Exchange Risk Management: Current Practices of U.S. Multinational Corporations," (Ph.D. dissertation, University of South Carolina, 1976), pp. 232-33.

11. The data were collected in Jadwani's study, "Multinational Corporation Exposure" by personal interviews, whereas in Jilling's "Foreign Exchange Risk Management," by mail questionnaire. Neither of the samples were randomly selected. Also they did not seek to measure the frequency in the use of a particular defensive strategy in each company. Their terminologies descriptive of the defensive strategies may have lent to different interpretations by the respondents. However, their studies are the only ones known to exist which make such a comparison possible.

12. See A.L. Pakkala, "Foreign Exchange Accounting of Multinational Corporations," *Financial Analysts Journal* 31 (March-April 1975), pp. 32-41, 76. Also see, M. Edgar Barrett and Leslie L. Spero, "Accounting Determinants of Foreign Exchange Gains and Losses," *Financial Analysts Journal* 31 (March-April 1975): 26-30.

13. Ibid.

14. For a more detailed report on FASB 8's impact on earnings of companies, see Rita M. Rodriguez, "FASB No. 8: What Has It Done for Us?" *Financial Analysts Journal* 31 (March-April 1975): 40-47.

15. Statement made by David Hawkins of the Harvard Business School quoted in John H. Allan, "Currency Swings Blur Profits," *New York Times* (June 20, 1976), Business and Finance Section, p. 1.

16. For a summary of the evidence which questions the efficient market hypothesis, see Thomas R. Dychman, David H. Downes, and Robert P. Magee, *Efficient Capital Markets and Accounting: A Critical Analysis* (Englewood Cliffs, N.J.: Prentice Hall, Inc., 1975), Chapter 3.

17. Joseph M. Burns, *Accounting Standards and International Finance, with Special Reference to Multinational Firms* (Washington, D.C.: American Enterprise for Public Policy Research, 1976), p. 15.

18. Robert M. Dunn, "Flexible Exchange Rates and Oligopoly Pricing: A Study of Canadian Market," *Journal of Political Economy* 79 (January-February 1979): 140-51.

19. This criterion was suggested by Rita M. Rodriguez, "FASB No. 8: What Has It Done for Us?" p. 47.

20. Cecil S. Ashdown, "Treatment of Foreign Exchange in Branch Office Accounting," *Journal of Accountancy* 34 (October 1922): 262-79.

21. Samuel R. Hepworth, "Reporting Foreign Operations," *Michigan Business Studies,* vol. 12, no. 5 (Ann Arbor: University of Michigan, 1956), p. 10.

22. Leonard Lorensen, *Accounting Research Study No. 12: Reporting Foreign Operations of U.S. Companies in U.S. Dollars* (New York: American Institute of Certified Public Accountants, 1972), p. 7.

23. R. MacDonald Parkingson, *Translation of Foreign Currencies* (Toronto: Canadian Institute of Chartered Accountants, 1972), pp. 1-35.

24. Financial Accounting Standards Board, *Statement of Financial Accounting Standards No. 8: Accounting for the Translation of Foreign Currency Transactions and Foreign Currency Financial Statements* (Stamford, Connecticut: Financial Accounting Standards Board, 1975), pp. 55-56.

25. For a detailed discussion of the developments of the different translation methods before FASB 8 was issued, see Robert I. Glover, "Selected Problems of Foreign Currency Translation," (Ph.D. dissertation, University of Kansas, 1975), pp. 38-79.

26. In fact, this method was not officially endorsed by the U.S. accounting profession until 1965. See Accounting Principles Board, *Accounting Principles Board Opinion No. 6: Status of Accounting Research Bulletin* (New York: American Institute of Certified Public Accountants, 1965), par. 18.

27. Robert Z. Aliber and Clyde T. Stickney, "Accounting Measures of Foreign Exchange Exposure: The Long and Short of It," *Accounting Review* 7 (January 1975), p. 45.

28. Ibid.

29. Ian H. Giddy, "Exchange Risk: Whose View?" *Financial Management* 6 (Summer 1977): 23-33.

30. Aliber and Stickney, "Accounting Measures of Foreign Exchange Exposure," p. 45.

31. Ian H. Giddy, "Exchange Risk," pp. 29-30.

32. See Michael C. Porter, "A Theoretical and Empirical Framework for Analyzing the Term Structure of Exchange Rate Expectations," *International Monetary Fund Staff Papers* 18 (November 1971): 613-42; Henry G. Gailliot, "Purchasing Power Parity as An Explanation of Long-term Changes in Exchange Rates," *Journal of Money, Credit and Banking* 2 (August 1970): 348-57; and Lawrence H. Officer, "The Purchasing-Power-Parity Theory of Exchange Rates: A Review Article," *International Monetary Fund Staff Papers* 23 (March 1976): 1-60.

33. Sidney M. Robbins and Robert B. Stobaugh, *Money in the Multinational Enterprise* (New York: Basic Books, 1973), p. 25.

34. Raymond Vernon, *Manager in the International Economy* (Englewood Cliffs, N.J.: Prentice Hall, 1972), p. 54-59.

35. Gunter Dufey, "Corporate Finance and Exchange Rate Variations," *Financial Management* 1 (Summer 1972): 51-57.

36. Ibid., p. 55.

37. Ibid., p. 52.

38. Ibid.

39. Aliber and Stickney, "Accounting Measures of Foreign Exchange Exposure," p. 52.

40. Donald Heckerman, "The Exchange Risks of Foreign Operations," *The Journal of Business* 45 (January 1972): 42-48.

41. Dufey, "Corporate Finance and Exchange Rate Variations," p. 52.

42. Alan C. Shapiro, "Exchange Rate Changes, Inflation, and the Value of the Multinational Corporation," *The Journal of Finance* 30 (May 1975): 485-502.

43. "Discussion," *The Journal of Finance* 30 (May 1975): 504-5.

44. Robert K. Ankrom, "Top Level Approach to the Foreign Exchange Problem," *Harvard Business Review* 52 (July-August 1974): 79-91.

45. Ibid., p. 81.

46. R.B. Shulman, "Are Foreign Exchange Risks Measurable," *Columbia Journal of World Business* 5 (May-June 1970): 55-60.

47. Ian H. Giddy, "What is FAS No. 8 Effect on the Market's Valuation of Corporate Stock Prices?" *Business International Money Report,* 26 May 1978, pp. 165, 168.

48. Alan C. Shapiro, "Economic Vs. Accounting Exposure Management: Are Shareholders Sophisticated?" *Business International Money Report,* 25 November 1977, pp. 372-73.

49. For a summary of the evidence which questions the efficient market hypothesis, see Dyckman *et al, Efficient Capital Markets and Accounting,* Chapter 3.

50. Burns, *Accounting Standards,* p. 14.

51. John H. Makin, "Flexible Exchange Rates, Multinational Corporations, and Accounting Standards," *Federal Reserve Bank of San Francisco Economic Review,* Fall 1977, pp. 44-45. See also his "Judging Standards' Impact on Market Behavior: Should FAS No. 8 Matter?" *Business International Money Report,* 30 June 1978, pp. 204-5, 208.

52. David B. Zenoff and Jack Zwick, *International Financial Management* (Englewood Cliffs, N.J.: Prentice Hall, 1969), pp. 105-14.

53. Vernon, *Manager in the International Economy,* pp. 45-59.

54. Robbins and Stobaugh, *Multinational Enterprise,* pp. 119-38.

55. Rita M. Rodriguez and E. Eugene Carter, *International Financial Management* (Englewood Cliffs, N.J.: Prentice-Hall, 1976), pp. 244-59.

56. Andreas R. Prindl, *Foreign Exchange Risk,* pp. 58-88.

57. Business International Corporation, "Hedging Foreign Exchange Risks," New York, 1971, (Monograph).

58. See Claude McMillan, "Swap as a Hedge in Foreign Exchange," *California Management Review* (Summer 1962), pp. 56-65; William M. Furlong, "Minimizing Foreign Exchange Losses," *Accounting Review* 41 (April 1966): 245-51; H.W. Allen Sweeney, "Protective Measures Against Devaluation," *Financial Executive* 36 (January 1968): 28-37; Gunter Dufey, "The Eurobond Market: Its Significance for International Financial Management," *Journal of International Business Studies* 1 (Spring 1970): 65-81; Gerald Kramer, "Borrowing on the International Capital Markets," *Columbia Journal of World Business* 9 (Spring 1974): 73-78; Joseph Wemhoff, "How To Refinance a Foreign Currency Debt Via the Reverse Swap Route," *Business International Money Report,* 21 July 1978, pp. 230-31. Business International Corporation has also often published short articles on these hedging methods in its weekly *Business International Money Report.*

59. Robert R. Ankrom, "Top Level Approach," pp. 84-87.

60. See Alan C. Shapiro and David P. Rutenberg, "Managing Exchange Risks in a Floating World," *Financial Management* 5 (Summer 1976): 49-51; Dennis E. Logue and George S. Oldfield, "Managing Foreign Assets When Foreign Exchange Markets are Efficient," *Financial Management* 6 (Summer 1977): 20-21; Giddy, "Exchange Risk: Whose View?" pp. 23-33.

61. See Robbins and Stobaugh, *Money in the Multinational Enterprise,* p. 130 and Steven W. Kohlhagen, "Evidence on the Cost of Forward Cover in a Floating System," *Euromoney,* September, 1975, pp. 138-41.

62. See Gunter Dufey, "Corporate Financial Policies and Floating Exchange Rates," (Paper presented at the Meeting of the International Fiscal Association, Rome, Italy, October 14, 1974); Joseph E. Finnerty, "Management of the Foreign Exchange Risk in a Multinational Firm," (Unpublished Paper, University of Massachusetts, 1976); Alan C. Shapiro, "Developing a Profitable Exposure Management System: The "Proactive' Approach," *Business International Money Report,* 17 June 1977, pp. 187-88 and 1 July 1977, pp. 204-5, 208.

63. For example, John S. Hughes, Dennis E. Logue, and Richard J. Sweeney, "Corporate International Diversification and Market Assigned Measures of Risk and Diversification," *Journal of Financial and Quantitative Analysis* 10 (November 1975): 627-38.

64. John H. Makin, "Portfolio Theory and the Problem of Foreign Exchange Risk," *Journal of Finance* 33 (May 1978): 517-34. See also Don S. Gull, "Composite Foreign Exchange Risk," *Columbia Journal of World Business* 10 (Fall 1975): 51-69.

65. Harry M. Markowitz, *Portfolio Selection: Efficient Diversification of Investments* (New York: John Wiley & Sons, 1959).

66. See Kenneth J. Arrow, "Comments," *Review of Economics and Statistics* 45 (Supplement February 1963): 24-27.

67. Ian H. Giddy and Gunter Dufey, "The Random Behavior of Flexible Exchange Rates: Implications for Forecasting," *Journal of International Business Studies* 6 (Spring 1975): 1-32.

68. With the exception of recent work by Makin. See Makin, "Portfolio Theory."

69. Bernard A. Lietaer, *Financial Management of Foreign Exchange: An Operational Technique to Reduce Risk* (Cambridge: MIT Press, 1971), p. 12-15.

70. Yutaka Imai, "Exchange Rate Risk Protection in International Business," *Journal of Financial and Quantitative Analysis* 10 (September 1975): 447-56.

71. James V. Jucker and Clovis de Faro, "The Selection of International Borrowing Sources," *Journal of Financial and Quantitative Analysis* 10 (September 1975): 381-408.

72. Martin L. Feldstein, "Uncertainty and Forward Exchange Speculation," *Review of Economics and Statistics* 45 (February 1968): 182-92.

73. Hayne E. Leland, "Optimal Forward Exchange Position," *Journal of Political Economy* 79 (March-April 1971): 257-69.

74. William R. Folks, Jr., "The Optimal Level of Forward Exchange Transactions," *Journal of Financial and Quantitative Analysis* 3 (January 1973): 105-10.

75. David B. Rutenberg, "Maneuvering Liquid Assets in a Multinational Firm: Formulation and Deterministic Solution Procedures," *Management Science* 16 (June 1970): B-671-84.

76. Alan C. Shapiro, "Management Science Models for Multicurrency Cash Management," (Ph.D. dissertation, Carnegie-Mellon University, 1971).

77. Alan C. Shapiro and David B. Rutenberg, "When to Hedge Against Devaluation," *Management Science* 2 (August 1974): 1514-30.

78. William R. Folks, Jr., "Decision Analysis for Exchange Risk Management," *Financial Management* 1 (Winter 1972): 101-11.

79. Steven C. Wheelwright, "Applying Decision Theory to Improve Corporate Management of Currency Exchange Risks," *California Management Review* 17 (Summer 1975): 41-49.

80. Zenoff and Zwick, *International Financial Management,* pp. 243-47.

81. William R. Folks, Jr., "The Analysis of Cross-Border Financing Decisions," *Financial Management* 5 (Autumn 1976): 19-27.

82. E. Eugene Carter and Rita M. Rodriguez, "Foreign Exchange Exposure: Models or Management," (Unpublished Working Paper, Graduate School of Business, Harvard University, August 10, 1977).

83. For example, the survey sponsored by the Financial Executives Institute. See J.H. Combes and J.W. Houghton, "Translating Foreign Currency," *Financial Executive* 41 (December 1973): 8-16.

84. Rodriguez, "FASB No. 8."

85. For example, Newton H. Hoyt, "The Management of Currency Exchange Risks by the Singer Company," *Financial Management* 1 (Spring 1972): 13-20; John Verroen, "How ITT Manages Its Foreign Exchange," *Management Services* 2 (January-February 1965): 27-33.

86. For example, address by Mr. M. Joseph Lambert at the Seminar on Management of Foreign Exchange Risks in New York City on May 15-16, 1978.

87. Jadwani, "Multinational Corporations' Exposure," pp. I-31 and I-32.

88. Robbins and Stobaugh, *Money in the Multinational Enterprise,* pp. 119-38.

89. Ibid.

90. Norman S. Fieleke, "The Hedging of Commercial Transactions between U.S. and Canadian Residents: A View from the U.S.," *Canadian-United States Financial Relationships* (Boston: Federal Reserve Bank of Boston, 1971), pp. 171-91; and "The Flotation of the Mark and the Hedging of Commercial Transactions between the U.S. and Germany: Experiences of Selected U.S. Non-Banking Enterprises," *Journal of International Business Studies* 4 (Spring 1973): 43-59.

91. Rita M. Rodriguez, "Foreign Exchange Risk Management in the U.S. Multinationals," (Unpublished Working Paper, Graduate School of Business, Harvard University, May, 1977).

92. Jilling and Folks, "Practices of American Corporations," n.p.

93. The results of which are available in the form of Working Papers such as the one indicated in the preceding footnote. A more comprehensive analysis was presented in Jilling, *Foreign Exchange Risk Management.* This discussion is based on his Ph.D. dissertation of the same title (University of South Carolina, 1976).

CHAPTER II

1. Jadwani, "Multinational Corporations' Exposure," p. IV-20.

2. Aliber and Stickney, "Foreign Exchange Exposure," p. 51.

3. Burns, *Accounting Standards,* p. 12.

4. Dufey, "Corporate Financial Policies and Floating Exchange Rates."

5. Ibid.

6. Shapiro, "Exchange Rate Changes," p. 248.

7. Lietaer, *Financial Management,* pp. 12-15.

8. Robert Stobaugh, Jr., "Financing Foreign Subsidiaries of U.S.-Controlled Multinational Enterprises," *Journal of International Business Studies* 1 (Summer 1970): 43-64.

9. Ibid, pp. 46-47.

10. Jadwani, "Multinational Corporations' Exposure," pp. V-8 and V-10.

11. Obie G. Whichard and Julius N. Freidlin, "U.S. Direct Investment Abroad in 1975," *Survey of Current Business* 56 (August 1976), Table 14.

12. Fieleke, "Hedging of Commercial Transactions (1971)"; and "Hedging of Commercial Transactions (1973)," pp. 171-91.

13. Jilling, "Foreign Exchange Risk Management."

14. As noted in "Implications of Floating Exchange Rates and FASB 8" in Chapter I, 1971-1972 represented the fixed rate period, whereas generalized floating started in 1973.

15. For the root of this definition, see Raymond Vernon, *Sovereignty at Bay* (New York: Basic Books, 1971), pp. 4-11.

16. James W. Vaupel and Joan P. Curhan, *The Making of Multinational Enterprise* (Boston: Harvard University Press, 1969), pp. 6-8. In describing these multinational corporations, Professor Vernon noted: "The 187 enterprises prove to be an extraordinary group, quite distinct in many respects from the rest of the U.S. corporate economy. . . . A group of enterprises of extraordinary size and high profitability, committed to activities that involve the relatively heavy use of skilled manpower. . . . The group holds a major position in the U.S. economy. . . . Their dominant position . . . pronounced as it is in relation to the U.S. economy as a whole, is even more evident in transactions between the U.S. economy and foreign countries." Vernon, *Sovereignty at Bay,* pp. 11-13.

17. Rodriguez, "FASB No. 8," pp. 40-47.

18. Jadwani, "Multinational Corporations' Exposure," pp. I-31 and I-32.

19. Fieleke, "Flotation of the Mark," p. 44.

20. Jilling, "Foreign Exchange Risk Management," pp. 68-69.

21. Ibid.

22. Ibid., Table 16.

23. Ibid., Table 54.

24. Ibid., Table 62.

25. Fieleke, "Flotation of the Mark," p. 44.

26. Rita M. Rodriguez, "Management of Foreign Exchange Risk in the U.S. Multinationals," *Journal of Financial and Quantitative Analysis* 9 (November 1974): 849-52.

CHAPTER III

1. In the seminar "International Treasury Operations Management," New York City, 28-29 March 1978, Mr. Edmund G. McElroy, Director of Cash Management of Avon Products, Inc. indicated that his company manages its foreign exchange solely on a cash flow basis, and simply disregards FASB 8.

2. It is interesting to note that Ankrom, "Top Level Approach" and Shulman, "Are Foreign Exchange Risks Measurable?" did not suggest that exposed earnings be included in the computation of the currency exposure.

3. Typically, gains/losses on foreign currency transactions are subject to income taxation whereas translation adjustments are not. For detailed analyses of the tax issue, see, for example, Gerald M. Blank, "Currency Devaluation: A Guide to Income Tax Consequences in 14 Countries," *Journal of Taxation* 35 (July 1971): 15-19; Donald R. Ravenscroft, "Taxation of Income Arising from Changes in Value of Foreign Currency," *Harvard Law Review* 82 (February 1969): 772-97.

4. Jilling, "Foreign Exchange Risk Management," pp. 209-11 and Appendix B, Exhibits 35 and 36.

5. Ibid., pp. 222-24.

6. Ibid.

7. 1974. See Rodriguez, "Management of Foreign Exchange Risk."

8. E. Eugene Carter and Rita M. Rodriguez, "Foreign Exchange Exposure: Models or Management," (Unpublished Paper, Graduate School of Business Administration, Harvard University, May 10, 1977), p. 16.

9. Excerpted from an address delivered in the seminar "Foreign Risk Management," New York City, 15-16 May 1978.

10. K. Larry Hastie and Roger W. Rosenwald, "Managing Foreign Currency Exposure," (Paper presented at the Annual Meeting of the Financial Management Association, Minneapolis, Minn., 13 October 1978). Mr. Hastie is Vice President and Treasurer of the Bendix Corporation.

11. For a discussion of the "naive investor" view, see Dyckman et al, *Efficient Capital Markets and Accounting,* pp. 2-4.

12. *Business Week,* 26 January 1976, as quoted in Jilling, "Foreign Exchange Risk Management," p. 104.

13. Dunn, "Flexible Exchange Rates," pp. 140-51.

14. Ibid., p. 149.

15. The estimates range from 17 percent to 14 percent per annum. If return on investments in non-exposed assets from the funds so generated is included, the effective cost is estimated to be from 9 to 4 percent annually. See Jadwani, "Multinational Corporations' Exposure," pp. III-20; Jilling, "Foreign Exchange Risk Management," p. 86.

16. Jadwani, Ibid., pp. IV-25 and IV-26; Jilling, Ibid., pp. 84-89.

17. This discussion is based on Zenoff and Zwick, *International Financial Management,* pp. 242-43.

18. For a description of another multinational firm's (Carborundum) inter-company netting system, see "Carborundum's System of Covering Current and Future Exposure," *Business International Money Report,* 6 May 1977, p. 138.

19. Jilling, "Foreign Exchange Risk Management," pp. 232-33.

20. See, for example, Zenoff and Zwick, *International Financial Management,* pp. 242-43; or Vernon, *Sovereignty at Bay,* pp. 4-11.

21. "Leads, Lags, and Netting: Countries' Regulations Show Little Change," *Business International Money Report,* 28 April 1978, p. 132.

22. See Jilling, "Foreign Exchange Risk Management," p. 278; Jadwani, "Multinational Corporations' Exposure," pp. IV-19 to 22.

CHAPTER IV

1. Jilling and Folks, "Practices of American Corporations," n.p.

2. Jilling, "Foreign Exchange Risk Management," Table 26-Appendix B.

3. See, for example, Ian H. Giddy and Gunter Dufey, "The Random Behavior of Flexible Exchange Rates: Implications for Forecasting," *Journal of International Business Studies* (Spring 1975): 1-32.

4. Gunter Dufey and Ian H. Giddy, "Forecasting Exchange Rates in a Floating World," *Euromoney,* November 1975, p. 33.

5. S.R. Bradford, "Measuring the Cost of Forward Exchange Contracts," *Euromoney,* August 1974, pp. 71-75; Giuliano Pelli, "Thoughts on the Cost of Forward Cover in a Floating System," *Euromoney,* October 1974, pp. 34-35; S.R. Bradford, "Thoughts on the Cost of Forward Cover in a Floating System—A Reply," *Euromoney,* November 1974, pp. 32-33. In this debate, the two writers presented their viewpoints on the proper way to measure the cost of forward exchange contracts. Their respective views are evident from Professor Kohlhagen's quote.

6. Steven W. Kohlhagen, "Evidence on the Cost of Forward Cover in a Floating System," *Euromoney,* September 1975, p. 138.

CHAPTER V

1. See Pakkala, "Foreign Exchange Accounting," p. 34.

2. This discussion of intervention policies is drawn from Arthur I. Bloomfield's "Foreign Exchange Policies of Industrialized Countries since March 1973," (Unpublished paper, University of Pennsylvania, n.d.).

3. As noted in Chapter II, this term signifies that the use of a strategy is increased by at least one scale; for example from "occasionally" to "usually."

4. Kohlhagen, "Evidence on the Cost of Forward Cover," p. 139.

5. Kolhlhagen, "Foreign Exchange Markets: 1971-1974," p. 37.

6. Kohlhagen, "Evidence of the Cost of Forward Cover," p. 141.

7. Jadwani, "Multinational Corporations' Exposure," pp. IV-1 through IV-57.

8. Ibid.

9. Fieleke, "Flotation of the Mark," pp. 47-53.

10. Jilling, "Foreign Exchange Risk Management," pp. 232-76 and Table 42-Appendix B.

11. Financial Accounting Standards Board, *Statement of FASB 8*, p. 55.

12. Ibid., p. 6.

13. Ibid.

14. Ibid., pp. 7-8.

15. Ibid., p. 11.

16. This should be distinguished from the translation method. Two of these companies translated inventory at historical rates.

17. It appears that this company has begun to hedge its balance sheet exposure since FASB 8, although it did not resort to this practice before.

18. It should be noted that when a company translated long-term debts at historical rates, its policy of income recognition of the currency effects on long-term debts was equivalent to that of a reserve account.

CHAPTER VI

1. Carter and Rodriguez, "Models or Management."

Appendix A

Interview Schedule

A. Organization

1. How is the responsibility of managing foreign exchange divided between the subsidiaries and the corporate finance department at the headquarters?

   Probe: 1.1 To what extent is the corporate finance department involved in the foreign exchange management decisions made at the subsidiaries? In France, West Germany, and England?

   1.2 What guidelines, if any, do you provide them?

2. At the headquarters, how is this responsibility divided among different departments and levels of management?

B. Information Systems

3. What balance sheet items and transactions do you include in the computation of your currency exposures?

   Probe: 3.1 Do you adjust this exposure figure to include transactions not yet recorded on the books, such as fixed foreign currency commitments, remittances to the parent company, or planned deliveries and purchases?

4. What reports do you receive from your subsidiaries whereby you obtain the data on the exposures in various currencies?

   Probe: 4.1 How often do the subsidiaries send in their reports?

   4.2 In what currencies are the exposed positions stated?

   4.3 Do these reports segregate the exposed items, such as A/R, A/P, bank loans, or are the exposed assets and exposed liabilities netted out?

   4.4 Do these reports show intra-company transactions?

   4.5 Is there any provision whereby the issuing subsidiary provides a forecast of its future exposures on the reports?

4.6   Do these reports show future exposed transactions not yet recorded on the books, such as fixed foreign currency commitments, or future deliveries and purchases?

5.   What are the sources of your exchange rate forecasts?

Probe: 5.1   (If both internal and outside sources are used) How much and for what kind of decisions do you rely on forecasts from the outside sources? Forecasts developed internally?

5.2   (Internal source) How do you make these forecasts?

5.3   How often do you revise your forecasts?

6.   How do you present your forecasts? Point estimate, range, probability distributions?

Probe: 6.1   How do you explain to the users of your forecasts the degree of uncertainty in your forecasts?

7.   As compared to fixed exchange rates, is it more or less difficult to forecast rate movements under floating exchange rates? In what respects?

Probe: 7.1   How do you overcome or cope with this difficulty?

C.   Evaluation of Defensive Strategies

8.   Given that you have an exposed position, and you want to hedge, possibly by forward contracts, how do you determine that the hedging costs are worthwhile?

Probe: 8.1   How do you compute the cost of a forward contract?

9.   Now, let's say you are considering obtaining a short-term bank loan for a subsidiary in Germany. You may borrow locally in German marks or in the Euro-currency markets. Or using intra-company accounts, you may tab the money markets in other countries, such as France or England. Naturally, you can always extend a dollar loan in the parent company's account. How do you evaluate these financing/hedging alternatives?

Probe: 9.1   What criteria do you use to rank these alternatives?

9.2   In this situation, as in a hedge versus no hedge problem, there is always a chance that your expectations of future rate movements will not materialize, both in the direction and the magnitude. How do you incorporate this element of risk into your analysis?

9.3   Do you explicitly state your estimate of the degree of risk? And how?

9.4   Do you use a mathematical model or computer program in the evaluation? What models?

10. Now, given that you have more than one way to hedge, and that you have ranked them in terms of the criteria that you just cited, who decides as to which defensive strategy(ies) is/are to be accepted?

Probe: 10.1   What are the criteria used to reach this conclusion?

10.2   Are there any foreign exchange management or hedging problems which require the approval of an authority higher than this person?

11. When you consider hedging, what factors, if any, do you feel limit the ways you can hedge?

Probe: 11.1   For instance, you consider, for hedging purposes, accelerating the collection of A/R, or changing the currency denominations on the invoices. Or you may want to adjust the level of inventory. How much influence would the marketing and production considerations have in such situations?

11.2   When you consider obtaining a local currency loan, would consideration for its effects, if any, on local banking relationships enter into your evaluation?

11.3   When a currency is under pressure to depreciate or appreciate, it is natural for a company to take out forward contracts to cover its exposed positions. And yet, this may contribute to the further weakening or strengthening of that currency. How does this sort of consideration enter into your decisions?

D. Objectives

12. What is/are the foreign exchange management objective(s) of this company?

Probe: 12.1   What is the allowed size of exposure in each of the currencies—French franc, German mark, and pound sterling?

12.2   Do you budget for foreign exchange losses and/or hedging expenses?

12.3   What is the philosophy or rationale underlying this objective?

12.4   Is this objective stated to you explicitly by the higher level of management?

12.5   (If not), do the higher level of management give you any guidelines to help you in your exposure management activities?

12.6   (If not), how do you feel this lack of guidelines affects you?

12.7   Earlier, you mentioned the rule-of-thumb, so to speak, that . . . How was this rule-of-thumb created?

E. Exposure Measurement

13. Earlier you said that currency exposure is measured by . . . Is this the basis whereby you assess the effects of foreign exchange on your company?

Probe: 13.1   By way of simplification, if this exposure is multiplied by the rate change, you will have an amount of exchange gain or loss. Is this the number you try to minimize?

14. Was this the same method used to calculate currency exposures before FASB 8 was issued?

Probe: 14.1   If not, was FASB 8 a reason for the change?

15. Analytically, why do you consider inventory exposed? Long-term debt?

F. Defensive Strategies

16. How do you take into consideration the problems of foreign exchange in your long-run plans?

Probe: 16.1   Do you have a formal long-run foreign exchange management plan?

16.2   How often do you make adjustments to your long-run plan?

17. What defensive measures or hedging techniques do you or your subsidiaries in France, West Germany, and England use to protect your currency exposures?

   Probe: 17.1 How do you hedge on foreign currency payments and receipts?

   17.2 Do you or your subsidiaries in France, Germany, or England borrow locally explicitly for exchange risk protection?

   17.3 Do you contract forward cover on fixed foreign currency commitments arising from contractual sale or purchase agreements? Other specific sale or purchase transactions not yet recorded on the books?

18. We have discussed division of responsibility, reporting systems, exchange rate forecasting, planning, and defensive strategies. These activities can be viewed as separate but interrelated parts of an overall foreign exchange management strategy. What would you say is/are the most important element(s) of your foreign exchange management strategy?

G. Floating Exchange Rates

19. How has this strategy changed as we went from the fixed exchange rate system to floating exchange rates?

20. What are the defensive strategies which you did/did not use before floating exchange rates, but now you do/do not use?

21. Are there any defensive strategies which you have used before and also after floating exchange rates? Which strategies? Are they now used more or less frequently?

22. In the present floating rate regime, there are currencies which move together in the same direction, such as those in the "snake" group. And there are those which move together but in opposite directions. Yet, there are those currencies whose movements are perfectly uncorrelated. This environment represents opportunities for diversification of risk across currencies, or inter-currency netting. To what extent do you use inter-currency netting as a defensive strategy?

   Probe: 22.1 Let's consider a situation in which you have a short

position in DM and this currency is expected to appreciate; so you have a potential loss. In French francs,
you have a long position, and this currency is also expected to appreciate such that you have a potential
gain in French francs which is equal or greater than the
potential DM loss. Do you take any actions to protect
the company against the DM loss?

22.2   How do you use intra-company or inter-subsidiary
accounts as a defensive strategy?

22.3   Do you use the adjustment of inventory levels at various
subsidiaries as a defensive strategy?

22.4   Do you use inter-subsidiary transfer pricing as a defensive strategy?

22.5   Would you say that by using inter-currency netting, the
amounts of your hedging on individual currencies has
been less than they would be otherwise?

23. In general, it can be said that floating exchange rates have increased the
degree of uncertainty in forecasting. How would you say this increased
uncertainty affects the amount of your hedging?

H. FASB 8

24. Before FASB 8 was issued, companies had a number of options as to
the translation of their foreign subsidiaries' financial statements as well
as the timing of income recognition as far as exchange gains or losses
are concerned. I understand that your company had opted to . . .

25. It has been observed in the press and professional literature that FASB
8 has caused significant volatility of quarterly reported earnings at a
number of companies. Such earnings volatility would not have occurred, so it was observed, if these companies had continued to use the
same methods of translation and income recognition that they had
previously used. How significant have been the effects of FASB 8 on
your company's quarterly earnings?

26. What are your views about the efficiency of the stock market for your
company's securities in general and in particular, its ability to understand the data regarding your company's foreign exchange gains and
losses?

Probe: 26.1   As you see it, how has the stock market reacted to
the fluctuations in your company's quarterly earnings?

26.2   Have you made any effort to explain the data regarding your company's foreign exchange gains/losses to the shareholders and securities analysts? How?

27. Have you contemplated any strategies to reduce or increase your currency exposures as a result of consideration for (potential) effects of FASB 8?

Probe: 27.1   Have you found that in considering future bank loans for your subsidiaries FASB 8 has become a factor for consideration? For example, you may prefer stable to weak currencies, or that stability of a currency is at least as important as its weakness, if not more?

27.2   I understand that you do sell forward on fixed foreign currency sale commitments. Have you considered buying the same currency forward simultaneously in the same amount and for the same term to maturity?

27.3   Because of the FASB 8 requirement that gains or losses on forward contracts are to be recognized currently, have you considered reducing the amounts of your forward sales or purchases of foreign currencies?

27.4   Intra-company accounts is a very cost-effective strategy to transfer exposed liabilities from a currency which has a history of violent movements to a more stable currency. Have you considered using intra-company accounts for this purpose?

27.5   Have you considered changing your credit policy such that increasing portions of your trade receivables and payables will be denominated in more stable currencies? And that you would like to shorten terms of payments on receivables and payables denominated in volatile currencies?

28. Have you taken in the present or in the past years any of the above actions?

Bibliography

Books

Accounting Principles Board. *Accounting Principles Board Opinion No. 6: Status of Accounting Research Bulletin.* New York: American Institute of Certified Public Accountants, 1965.

Burns, Joseph M. *Accounting Standards and International Finance, With Special Reference to Multinational Firms.* Washington, D.C.: American Enterprise for Public Policy Research, September 1976.

Dyckman, Thomas R., Downs, H. David; and Magee, P. Robert. *Efficient Capital Markets and Accounting: A Critical Analysis.* Englewood Cliffs, New Jersey: Prentice Hall, 1975.

Financial Accounting Standards Board. *Statement of Financial Accounting Standards No. 8: Accounting for the Translation of Foreign Currency Financial Statements.* Stamford, Connecticut: Financial Accounting Standards Board, 1975.

International Monetary Fund. *International Monetary Fund, Annual Report of the Executive Directors for the Fiscal Year Ended April 30, 1976.* Washington, D.C.: International Monetary Fund, no date.

_____ . *International Monetary Fund, Annual Report of the Executive Directors for the Fiscal Year Ended April 30, 1977.* Washington, D.C.: International Monetary Fund, no date.

Lietaer, Bernard A. *Financial Management of Foreign Exchange: An Operational Technique to Reduce Risk.* Cambridge: M.I.T. Press, 1971.

Lorensen, Leonard. *Accounting Research Study No. 12: Reporting Foreign Operations of U.S. Companies in U.S. Dollars.* New York: American Institute of Certified Public Accountants, 1972.

Markowitz, Harry M. *Portfolio Selection: Efficient Diversification of Investments.* New York: John Wiley & Sons, 1959.

Parkinson, R. MacDonald. *Translation of Foreign Currencies.* Toronto: Canadian Institute of Chartered Accountants, 1972.

Prindl, Andreas R. *Foreign Exchange Risk.* New York: John Wiley & Sons, 1976.

Ravenscroft, Donald R. *Taxation and Foreign Currency: The Income Tax Consequences of Foreign Exchange Transactions and Exchange Rate Fluctuations.* Cambridge: International Tax Program, Law School of Harvard University, 1973.

Robbins, Sidney M., and Stobaugh, Robert M. *Money in the Multinational Enterprise: A Study in Financial Policy.* New York: Basic Books, 1972.

Robichek, Alexander A., and Meyers, Stewart C. *Optimal Financing Decisions.* Englewood Cliffs, New Jersey: Prentice Hall, 1965.

Rodriguez, Rita M., and Carter, Eugene. *International Financial Management.* Englewood Cliffs, New Jersey: Prentice Hall, Inc., 1976.

Vaupel, J.W., and Curhan, J.P. *The Making of Multinational Enterprise.* Boston: Harvard Business School, 1967.

Vernon, Raymond. *Manager in the International Economy.* 2nd Edition. Englewood Cliffs, New Jersey: Prentice Hall, Inc., 1972.

_____ . *Sovereignty at Bay: The Multinational Spread of U.S. Enterprises.* New York: Basic Books, 1971.

Zenoff, David B., and Zwick, Jack. *International Financial Management.* Englewood Cliffs, New Jersey: Prentice Hall, Inc., 1969.

Articles

Aliber, Robert Z. and Stickney, Clyde P. "Accounting Measures of Foreign Exchange Exposure: The Long and Short of It." *Accounting Review* 50 (January 1975), pp. 44-57.

Aliber, Robert Z. "Exchange Risk, Political Risk and Investor Demand for External Currency Deposits." *Journal of Money, Credit, and Banking* 7 (May 1975), pp. 162-179.

Allan, John H. "Currency Savings Blur Profits." *New York Times* 20 June 1976, Business and Finance Sec., p. 1.

Ankrom, Robert K. "Top-Level Approach to the Foreign Exchange Problem." *Harvard Business Review* 52 (July-August 1974), pp. 79-90.

Arrow, Kenneth J. "Comments." *Review of Economics and Statistics* 45 (February 1963), pp. 24-27.

Ashdown, Cecil S. "Treatment of Foreign Exchange in Branch Office Accounting." *Journal of Accounting* 24 (October 1922), pp. 262-79.

Barrett, M. Edgar and Spero, Leslie L. "Accounting Determinants of Foreign Exchange Gains and Losses." *Financial Analysts Journal* 31 (March-April 1975), pp. 26-30.

Beaver, William H. "What Should be the FASB's Objectives." *Journal of Accountancy* 136 (August 1973), pp. 49-56.

Blank, Gerald M. "Currency Devaluation: A Guide to Income Tax Consequences in 14 Countries." *Journal of Taxation* 25 (July 1971), pp. 15-19.

Bradford, S.R. "Measuring the Cost of Forward Exchange Contracts." *Euromoney* (August 1974), pp. 71-75.

_____. "Thoughts on the Cost of Forward Cover in a Floating System—A Reply." *Euromoney* (November 1974), pp. 32-33.

Business International Corporation. "Hedging Foreign Exchange Risks." New York, 1971. (Monograph.)

"Carborundum's System of Covering Current and Future Exposure," *Business International Money Report,* May 6, 1977, pp. 137-38.

Clague, Llewellyn and Grossfield, Rena. "Export Pricing in a Floating Rate World." *Columbia Journal of World Business* 9 (Winter 1974), pp. 17-22.

Combes, J.H. and Houghton, J.W. "Translating Foreign Currency." *Financial Executive* 41 (December 1973), pp. 8-16.

Danert, Gunter. "Inter-company Strategies of Multinational Companies and National Economic Policy." *Financial Executive* 45 (October 1977), pp. 46-56.

deVries, Margaret. "The Magnitude of Exchange Devaluation." *Finance and Development* 5 (June 1968), pp. 8-12.

Deldridge, Richard. "Foreign Exchange Dealings in Banks." *The Arthur Anderson Chronicle* 35 (April 1975), pp. 30-54.

"Discussion." *The Journal of Finance* 30 (May 1975), pp. 503-07.

Dufey, Gunter. "The Eurobond Market: Its Significance for International Financial Management." *Journal of International Business Studies* 1 (Spring 1970), pp. 65-81.

_____. "Corporate Finance and Exchange Rate Variations." *Financial Management* 1 (Summer 1972), pp. 52-57.

_____, and Giddy, Ian H. "Forecasting Exchange Rates in a Floating World." *Euromoney* (November 1975), pp. 28-36.

Dunn, Robert M., Jr. "Flexible Exchange Rates and Oligopoly: A Study of Canadian Markets." *Journal of Political Economy* 79 (January-February 1970), pp. 140-151.

Evans, Thomas G. "Some Concerns about Exposure After the FASB's Statement No. 8" *Financial Executive* 44 (November 1976), pp. 28-30.

Feldstein, Martin S. "Uncertainty and Foreward Exchange Speculation." *Review of Economics and Statistics* 45 (February 1968), pp. 182-92.

Fieleke, Norman S. "The Hedging of Commercial Transaction Between U.S. and Canadian Residents: A View from the U.S." *Canadian-United States Financial Relationships.* Boston: Federal Reserve Bank of Boston, 1971, pp. 171-91.

_____. "The 1971 Flotation of the Mark and the Hedging of Commercial Transactions between the U.S. and Germany: Experiences of Selected U.S. Non-Banking Enterprises."

Journal of International Business Studies 4 (Spring 1973), pp. 43-59.

_____ . "Exchange Rate Flexibility and the Efficiency of the Foreign Exchange Markets." *Journal of Financial and Quantitative Analysis* 3 (September 1975), pp. 409-28.

Flower, J.F. "Coping with Currency Fluctuations in Company Accounts." *Euromoney* (May 1974), pp. 14-19.

_____ . "Coping with Currency Fluctuations in Company Accounts." *Euromoney* (June 1974), pp. 45-46.

Folks, William R., Jr. "Decision Analysis for Exchange Risk Management." *Financial Management* 1 (Winter 1972), pp. 101-12.

_____ . "The Optimal Level of Forward Exchange Transactions." *Journal of Financial and Quantitative Analysis* (January 1973), pp. 105-10.

_____ . "The Analysis of Cross-Border Financing Decisions." *Financial Management* 5 (Autumn 1976), pp. 19-27.

Folks, William R., Jr. and Stansell, Stanley R. "The Use of Discriminant Analysis in Forecasting Exchange Rate Movements." *Journal of International Business Studies* 6 (Spring 1975), pp. 33-50.

Franck, Peter and Young, Allan. "Stock Price Reaction of Multinational Firms to Exchange Realignments." *Financial Management* 1 (Winter 1972), pp. 66-73.

Frenkel, Jacob A. "Covered Interest Arbitrage: Unexploited Profits?" *Journal of Political Economy* 83 (April 1975), pp. 325-36.

Furlong, William L. "Minimizing Foreign Exchange Losses." *Accounting Review* 41 (April 1966), pp. 245-51.

Gailliot, Henry J. "Purchasing Power Parity as an Explanation of Long Term Changes in Exchange Rates." *Journal of Money, Credit and Banking* 2 (August 1970), pp. 348-57.

Gaskins, J. Peter. "Taxation of Foreign Source Income." *Financial Analysts Journal* 29 (September-October 1973), pp. 55-64.

Gesterner, David. "Strategies in Managing International Sales." *Harvard Business Review* 52 (September-October 1973), pp. 103-8.

Giddy, Ian H. and Dufey, Gunter. "The Random Behavior of Flexible Exchange Rates: Implications for Forecasting." *Journal of International Business Studies* 6 (Spring 1975), pp. 1-32.

Giddy, Ian H. "Exchange Risk: Whose View?" *Financial Management* 6 (Summer 1977), pp. 23-30.

_____ . "What is FASB No. 8's Effect on the Market's Valuation of Corporate Stock Prices?" *Business International Money Report* (26 May 1978), pp. 165, 168.

Gull, D.S. "Composite Foreign Exchange Risk." *Columbia Journal of World Business* 10 (Fall 1975), pp. 51-69.

Hanoch, Giara and Haim, Levy. "Efficient Portfolio Selection with Quadratic and Cubic Utility." *The Journal of Business* 43 (April 1970), pp. 181-89.

Hawkins, David J. "Controlling Foreign Operations." *Financial Executive* 33 (February 1965), pp. 25-26.

Heckerman, Donald. "The Exchange Risks of Foreign Operations?" *Journal of Business* 45 (January 1972), pp. 42-48.

Hepworth, Samuel R. "Reporting Foreign Operations." *Michigan Business Studies,* Vol. 12, No. 5. Ann Arbor, Michigan: Bureau of Business Research, Graduate School of Business, The University of Michigan, 1956.

Hertz, David B. "Risk Analysis in Capital Investment." *Harvard Business Review* 42 (January-February 1964), pp. 95-106.

Horst, Thomas. "The Theory of the Multinational Firm: Optimal Behavior Under Different Tariff and Tax Rates." *Journal of Political Economy* 79 (September-October 1971), pp. 1059-71.

Hoyt, Newton H. "The Management of Currency Exchange Risks by the Singer Company." *Financial Management* 1 (Spring 1972), pp. 13-20.

Hughes, John S.; Logue, Dennis E.; and Sweeney, Richard James. "Corporate International Diversification and Market-Assigned Measures of Risk and Diversification." *Journal of*

Financial and Quantitative Analysis 10 (November 1975), pp. 627-38.

Imai, Yutaka. "Exchange Rate Risk Protection in International Business." *Journal of Financial and Quantitative Analysis* 10 (September 1975), pp. 447-56.

Ishimaya, Yoshihidi. "The Theory of Optimum Currency Areas: A Survey." *International Monetary Fund Staff Papers* 26 (July 1975), pp. 344-83.

Jucker, James V. and deFaro, Clovis. "The Selection of International Borrowing Sources." *Journal of Financial and Quantitative Analysis* 10 (September 1975), pp. 381-408.

Kohlhagen, Steven W. "Evidence on the Cost of Forward Cover in a Floating System." *Euromoney* (September 1975), pp. 138-41.

———. "The Performance of the Foreign Exchange Markets: 1971-74." *Journal of International Business Studies* 6 (Fall 1975), pp. 33-39.

Kramer, Gerald. "Borrowing on the International Capital Markets." *Columbia Journal of World Business* 9 (Spring 19⌐⌐), pp. 73-77.

"Leads, Lags and Netting: Countries Regulations Show Little Change." *Business International Money Report* (28 April 1978), pp. 132-33.

Leff, Nathaniel H. "International Sourcing Strategy." *Columbia Journal of World Business* 9 (Fall 1974), pp. 71-79.

Leland, Hayne E. "Optimal Forward Exchange Positions." *Journal of Political Economy* 79 (March-April 1971), pp. 257-69.

Lietaer, Bernard A. "Managing Risks in Foreign Exchange." *Harvard Business Review* 48 (March-April 1979), pp. 127-38.

Lintner, John. "Security Prices, Risk, and Maximal Gains from Diversification." *Journal of Finance* 20 (December 1965), pp. 587-613.

Logue, Dennis E. and Oldfield, George S. "Managing Foreign Assets When Foreign Markets Are Efficient." *Financial Management* 6 (Summer 1977), pp. 16-22.

McMillan, Claude. "The Swap as a Hedge in Foreign Exchange." *California Management Review* (Summer 1962), pp. 57-65.

Makin, John. "Portfolio Theory and the Problem of Foreign Exchange Risk." *Journal of Finance* 33 (May 1978), pp. 517-34.

———. "Judging Standards' Impact on Market Behavior: Should FASB No. 8 Matter." *Business International Money Report.* (30 June 1978), pp. 204-8.

———. "Flexible Exchange Rates, Multinational Corporations, and Accounting Standards." *Federal Reserve Bank of San Francisco Economic Review* (Fall 1977), pp. 44-45.

Ness, Walter, Jr. "U.S. Corporate Income Taxation and the Dividend Remittance Policy of Multinational Corporations." *Journal of International Business Studies* 6 (Spring 1975), pp. 67-77.

———. "A Linear Programming Approach to Financing the Multinational Corporation." *Financial Management* 1 (Winter 1972), pp. 81-100.

Neuman-Etienne, Ruediger. "A Framework for Financial Decisions in Multinational Corporations—A Summary of Recent Research." *Journal of Financial and Quantitative Analysis* 9 (November 1974), pp. 859-74.

Officer, Lawrence H. "The Purchasing Power Parity Theory of Exchange Rates: A Review Article." *International Monetary Fund Staff Papers* 23 (March 1976), pp. 1-60.

Olstein, Robert A., and O'Glove, Thornton L. "Devaluation and Multinational Reporting." *Financial Analysts Journal* 29 (September-October 1973), pp. 65-84.

Pakkala, A.L. "Foreign Exchange Accounting of Multinational Corporations." *Financial Analysts Journal* 31 (March-April 1975), pp. 32-41, 76.

Pelli, Guiliano. "Thoughts on the Cost of Forward Cover in a Floating System." *Euromoney* (October 1974), pp. 34-35.

Petty, J. William, II and Walker, Ernest W. "Optimal Transfer Pricing for the Multinational Firm." *Financial Management* 1 (Winter 1972), pp. 74-84.

Peterson, S.C. "Impact of Accounting Methods on Foreign Exchange Management." *Euromoney* (June 1974), pp. 50-54.

Poole, William. "Speculative Prices as Random Walk: An Analysis of Ten Time Series of Flexible Exchange Rates." *Southern Journal of Economics* 33 (April 1967), pp. 468-78.

Porter, Michael C. "A Theoretical and Empirical Framework for Analyzing the Term Structure of Exchange Rate Expectations." *International Monetary Fund Staff Papers* 18 (November 1971), pp. 613-45.

Ravenscroft, Donald R. "Taxation of Income Arising From Changes in Value of Foreign Currency." *Harvard Law Review* 82 (February 1969), pp. 772-97.

Robbins, Sidney M., and Stobaugh, Robert B. "Financing Foreign Affiliates." *Financial Management* 1 (Winter 1972), pp. 56-65.

Robichek, Alexander A.; Teichroew, D.; and Jones, J.M. "Optimal Short Term Financing Decision." *Management Science* 12 (September 1965), pp. 1-30.

Robichek, Alexander A. and Eaker, Mark R. "Debt Denomination and Exchange Risk in International Capital Markets." *Financial Management* 5 (Autumn 1976), pp. 11-18.

Rodriguez, Rita M. "Management of Foreign Exchange Risks in the U.S. Multinationals." *Journal of Financial and Quantitative Analysis* 9 (November 1974), pp. 849-57.

_____. "FASB No. 8: What Has It Done for Us?" *Financial Analysts Journal* (March-April 1977), pp. 40-47.

Rutenberg, David P. "Maneuvering Liquid Assets in a Multinational Company: Formulation and Deterministic Solution Procedures." *Management Science* 16 (June 1970), pp. 671-84.

Schmitz, M.N. "Taxation of Foreign Exchange Gains and Losses." *Management Accounting* 63 (July 1976), pp. 49-51.

Schwab, Bernard and Lusztig, Peter. "Apportioning Foreign Exchange Risk Through the Use of Third Currencies: Some Questions of Efficiency." *Financial Management* 7 (Fall 1978), pp. 25-30.

Scott, George M. "Currency Exchange Rates and Accounting Translation: A Mis-marriage?" *ABACUS: A Journal of Accounting and Business Studies* 11 (June 1975), pp. 58-70.

Shapiro, Alan C. "Optimal Inventory and Credit Granting Strategies Under Inflation and Devaluation." *Journal of Financial and Quantitative Analysis* 8 (January 1973), pp. 37-46.

_____. "Exchange Rate Changes, Inflation and the Value of the Multinational Corporation." *Journal of Finance* 30 (May 1975), pp. 485-502.

_____. "Evaluating Financing Cost for Multinational Subsidiaries." *Journal of International Business Studies* 6 (Fall 1975), pp. 25-32.

_____. "Developing a Profitable Exposure Management System: The 'Proactive' Approach." *Business International Money Report* (27 June 1977), pp. 187-88; and (1 July 1977), pp. 204-5, 208.

_____. "Economic vs. Accounting Exposure Management: Are Shareholders Sophisticated?" *Business International Money Report* (25 November 1977), pp. 372-73.

_____. "How Chancy are MNCs? Worldwide Diversification May Lower Financial Risk." *Business International Money Report* (10 March 1978), pp. 75-76.

_____. "Capital Budgeting for the Multinational Corporation." *Financial Management* 7 (Spring 1978), pp. 7-16.

_____. "Managing Exchange Risks in a Floating World." *Financial Management* 5 (Summer 1976), pp. 48-57.

Shapiro, Alan C. and Rutenberg, David P. "When to Hedge Against Devaluation." *Management Science* 20 (August 1974), pp. 1514-29.

Shulman, James. "When the Price is Wrong—by Design." *Columbia Journal of World Business* 2 (May-June 1967), pp. 69-76.

_____. "Corporate Treatment of Exchange Risk." *Journal of International Business Studies* 1 (Spring 1979), pp. 83-88.

Shulman, R.B. "Are Foreign Exchange Risks Measurable?" *Columbia Journal of World Business* 5 (May-June 1970), pp. 55-60.

Stobaugh, Robert, Jr. "Financing Foreign Subsidiaries of U.S.-Controlled Multinational Enterprises." *Journal of International Business Studies* 1 (Spring 1970), pp. 43-64.

Stonehill, Arthur and Stitzel, Thomas. "Financial Structure and Multinational Corporation." *California Management Review* 12 (Fall 1969), pp. 91-96.

Sweeney, H.W. Allen. "Protective Measure Against Devaluation." *Financial Executive* 36 (January 1968), pp. 28-37.

Foreign Exchange Management in Multinational Firms

Teck, Alan. "Control Your Exposure to Foreign Exchange." *Harvard Business Review*
52 (January-February 1974), pp. 66-74.
Thomas, Lloyd B. "Behavior of Flexible Exchange Rates: Additional Tests from the Post-
World War I Episode." *Southern Economic Journal* 40 (October 1973), pp. 167-82.
Underwood, Trevor G. "Unfinished Business: Making Floating Exchange Rates Work."
Euromoney (October 1974), pp. 68-71.
Upson, Roger B. "Random Walk and Forward Exchange Rates: A Spectral Analysis."
Journal of Financial and Quantitative Analysis 7 (September 1972), pp. 1897-1906.
Verroen, John. "How ITT Manages Its Foreign Exchange." *Management Services* 2 (Janu-
ary-February 1965), pp. 27-33.
Watts, John H., II. "Strategies for Financial Risk in Multinational Operations." *Columbia
Journal of World Business* 6 (September-October 1971), pp. 15-23.
Walton, Horace. "Foreign Currency: To Hedge or Not to Hedge." *Financial Executive*
42 (April 1974), pp. 48-55.
Wemhoff, Joseph. "How to Refinance a Foreign Currency Debt Via the Reverse Swap
Route." *Business International Money Report* 21 July 1978, pp. 230-31.
Wheelwright, Steven C. "Applying Decision Theory to Improve Corporate Management
of Currency Exchange Risks." *California Management Review* 17 (Summer 1975),
pp. 41-49.
Whichard, Obie G. and Freidlin, Julius N. "U.S. Direct Investment Abroad in 1975." *Survey
of Current Business* 56 (August 1976), pp. 40-63.
Wooster, John T. and Thoman, G. Richard. "New Financial Priorities for MNC's." *Harvard
Business Review* 52 (May-June 1974), pp. 58-68.
Wyman, Harold E. "Analysis of Gains or Losses from Foreign Monetary Items: An Application of Purchasing Power Parity Concepts." *Accounting Review* 51 (July 1976),
pp. 545-58.

Doctoral Dissertations
Aggarwal, Raj Kumar. "The Management of Foreign Exchange: Optimal Policies for a
Multinational Company." D.B.A. Dissertation, Kent State University, 1975.
Ayarslan, Solmaz. "A Dynamic Stochastic Model for Current Asset and Liability Manage-
ment of a Multinational Corporation." Ph.D. Dissertation, New York University, 1976.
Brooks, Robert. "Expectations and Forward Exchange." Ph.D. Dissertation, University of
Washington, 1972.
Glover, Robert Ivy. "Selected Problems of Foreign Currency Translation." Ph.D. Disserta-
tion, University of Houston, 1975.
Graham, Lynford Earle. "An Investigation into the Accounting Problems Involved in Pre-
senting Financial Statements for the U.S.-Based Company with Foreign Operations."
Ph.D. Dissertation, University of Pennsylvania, 1976.
Jadwani, H.J. "Some Aspects of the Multinational Corporations' Exposure to Exchange
Rate Risk." D.B.A. Dissertation, Harvard Business School, 1971.
Jilling, Michael. "Foreign Exchange Risk Management: Current Practices of U.S. Multina-
tional Corporations." Ph.D. Dissertation, University of South Carolina, 1976.
Kwan, Cheuken. "Multinational Common Stock Portfolio Selection Model with Exchange
Risk Adjustments." Ph.D. Dissertation, University of California, Los Angeles, 1974.
Obersteiner, Erich. "Decision Model for the Allocation of Foreign Funds to Dividend
Remittances and Foreign Investment in Multinational Corporate System with Wholly-
Owned Manufacturing Subsidiaries." Ph.D. Dissertation, Columbia University, 1972.
Salmi, Timo Yrjo. "Joint Determination of Trade, Production, and Financial Flows in the
Multinational Firm Assuming Risky Currency Exchange Rates: A Two-State Linear
Programming Model Building Approach." D.Sc. Dissertation, Helsinki School of Eco-
nomics (Finland), 1975.
Shapiro, Alan C. "Management Science Models for Multicurrency Cash Management."
Ph.D. Dissertation, University of Pennsylvania, 1971.
Tsoa, Eugene Yu-seng. "A Study of Actual Deviations from the Interest Parity Theory
for Forward Exchange Theory and Empirical Evidence." Ph.D. Dissertation, University
of Notre Dame, 1975.

Speeches
Dufey, Gunter. "Corporate Financial Policies and Floating Exchange Rates." Paper presented at the Meeting of the International Fiscal Association in Rome, Italy, October 1974.
Elsaid, Hussein H., and Issa, A.D. "The Measurement of Risk and Return by U.S. Multinational Corporations." Paper presented at the Annual Meeting of the Financial Management Association in Minneapolis, Minnesota, 12 October 1978.
Hackett, J.T. "Adapting Financial Policies to Changing Circumstances." Paper presented at the Annual Meeting of the Financial Management Association in Minneapolis, Minnesota, 12 October 1978.
Hastie, K. Larry and Rosenwald, Roger W. "Managing Foreign Currency Exposure." Paper presented at the Annual Meeting of the Financial Management Association in Minneapolis, Minnesota, 13 October 1978.
Lambert, Joseph. Remarks presented at the seminar "Management of Foreign Exchange Risks," New York City, 15-16 May 1978.
McElroy, Edmund G. Remarks presented at the seminar "International Treasury Operations Management," New York City, 28-29 March 1978.
Militello, Frederick C. "Conceptual and Practical Problems of Foreign Exchange Exposure Analysis." Paper presented at the Annual Meeting of the Financial Management Association in Minneapolis, Minnesota, 13 October 1978.

Unpublished Materials
Bloomfield, Arthur. "Foreign Exchange Policies of Leading Industrialized Countries Since March 1973." University of Pennsylvania, no date.
Carten, E. Eugene and Rodriguez, Rita M. "Foreign Exchange Exposure: Models or Management." Graduate School of Business Administration, Harvard University, 1977.
Finnerty, Joseph E. "Management of the Foreign Exchange Risk in a Multinational Firm." University of Massachusetts, 1976.
Jilling, Michael and Folks, William R., Jr. "Practices of American Corporations in Foreign Exchange Risk Management: A Statistical Summary." Working Paper I: Foreign Exchange Risk Management Project, University of South Carolina, no date.
———. "The Emergence of the Foreign Exchange Risk Management Function." Working Paper II: Foreign Exchange Risk Management Project, University of South Carolina, no date.
———. "A Survey of Corporate Exchange Rate Forecasting Practices." Working Paper III: Foreign Exchange Risk Management Project, University of South Carolina, no date.
Rodriguez, Rita M. "Foreign Exchange Risk Management in the U.S. Multinationals," Graduate School of Business Administration, Harvard University, May 1977.

Index

Date Due

JUL 22 '94			

BRODART, INC.   Cat. No. 23 233   Printed in U.S.A.